D1798236

A guide to the third and fourth Egyptian rooms : predynastic antiquites, mummied birds and animals, portrait statues, figures of gods, tools, implements and weapons, scarabs, amulets, jewellery, and other objects connected with the funeral rites of the an

British Museum. Dept. of Egyptian and Assyrian Antiquities, Budge, E. A. Wallis (Ernest Alfred Wallis), Sir, Hall, H. R. (Harry Reginald)

BIBLIOLIFE

Copyright © BiblioLife, LLC

BiblioLife Reproduction Series: Our goal at BiblioLife is to help readers, educators and researchers by bringing back in print hard-to-find original publications at a reasonable price and, at the same time, preserve the legacy of literary history. The following book represents an authentic reproduction of the text as printed by the original publisher and may contain prior copyright references. While we have attempted to accurately maintain the integrity of the original work(s), from time to time there are problems with the original book scan that may result in minor errors in the reproduction, including imperfections such as missing and blurred pages, poor pictures, markings and other reproduction issues beyond our control. Because this work is culturally important, we have made it available as a part of our commitment to protecting, preserving and promoting the world's literature.

All of our books are in the "public domain" and some are derived from Open Source projects dedicated to digitizing historic literature. We believe that when we undertake the difficult task of re-creating them as attractive, readable and affordable books, we further the mutual goal of sharing these works with a larger audience. A portion of BiblioLife profits go back to Open Source projects in the form of a donation to the groups that do this important work around the world. If you would like to make a donation to these worthy Open Source projects, or would just like to get more information about these important initiatives, please visit www.bibliolife.com/opensource.

BRITISH MUSEUM.

A GUIDE

TO THE

THIRD AND FOURTH

EGYPTIAN ROOMS.

**Predynastic Antiquities,
Mummied Birds and Animals, Portrait Statues, Figures of Gods, Tools,
Implements and Weapons, Scarabs, Amulets, Jewellery, and
other Objects connected with the Funeral Rites
of the Ancient Egyptians.**

WITH 8 *PLATES AND* 131 *ILLUSTRATIONS IN THE TEXT*

PRINTED BY ORDER OF THE TRUSTEES.

1904.
[*All rights reserved*]

THIS Guide contains a description of the pre-dynastic and archaic antiquities, portrait statues, and figures of the gods, tools, implements and weapons, scarabs, amulets, jewellery, porcelain objects of all kinds, furniture, and other miscellaneous objects connected with the Funeral Rites of the Ancient Egyptians, dating from B.C. 4500 to A.D. 250.

With the view of making the important and comprehensive collection of scarabs exhibited in the Fourth Egyptian Room more useful to collectors, for purposes of comparison and verification, the cartouches containing the names and prenomens of all the principal kings who are commemorated on scarabs have been given in hieroglyphic type, together with transliterations into English letters.

The visitor should note that the descriptions are numbered according to the numbers painted in red on the top left-hand corners of the labels and plinths.

In the preparation of this Guide I have been helped by Mr. H. R. Hall, M.A., Assistant in the Department.

E. A. WALLIS BUDGE.

DEPARTMENT OF EGYPTIAN AND ASSYRIAN
ANTIQUITIES, BRITISH MUSEUM,
June 11, 1904.

LIST OF PLATES

AND

ILLUSTRATIONS IN THE TEXT.

—

I.—PLATES.

II.—ILLUSTRATIONS IN THE TEXT.

THE GODS AND GODDESSES OF MEMPHIS.

THE GODS OF THE COMPANY OF OSIRIS.

THE EGYPTIAN ALPHABET.

𓄿	A		𓉗	H
𓇋	A		𓎛	H
⟋	A		𓐍	KH
𓏭 or \\	I		—•— or 𓊃	S
𓅱 or ☉	U		𓈙	SH
𓃀	B		𓎡	K
𓊪	P		𓈎	Q
𓆑	F		𓎼	K
𓅓 or ⟷	M		𓏏	T
∿∿∿ or 𓈖	N		𓂧	Ṭ or DH
⟷ or 𓂋	R and L		𓇋 or 𓍿	TH
		𓆓	TCH	

A GUIDE

THIRD AND FOURTH EGYPTIAN ROOMS.

THIRD ROOM.

THE collections of Egyptian antiquities exhibited in this room are of a miscellaneous character, and the greater number of them illustrate in a very important manner the funeral ceremonies of the ancient Egyptians, and afford us an idea of the contents of the tombs of the best periods of dynastic civilization. The oldest objects here displayed will be found in **Table-Cases L and M,** where is exhibited a valuable collection of **predynastic antiquities,** which date from the latter part of the Neolithic Period, before B C. 4500, and from the time of the first six dynasties. They should be examined in connexion with the Predynastic and Archaic Egyptian antiquities exhibited on the **Landing of the North-West Staircase,** and with the magnificent group of early jars in stone of many varieties in **Wall-Cases 194–197** of the Fourth Egyptian Room. At the west end of the Third Room are the **mummies of sacred animals** and birds ; at the east end is a fine group of **funeral chests,** etc, from B.C. 2600 to the Roman Period ; on the north side are **sepulchral boats,** painted and inscribed wooden **stelæ,** and a very fine collection of

B

typical portrait figures of Egyptian kings, officials, priests, etc, from B.C 4000 to A D 100; and on the south side is, perhaps, the largest and most representative collection of figures of Egyptian gods in the world   A good series of weapons, tools, and implements of various kinds is to be seen in Table-Cases B and K, and an extremely interesting group of frescoes from Egyptian tombs of the XVIIIth dynasty is in Cases D and I   The art of writing in all its branches is illustrated by the palettes, ink-wells, coloured earths, pens, papyrus, and the drafts of literary compositions in the hieratic character in Table-Case C.   Fine specimens of Egyptian linen work, which date from the first portion of the XVIIIth dynasty, about B.C 1700, and come down to so late a period as A D 900, are exhibited in Table-Cases E and J, and the rare example of silk-work (No 25) in Table-Case J is of special interest   In Table-Case H are selections from the figures of gods in gold, silver, and bronze, and several specimens of fine metal work inlaid in gold ; with these are exhibited figures of Egyptian sacred animals, e.g., an Apis Bull (No 37,448), with his characteristic marks, and a rock-crystal figure of the hippopotamus goddess Thoueris (No. 24,395), which date from the XIIth dynasty, or earlier   Of the series of glass vessels the most important are those of Thothmes III. (No 4762) and Amen-hetep II. (No. 36,342)   The Egyptian wig and the reed-case in which it was found are objects of great rarity   Of interest too are the funeral offerings, which consist of pomegranates, figs, dates, and raisins, crushed wheat, or barley, bread cakes, ornamental pastry (e.g., a cake in the form of a crocodile's head, No 5362), and a duck, and bread cakes (No 5340), and reed stand.   On Cases F and G is mounted a series of reproductions of all the important vignettes of the Book of the Dead as found in the Papyrus of Ani.   This work was written at Thebes, about B C 1450, for the scribe Ani, who held the important office of Registrar for the offerings made at Thebes and Abydos, and is the fullest and finest illustrated funeral papyrus known   The first section of the papyrus was probably written by Ani himself.   One of its most interesting chapters, the 175th, of which only one other copy, and that imperfect, is extant. is important because it

PLATE I.

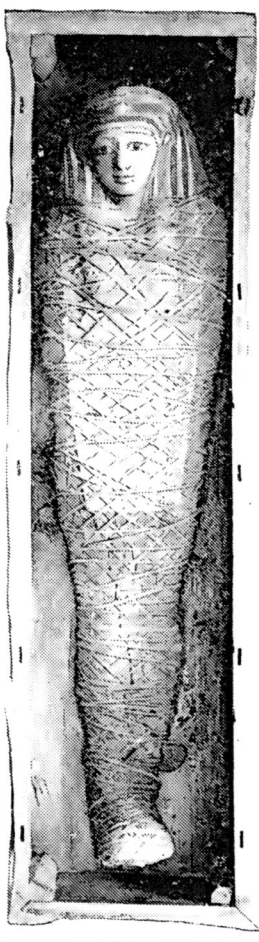

Coffin and mummy of the Christian period, about A.D. 400.
[No. 24,800.] (See page 3.)

contains a definite assertion concerning the Egyptian belief in immortality. In answer to the question asked by Ani, "How long shall I live"? the god Thoth replies: "It hath been decreed that thou shalt live for millions of millions of years, a life of millions of years."

CASE GG. 1. Roughly made coffin with mummy of **Khensu-Tehuti** 𓅬 𓏏 𓆓 𓊹, the son of Saipem (?), a singer, enclosed in a painted cartonnage case. On the outside of the coffin are figures of the goddess Nut and the four children of Horus. About A.D. 200 [No. 6599]

No. 2. Wooden coffin with vaulted cover containing the mummies of a Greek or Roman lady and her three children On one end of the coffin is represented the mummy of the deceased lying upon its bier in a boat, protected by Isis and Nephthys; and at the other end the deceased and her soul offer incense to Osiris in the presence of Isis and Nephthys. About A.D. 250 [No. 29,783.]

CASE HH. 1, 2. Two mummies of Greek or Roman ladies wrapped in linen shrouds ornamented with portraits of the deceased, and with rough copies of ancient Egyptian symbols and figures of the gods About A.D. 100. From Thebes [Nos. 6709, 6712.]

No 3. Rectangular wooden coffin containing a mummy with gilded and painted cartonnage case, the swathing is in a late style. This mummy is the most modern in the Collection About A.D. 400. From Upper Egypt **(See Plate I** ; [No. 24,800.]

TABLE-CASE A. Here is exhibited a large collection of **sandals** and **shoes** which belong to the period that falls between B.C. 1600 and A D 200 The greater number of them are made of papyrus, of various degrees of thickness, a few are of wood, and the remainder are made of leather of various kinds, chiefly gazelle skin The leather sandals and shoes are of the Roman and Coptic periods. The most interesting are :—

No. 1. Papyrus sandals, with painted toes, for ceremonial use. [No. 36,201.]

No. 4   Pair of large papyrus sandals with side flaps: the toes are painted, and, curving backwards, are fastened to the latchets.   [No. 4464.]

No 7   Pair of papyrus sandals, elaborately plaited, with painted toes and thick latchets.   From Memphis (Sakkára?)   Presented by Dr Gideon Mantell, 1843
[No. 4456]

Nos 9, 10.   Two pairs of thick, elaborately plaited, sandals with rounded toes; in No 9, part of the papyrus toe strap still remains   [Nos. 4424, 4425, 4434, 4435.]

No 16   Thickly plaited papyrus sandal, with painted turned up toe, and latchet and the strap complete   Well preserved   [No 4451.]

No 18   Pair of finely plaited papyrus sandals, with thick padding ; on the upper part the plaiting is horizontal, and on the lower part cross-hatched.   [Nos 4420, 4421]

No 21   Sandal made of palm fibre   Presented by the Trustees of the Christy Collection, 1865.   [No. 36,209]

No 22   Papyrus sandal, with flat heel attached.
[No 4446]

No 28.   Papyrus sandal for a baby   [No 22,000.]

No 29   Pair of child's sandals, with latchets.
[No. 36,217.]

No 32   Pair of sandals, made to the shape of the foot, carefully woven of a fine fibrous material ; they were held on the feet by means of a double cord, which was fastened in the sandals at a point near the joining of the first and second toes, and passed round the ankles.   Presented by Dr Gideon Mantell, 1843.   [Nos 4418, 4419.]

No 39   Pair of red and green leather sandals, with painted toes.   They were kept on the feet by means of a strap which passed over the instep, and was fastened by the heel.   XIXth dynasty.   [Nos 4397, 4398]

No 41   Red and green leather sandal for the left foot, with a flat covering for the instep, ornamented with green leather hollow work.   [No 36,200]

No. 42.   Heavy leather boot, of a late period
[No. 4415]

No. 43   Pair of white leather sandals, with tooled ornamentation.   [Nos 4377, 4378.]

Nos. 45, 46   Pair of wooden sandals, painted with dotted patterns in black on a white ground.
[Nos. 12,551, etc]

No. 49.   Pair of model sandals, which formed a sepulchral offering made in a tomb.   [Nos 36,215, 36,216]

No. 57   Pair of leather shoes for a child, with forestraps.   From Thebes.   Greek period
[Nos. 4402, 4403]

No. 65   Leather shoes, with embroidered ornament in the form of a rosette over the toe   Coptic period
[No 4416]

No. 67   Pair of leather slippers, with gilded leathern tongued ornamentation over the toes.   Late Roman period
[No. 20,942]

No 68   Pair of black leather shoes, with turned-up sides, ornamented with gilded leather.   At the toes are tassels formed of various coloured silks.   [No. 32,604]

No. 73   Pair of red and green leather sandals for a child.   [No 4386]

No. 84.   Pair of fine, green leather shoes, for a child. From Thebes.   Greek period.   [Nos. 4408, 4409.]

No. 85   Fragment of a white leather sandal, with an inscription in hieratic stating that it was made for a deceased person called Iuf   XVIIIth dynasty.   [No 36,196.]

No 91   Part of a leather sandal, stuffed with hair. From Thebes.   Presented by Sir J. G. Wilkinson, 1835.
[No 4394]

No. 92   Large leather garter   Roman period.
[No 21,719.]

TABLE-CASE B. In this case are grouped several series of Egyptian **arms** and **weapons**; the earliest date from the time of the IIIrd or IVth dynasty, and the latest belong to the Roman period.   The most important are : —

Nos. 1–3.   Iron axe-heads of uncertain date
[Nos. 36,288, 36,775, 20,762]

No. 4.   Bronze **axe-head**, incised with the figure of a boat, an inscription of two lines in hieroglyphics, and the cartouche of **Amen-ḥetep II.** 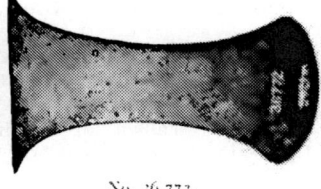   XVIIIth dynasty.   [No. 37,447.]

No. 5.   Bronze **axe-head** inscribed with the cartouches of **Kames,** a king of the XVIIth dynasty.   Presented by the Rev. W. J. Sparrow-Simpson, M.A., 1875.   [Nos. 36,772.]

No. 37,447.   No. 36,772.

No. 6.   Cast of a similar axe-head of **Kames,** in the possession of Sir John Evans, K.C.B.   [No. 36,810.]

Nos. 7-18.   A collection of fine bronze axe-heads of various types and periods.   [Nos. 6050, etc.]

Nos. 19, 20.   Two models of axe-heads in bronze.
[Nos. 6073, 6074.]

Nos. 21, 22.   Two bronze heads of battle-axes.
[Nos. 6051, 30,087.]

No. 26.   Bronze halbert blade.   [No. 27,493.]

Nos. 27-29.   Three large bronze ceremonial **halbert** blades, of crescent shape, riveted on to a bronze shaft, in which wooden handles were fitted.   A portion of the handle may be seen in No. 29.
[Nos. 36,776, 32,204, 32,203.]

No. 30.   Bronze **axe-head** fastened to the original handle by thongs of gazelle skin ; on the blade is the prenomen of **Thothmes III.**

[No. 36,770.]

Nos. 31, 32.   Two bronze models of axe-heads, fastened into original wooden handles by means of strips of linen.
[Nos. 6058, 6059.]

No. 33.   Painted wooden **model** of an **axe.**
[No. 6069.]

No. 34.   Bronze axe-head, set in its original wooden handle; in the hollow-work of the axe-head is the figure of a horseman riding over a plain. The leather thongs are covered with bitumen.
[No. 36,766.]

No. 35.   Hollow-work bronze axe-head ; scene, two bulls fighting.
[No. 36,764.]

No. 36.   Cast of a hollow-work axe-head ; scene, a lion chasing a gazelle. The original is in the possession of the Marquess of Bath.   [No. 36,811.]

No. 37.   Flint dagger, in its original wooden handle, with fragments of its original leather sheath.   [No. 22,816.]

Nos. 38, 39.   Two bronze ribbed **dagger-blades.**   [Nos. 36,308, 30,086.]

Nos. 40 and 43.   Two bronze dagger blades, of spatular shape. On No. 43 is incised a scene with a bird flying over plants.   [Nos. 32,211, 27,392.]

Nos. 41, 42.   Two bronze ribbed **spear-heads,** with tangs.

No. 22,816.

[Nos. 36,306, 36,307.]

No. 44.   Bronze dagger, set in an ivory handle made in the form of a papyrus sceptre.   [No. 30,734.]

No. 45.   Bronze **dagger,** set in a handle which is gold plated, and has a band of spiral decorations.   XVIIth or XVIIIth dynasty.   [No. 36,769.]

Nos. 46, 47.   Bronze dagger-blades or swords, with hollow-work handles, perforated to receive the rivets of the ivory or gold plates which were fastened to them.
[Nos. 26,261, 34,263.]

Nos 48, 49 Two bronze daggers, with handles of similar workmanship, in No. 49 the ivory inlay is wanting from the handle   [Nos 5425, 30,463]

Nos 50 54 Five bronze daggers, the handles of which were inlaid and riveted; the ends terminate in crescent-shaped pieces of ivory XVIIIth dynasty

[Nos. 30,732, etc.]

No 55 **Model** wooden **dagger.**   [No. 15,785]

No 56 Large wooden **box** containing a number of **reed arrows,** having square **flint heads.** From Kûrna Presented by the late Sir A Wollaston Franks, K C B, 1887

[No 20,648]

No. 57 **Wooden scabbard** for a dagger.

[No 5428]

No. 58 Green **stone dagger,** fashioned in modern times from a predynastic green schist or slate object

[No 30,090]

Nos. 60, 61 Two heavy stone objects; **polishers.** From Philæ   [Nos. 36,299, 36,300.]

No. 62 Portion of a bronze **sword-blade.**

[No 36,768]

No 63 Iron **spear-head.**   [No 36,765]

Nos 64, 65 Bronze **ferrules,** split and perforated

[Nos. 29,187, 29,188]

Nos 66-76 Bronze spear and **javelin-heads.**

[Nos 5421, etc]

No. 77 Bronze spear-head.   [No 36,822]

Nos. 78, 79. Iron **socketed spear-heads.**

[Nos 5423, 23,943.]

No 80. Iron **javelin-head, tanged.**   [No. 20,905]

Nos 81-94. Bronze **arrow-head, tanged,** some having barbs.   [Nos 5457, etc]

No. 95. Barbed and tanged arrow-head of iron.

[No 36,803]

Nos 95 112. Socketed arrow heads of bronze, of various periods   [Nos. 36,795, etc]

Nos 119-122   Lower ends, in bronze, of **ceremonial standards.**   [Nos. 35,907, etc.]

Nos 123-125.   Bronze **fish-hooks.**
[Nos. 15,931, etc.]

Nos 126-139.   Bronze **armour scales,** with metal pegs.   [Nos. 21,699, etc.]

No 140.   Long bronze ferrule.   [No. 32,582.]

No 141.   Copper, or bronze, **sling bullet.**
[No 37,930.]

No. 142.   **Sickle-shaped** iron **knife.**   [No 23,555.]

No 144.   Sickle-shaped bronze knife.   [No. 24,637.]

Nos. 145-153   Bronze **halbert blades.**   XVIIIth or XIXth dynasty.   [Nos 32,210, etc]

No. 154   **Socketed iron adze** or chisel-head.
[No. 36,289.]

Nos 155-166.   Socketed **adze, axe,** and **chisel-heads,** in copper and bronze.   [Nos. 6070, etc.]

Nos. 167-185.   A fine series of flat bronze axe-heads, many of which are perforated with several holes for the leather lacings which attached them to wooden handles. Of special interest is No. 166   Nos. 174, 177, 180, 183, 185 belong to the period of the Ancient Empire.
[Nos. 32,205, etc.]

No. 186.   Semicircular, flat axe-head, let into a wooden handle and fastened at the top by a bronze bolted ferrule, XVIIIth dynasty   [No. 30,083]

No. 187.   Bronze hollow-work ornamental axe-head. Scene, a bird perched on a papyrus plant.
[No. 24,636.]

No. 188   A set of three **model axe-heads,** with ears for insertion in wooden handles   [Nos 15,683-15,685]

Nos 189, 190.   Two bronze **adze blades.**
[Nos. 29,429, 26,430.]

No 191.   **Cast** of a magnificent **socketed bronze spear-head,** in the possession of Sir John Evans, K C.B On the blade are inscribed the name and titles of **Kames,** a king of the XVIIth dynasty, about B.C. 1700. Presented by Sir John Evans, K.C.B.   [No 36,808.]

No. 192   A leather **strap**, a portion of a soldier's equipment.   [No 5414.]

No. 193.   Leather **belt**, with embossed ornamentation, and carefully sewn.   Late period.   [No 36,778.]

No 194.   Leather strap, with embossed ornamentation and thongs.   [No 23,347.]

Nos 195–199. **Reed-arrows**, with bronze heads, which have been fastened on with strips of linen. No 196 is noteworthy.   [Nos 12,552, etc]

No. 200.   A collection of reed arrows, with flint heads.
                                        [Nos 5433, etc.]

No. 201   A bronze **kherp** sceptre ⌇ , XIIth dynasty
                                        [No 22,842]

No 202   Bronze **khepesh** ⌐ sword   [Presented by the Egypt Exploration Fund, 1887   [No 27,490.]

No 203   Curved bronze **scimitar**. A fine specimen
                                        [No 26,263.]

No 204   Fragment of a **linen cuirass** of a soldier. From Sakkâra.   [No. 37,124.]

No 205.   A **roll of leather**.   [No. 5399.]

No. 207. **Bronze tool** or implement with a cutting edge, having recurved ends The handle terminates in a goat's head.   [No 5466.]

TABLE-CASE C. In the upper portion of this Table-Case is exhibited a long and important series of slices of calcareous stone, and wooden boards plastered with lime, inscribed chiefly in the hieratic character with **drafts of literary compositions, hymns, school exercises**, etc , and with **sketches** made to scale of hieroglyphics, figures of kings, gods, etc These objects belong to various periods, but the greater number of them date from the XVIIIth, XIXth, and XXth dynasties, *i e*, from B.C. 1600 to B.C. 1100, and were found in tombs at Thebes. The most noteworthy are :—

Nos. 1, 5. Coloured representations of deceased persons adoring **Mer-seker,** the lady of the desert and goddess of the tombs at Thebes. [Nos. 8508, 8510.]

No. 4. Figure in outline of a queen (**Nefert-iti,** wife of **Khu-en-Aten ?)** nursing a child ; below is a figure of an Asiatic slave (?), with curiously dressed hair, holding a mirror. [No. 8506.]

No. 7. Plastered board, inscribed on both sides in hieratic with a series of sentences, extracts, etc, from literary works, it is perforated at one end, and was intended to be hung up in a school as a copy from which pupils might work. [No. 5645.]

No 8. Slab inscribed in hieratic with directions for building a royal tomb. [No. 5629.]

No. 10. Working scale-drawing for a bas-relief or statue of King **Thothmes III.** ; on one side is a series of **trial sketches** of hieroglyphics [No. 5601.]

No. 13. Plastered board inscribed with a copy, in the hieratic character, of a number of the rhetorical " Instructions " of Khā-kheper-Rā-senb, surnamed Ānkh, a famous author of the XIIth dynasty. This copy was made in the XIXth dynasty. [No. 5646.]

No. 17. Slice of limestone with a figure of the god Amen-Rā in relief ; he is called " king of the gods, lord of heaven, prince of Thebes " ; from the Tombs of the Kings. [No. 2.]

No. 18. Limestone slab with two figures of the god Osiris on obverse, and portions of six lines of hieratic on the reverse. [No. 8505.]

No 19. Slab of limestone inscribed in hieratic with five lines of a metrical composition , the members of the phrases are marked by red dots. [No. 5632.]

No. 20. Plastered board inscribed in hieratic with a number of sentences, probably written as a **school exercise.** Among the sentences occurs a series of names of persons and countries described in the text as " copying the

names of Keftiu." " Keftiu " is a geographical expression and means " Hinder-lands," *i.e*, the southern coast of Asia Minor and the Island of Crete. This copy was made at the end of the XVIIIth dynasty, when the Egyptians were in close communication with the inhabitants of the northern Mediterranean coast   [No. 5647.]

No 21. Slab of limestone inscribed in hieratic with a draft of a **legal document,** which refers to a robbery of weapons from the Royal Arsenal by the Chief of the Treasury, in the time of the XXth dynasty; the name of a royal tomb is given   [No 5631.]

No. 22 Slab of limestone inscribed in hieratic with a draft referring to the alterations which were made in the tombs of the parents of the writer by Thothmes, governor of the Thebaid , the original **grant of land** for the tombs had been made by King Amen-hetep III. The draft is dated in the seventh year of **Heru-em-heb,** king of Egypt, about B.C 1400.   [No 5624]

No 23. Portion of a plastered board inscribed in hieratic with a list of persons, objects, and numbers

[No 29,512.]

No. 26 Model for a large relief of **Rameses II.,** with the royal cartouches , on the back, in relief, is a figure of **Ketesh,** a goddess of Semitic origin. This object is probably an exercise of a sculptor's pupil.   [No 308.]

No. 27 Scale model of a head for a bas-relief

[No. 14,401.]

No 30. Limestone fragment inscribed with a portion of a text relating to a robbery of food   [No. 5637.]

No. 31 Slab inscribed with a portion of a text in linear hieroglyphics, which somewhat resemble their hieratic forms.   [No 5640]

No 33 Slab inscribed on both sides, in hieratic, with a portion of a document relating to the same matter as that referred to in No 22.   [No 5625.]

No 35 Limestone slab inscribed in hieratic with a portion of a Chapter (XLII.) from the Book of the Dead.

[No. 29,555.]

No 36. Limestone slab inscribed on both sides with a text in the demotic character.   [No. 29,511.]

No 38. Limestone slab inscribed on both sides with a list of personal properties and valuations of the same

[No 5633.]

No 39 Limestone slab with the heads of two kings, a winged lion, with the **head of Bes** in relief, on the reverse are figures of the birds 𓅬, 𓅭, in relief. This object is the exercise of a sculptor.   [No 13,324.]

No. 41. Slab inscribed in hieratic with a draft of some of the "**Instructions**" of **Amen-em-hāt I.**, king of Egypt, about B C. 2500, which were addressed to his son Usertsen This copy was written either under the XVIIIth or XIXth dynasty.   [No. 5638]

No. 42. Rough slab with a hieratic draft of an inscription, made under the Middle Empire.   [No 5641.]

No 43. Portion of a sepulchral stele, inscribed with parts of two lines of hieroglyphic text, and with four lines of demotic written in ink.   [No. 5650]

No 45. Portion of a slab inscribed in hieratic with the record of a series of **observations of the** "**star** of the waters," apparently one of the thirty-six Dekans, or Zodiacal Stars, from the fifth day of Phamenoth to the seventh day of Paoni, of the third year of the reign of a king whose name is not given   XIXth dynasty (?).   [No 5635.]

No 46. Slab inscribed in hieratic with a list of objects and their values, the purchase of a bull is mentioned

[No 5649]

No. 47 Fragment of a vase, *i.e.*, an ostrakon, inscribed in hieratic with an inventory or **list of objects,** with their quantities and values   [No 5643.]

No 48 Portion of a baked clay brick, or tablet, incised in hieratic with a part of the text of the CLIst Chapter of the Book of the Dead, which mentions the god *Khas* (?)

[No 29,547]

No. 51   Slab inscribed on both sides in hieratic with copies of a number of laudatory remarks on the profession of the scribe in Egypt ; they form part of the text commonly known as the "**Hymn in praise of learning**"

[No 29,550]

No 52   Slab inscribed in hieratic with the draft of a **hymn** in praise of Amen-Rā, the great god of Thebes

[No 29,559]

No 55   Slab inscribed in hieratic with the draft of a **metrical composition** of a religious character

[No 5639]

No 56   Slab inscribed in hieratic with part of a **letter,** or memorandum, of objects delivered to the police of western Thebes on the thirteenth of the month Paoni.

[No 5630]

No 57   Slab, with rough figure of the god **Åmen-Rā** traced upon it in outline   [No 1]

No 59   Limestone fragment, with two rows of hieroglyphics inscribed upon it in ink   Ptolemaic period.

[No 29,552]

No. 60   Limestone slab inscribed on both sides in hieratic with a **list of the articles of food,** etc , which were issued for the service of the gods Horus, Thoth, Hathor, and Mut, in the reign of a king called Amen-hetep

[No. 29,560]

No. 61   Limestone slab inscribed in hieratic with a **draft of the orders** issued by an officer of the palace of Amen-hetep III to Sebek-hetep, priest of Bast, or Sekhet, relating to the offerings, or supplies, for the service of the king's tomb.   [No 5627]

Section 1 of this Table-Case contains a collection of scribes' **palettes** of various periods. The palette is formed of a rectangular piece of wood provided with a number of hollows round an oval, in which the various coloured inks, or paints, were placed   The ink or colour was traced on the papyrus or other object by means of reed pens, which were kept in a hollow sunk longitudinally in the other portion

of the palette. The most interesting of the palettes here
exhibited are :—

No 1. Wooden palette of **Ba-nefer** [hieroglyphs],
a scribe of the royal granaries, and religious official, who
flourished in the reign of **Pepi II.**, king of Egypt, about
B.C. 3200.   [No. 12,782.]

No 2. Palette inscribed with the prenomen of
Áāḥmes I., the first king of the XVIIIth dynasty, about
B.C. 1700, [hieroglyphs].   [No 12,784.]

No. 3. Wooden palette of **Rā-meri** [hieroglyphs], with
a mention of the scribe **Tununa** [hieroglyphs] :
the deceased flourished in the reign of Thothmes IV.,
B.C 1470.   [No 5512.]

No 4 Wooden palette of the "scribe Pa-mer-ahau, of
renewed life," [hieroglyphs]. On the upper
portion is a cartouche with the inscription, "Beautiful god,
Neb-Maāt-Rā, beloved of Thoth, the lord of divine words."
The owner of the palette, we thus see, was employed in the
service of **Amen-ḥetep III.**, king of Egypt, B.C 1450.
                                              [No. 5513.]

No 5 Green slate palette of Amen-mes [hieroglyphs], a
scribe in the service of **Seti I.**, king of Egypt, about
B.C. 1370. On the upper part is a scene in which the
deceased is represented in the act of worshipping Osiris.
                                              [No 12,778.]

No. 6. Wooden palette of a scribe who lived in the
reign of **Rameses II.**, B.C. 1330. Presented by Sir J.
G. Wilkinson.   [No. 5514.]

No. 7. Wooden palette of the royal scribe of the altar
of some god ; the name of the deceased is erased
                                              [No. 12,786.]

No 10. Steatite palette, with an inscription of the royal scribe **Sa-Ámen.** Modern imitation

[No. 36,826.]

No 11. Stone model of a palette.   [No. 5525.]

No 13. Portion of a wooden palette inscribed with a funeral text addressed to the god Sebek, who is asked to give the "breath of life" to the double of the deceased, whose name is broken away.   [No. 5516.]

Section 2.

No. 17   Green slate palette of **Uáái** ⌇⌇ 𓂝 𓏤, inscribed with an address to Osiris, Thoth, and Sesheta, and a prayer for sepulchral offerings.   [No. 12,779.]

No 18. Wooden palette of the chief scribe **Ptaḥ-mes** 𓁟𓋴𓏤𓈖𓏤, XIXth dynasty. On the lower part are a few words in hieratic.   [No. 5515.]

No. 23. Fragment of a model of a palette, with hieroglyphics inlaid in lapis-lazuli   [No. 24,576.]

No. 28. Wooden palette, inscribed in hieratic.

[No. 5524.]

No 30. Wooden **box for** a pair of **small scales,** with sunk divisions in which the weights were placed. Coptic period.   [No. 26,845.]

Section 3 of this Table-case contains specimen rolls of **blank papyrus** ready for writing upon, to give the visitor an idea of the appearance of papyrus when new. By the side of them is a sheet of modern Sicilian papyrus made from the variety of the papyrus plant which grows at Syracuse Here, too, are exhibited specimens of **clay seals,** with impressions of names in hieroglyphics upon them, for attaching to papyri (Nos. 42–52), and also a number of thick **reed pens** of the Roman period, which are identical with those used at the present time in the East for writing Arabic, etc, and **reed cases** for holding the same

No 53 Specimens of blue **colour used in writing**; No 54, shell, used as a **paint pot,** with traces of black colour still remaining ; No. 55, a group of blue-glazed faïence ink or paint pots, mounted on a stand. XXVIth dynasty ; No. 56, basalt **slab for grinding paint,** which was made for **Tui** (⌐ ♀ ᛁᛁ), a wife of Rameses II., No. 57, basalt slab for grinding paint, with muller   Presented by Sir J. G. Wilkinson   [Nos. 5547, etc.]

No. 58. Bronze **ink pot,** with chain   Roman period.
[No. 5533.]

No. 59. Bronze scribe's **pen case.** Roman period.
[No. 36,827]

Nos. 60–68. **Inscribed** wooden **tesseræ,** or labels for mummies, etc. ·—

No. 60. Wooden tablet, inscribed in hieratic with a funeral text invoking the protection of *ushabtiu* figures on behalf of **Nesi-Khonsu,** the daughter of Ten-Hen-Tehuti XXth dynasty.   [No. 16,672.]

No. 61. Tessera with demotic inscription.
[No. 29,532.]

No. 62. Stone mummy tessera, inscribed in demotic.
[No. 29,533]

No. 63. Wooden mummy tessera, inscribed with the name of Pekysis, who died aged forty-six years   On the reverse is a figure of the god Anubis in black outline.
[No. 9895.]

No. 64. Tessera, inscribed with an account of the payment of 70 drachmæ to Tathautis and Taaibis, the daughters of Zminis, and others   Dated the seventeenth day of Epiph, in the thirty-first year of the reign of king Ptolemy II. Philadelphus, B.C. 255   [No. 29,530.]

No. 65. Mummy tessera of **Harpokration** and Taeouobsis   [No. 9894.]

No. 66. Mummy tessera of **Theano,** who died aged sixty-four years. She died on the twenty-eighth of Payni, in the twenty-second year of Commodus   [No. 2890]

No. 67. Mummy tessera of **Senphatres,** the Theban, the son of Cleopatra   At the end are the words, "To Tuphion," which show that the tessera was an address label attached to the mummy, which was sent by water from Thebes (?) to Tuphion.   [No. 29,531.]

C

No. 68   Mummy tessera of **Heras,** son of Herakleides, the agoranomos, or "inspector of the market"

[No 9891.]

No 69   Three wooden tablets, covered with wax, and inscribed in Greek (?), in the cover is a cavity for the stilus   Such tablets were only used by Greeks and Romans   [Nos. 26,801–26,803]

No 70   Wooden leaf, from a similar tablet, with inscription.   [No. 27,393.]

No. 71.   **Pugillaria,** or **wax tablets,** inscribed with part of a metrical inscription in Greek as a school exercise, the stilus and signet found with them are attached

[No 29,527.]

Nos. 72 75.   Prepared boards, inscribed with **school exercises** in Coptic ; chiefly of a religious character

[No. 5986 ff.]

Nos. 76–80   Ostraka, or potsherds, inscribed in demotic

[No. 5680 ff.]

Nos 81–84.   **Ostraka,** with bilingual inscriptions in Greek and demotic, containing **receipts,** or **acquittances,** for payments of taxes, and dating from the Ptolemaic period.   The most interesting (No 83) is a receipt for the payment into the office of Coptos of moneys due for the "apomoira," or tax on vines, and "eparourion," or land tax 2nd century B C.   [Nos. 12,623, etc]

No 85.   Receipt for money paid by **Aristoteles** on the sixteenth of Pakhanes (Pachons), in the thirteenth year of the reign of a king   4th–3rd century B C.   [No. 25,530]

No. 86.   Receipt for the **fish tax** of the thirty-first year of Ptolemy Philadelphus   B C. 255.   [No. 12,634]

No. 87.   Ostrakon, inscribed with a **school exercise,** consisting of lines 105–117, and 128–139 of the **Phœnissæ** of **Euripides.**   2nd century B.C   [No. 18,711]

No 88.   Receipts for five ardebs of corn, paid by **Bion** to the landowners Herakleides and his brethren as rent Dated in the fortieth year of Ptolemy IX   B.C. 130.   From Thebes.   [No. 25,910.]

No 89   Receipt for taxes paid to the office at Coptos by **Paniskos**. 2nd century B.C.   [No 29,691.]

No. 90.   Ostrakon, inscribed with a list of beginnings of **epigrams**. 2nd century B.C.   [No 25,736.]

Nos. 91, 92.   Ostraka, inscribed with lists of names and amounts in uncial characters.   1st century A D.
[Nos. 26,011, 31,631.]

No 93.   Receipt for eight drachmæ of silver paid for **poll tax** of the third year of **Gaius**, A.D. 39, by Petesoukhos, son of Pasenis.   [No 14,116.]

No. 94   Receipts for eight drachmæ of silver paid by **Tyrannos**, the blacksmith, to Rufonius, as **palm tax**. Dated in the fifteenth year of the reign of **Claudius**, A D. 54
[No. 5828.]

No 95.   **Receipt for taxes** paid by **Psametis**, son of Senpsaeris, to Sakhomneus and his partners.   Dated in the seventh year of **Nero**, A.D. 60   [No. 18,719.]

No 96   Receipt for **poll tax** paid by Phenophis, son of Pakhompauonnophis, in the sixth year of **Vespasian**, A.D. 74.   Signed by Melanthis.   [No 14,041.]

No 97.   Receipt for taxes paid in the third year of **Titus**, A D 81.   From Thebes.   [No. 19,464]

No. 98.   **Letter** from **Sabinus** to Ptolemaios (?) concerning the arrival of a large boat at Philæ.   From Dakkeh.   [No. 14,004.]

No 99.   **Receipt** for **port dues** paid by **Harpaesis**, the goose-herd, to Antonius Malchæus, the harbour master of Syene, from the thirtieth of Khoiak to the thirtieth of Pharmouthi, in the seventeenth year of **Trajan**, A.D. 114.
[No. 5970]

No 100.   **Letter** from **Salutarius** to Panōkh, informing him that he has ordered Paesis to send him some drugs. From Elephantine.   [No. 14,186.]

No 101.   Receipt for twenty drachmæ and two obols, paid by **Panubdis**, son of Petorzmêthês, to Herakleides and Isidoros, farmers of the taxes of the Holy Gate at

Syene, on the tenth Mesoré Dated in the fourth year of **Antoninus**, A.D. 141 The above sum was paid for the *kheironaxion*, or "trade tax" From Elephantine

[No 5801.]

No 102 Receipts for the payment of ten drachmæ, seven obols, for the poll tax, paid by the same person to the same tax-farmers in the following year. [No. 5802.]

No. 103 Receipt for the **palm tax** paid by **Petorz-méthès** to Phanophis, the tax-gatherer of Elephantine, in the nineteenth year of **Antoninus**, A D. 155.

[No 5813.]

No 104 Receipt, signed by **Julius Fronto**, in the third year of **Pertinax**, A D. 195 [No 14,022.]

No 105 Memorandum, or list of names of persons. 4th or 5th century A D.

No 106 **List of moneys** due to Bésodôra, Maria, Senemout, and Thatrea, on the twelfth day of Thoth, twenty-first day of Tybi, sixteenth day of Tybi, and tenth day of Mecheir respectively, of the sixth year of an Indiction 4th or 5th century A D. [No 19,945.]

No 108 Model of a man made of wax, papyrus, and hair, which was intended to be burned slowly in a fire in order to produce some evil effect upon the person whom it represented, or to provoke his love for the man or woman who had it made. The papyrus inside figures of this class is usually inscribed with a spell or charm in which the name of the person whom it is sought to influence is duly mentioned ; and it was believed by those who dealt in "black magic," both in Egypt and elsewhere, that if the figure was slowly burned in a fire whilst the curse or spell was recited in a certain tone and manner, either by a professional magician or by a private individual, under certain circumstances an irresistible effect was produced. The use of magical wax figures is often referred to in Egyptian literature, but the present example appears to be one of the first which has been recovered from Egypt It was found at Akhmim [No. 37,918]

STANDARD-CASE D. Contains a series of **frescoes** from Egyptian tombs of the XVIIIth dynasty from Thebes The scenes are painted upon a thin layer of plaster laid upon a backing of coarse mortar which covers the inequalites of the surface of the walls of the tomb. The scenes usually depicted on the tombs of the period are of two classes, and represent either the reception of envoys and tribute for the king by the deceased officials, or agricultural operations on their estates. Besides these we always find pictures of the deceased and his wife seated with tables of offerings before them. The tombs of this class were highly decorated with frescoes painted in bright colours, and the 100fs were generally ornamented with designs of a geometrical or floral character.

No. 1. Fresco from the **tomb of Sebek-ḥetep** at Shêkh ʻAbd al-Kûrna at Thebes. This scene represents the **presentation of tribute** by Semitic envoys from Rethennu, or Northern Syria, who offer vessels of gold, silver and bronze ; the vessels are of Egyptian type, and were probably of Phœnician workmanship. The last envoy in the upper register brings a tusk of ivory, which is provided with a case or cap of gold and bronze made in the form of the head of a goddess, surmounted by a hand. The last envoy in the lower register carries in his left hand a dish containing the head and neck (*protome*) of an eagle in gold. In the same register a man bears a red leather quiver on his right arm.　　　　　　　　　　　[No. 37,991.]

No 2. Painted fresco, representing a **table of funeral offerings,** such as was usually placed before a man of high rank The inscription in the left-hand corner contains a prayer to Rā, Seb, and the Great Company of the gods, for funeral offerings. On the right of the altar are the remains of a seated figure of the deceased, whose name is wanting, and on the left was the figure of his son, "the superintendent of the choir men of the god" (Åmen), who made the offerings, and was called **Mes.**　　　[No. 37,985.]

No. 3. Representation of an **ornamental lake,** or rectangular basin of water in a garden at Thebes, surrounded by palms, pomegranate trees, sycamores, and choice trees of an ornamental character The sides of the lake are fringed with reeds, and lilies grow in the waters, which are stocked with fish and water fowl   In the upper right-hand corner is a woman who stands by the side of a number of baskets of freshly gathered pomegranates and other fruit.

[No. 37,983.]

No. 4   Scene representing a **feast.** In the upper register are seated three Egyptian gentlemen and their wives, who are waited upon by male and female slaves, from whom they are accepting wine, flowers, and garlands. In the lower register are seated eight ladies, who are waited upon by a female slave who is bringing them wine ; to the right of this group is the first figure of a group of men, who are being waited upon by a male slave   To the left are two tables laden with delicacies.   [No. 37,986.]

No 5   Scene representing an Asiatic **bearing tribute,** a gold bowl, filled with small silver bowls, and a long metal vase, and driving before him two small horses.   Behind him is a woman carrying a vase in one hand and a child in the other.   [No. 37,987.]

No 6.   Scene representing the **inspection of a farm** by the overseer of an estate, who examines the crops and tastes the grain to see if it is ripe   Next are represented two chariots, each with its pair of horses and its charioteer   The horses in the upper register are restive, and are being held in tightly by their driver ; those in the lower register are feeding on the leaves of a tree, whilst their driver is resting in the chariot   [No. 37,982.]

TABLE-CASE E. Here is a large and miscellaneous collection of **wooden weapons,** sticks, stones, etc, and **tools and implements,** *e.g.,* **carriers' yokes, wool-combs, carders, spindles, spindle-whorls** of wood and ivory, bronze **needles, awls,** etc, as well as a representative collection of **linen fabrics,** both plain and ornamented, with fringes and embroidery, of various periods, from the beginning of the XVIIth dynasty, about B.C. 1700, to the Byzantine period, about A.D. 600   The most important objects are :—

No. 1.   **Fringed linen winding-sheet** or shroud, which belonged to a singing-woman of Queen **Āāhmes-nefert-ari**

⟨ 𓅬 𓏴 𓂋 𓈖 ⟩, called **Teḥuti-sat** 𓅓 𓅓 𓏏, about B.C. 1650. This very interesting object shows that the Egyptians were in the habit of marking the linen of the dead with indelible ink, it came from the famous hiding place of the royal mummies, Dêr el-Baḥari.

[No. 37,105]

No. 3. **Fringed mummy bandage**, with coloured thread woven at the ends, it measures 16 feet 10 inches in length   [No 6518]

No. 4. Large, coarsely woven **linen sheet**, with deep fringe.   [No. 37,101.]

No. 5. Finely woven **linen sheet**, dated in the fourth month of the season SHAT, of the 16th year of the reign of a king; it was probably intended by one of the kings of the XXIst dynasty for the re-dressing of the mummy of an earlier monarch   [No 6641]

No 6. Square of very finely woven linen, inscribed with the name of **Teḥuti-sat**.   [No 37,104

No 9. Portion of linen cloth, fringed, and ornamented with bands of blue thread   Presented by A Sussex Millbank, Esq   [No 6519]

No 10. Portion of a linen bandage, bleached by modern process.   Presented by Ch. Dodd, Esq., 1837.

[No 6524]

Nos. 11, 12. Portions of two bandages inscribed in a character half linear hieroglyphic and half demotic, with portions of the Saite recension of the Book of the Dead. Ptolemaïc period   [Nos 37,108, 6,644.]

No 13. Roll of fine linen inscribed with the cartouches of King **Piānkhi II., Seneferef-Rā** 𓈖 ⟨ 𓊨 𓈖 𓅭 𓋴 ⟩ 𓅭 𓏥 ⟨ 𓐍 𓊪 𓋴 ⟩ B C 700. At the bottom of the line of text is the date ⟨ 𓈖 𓏏 𓈖 ⟩   [No 6640.]

Nos. 14 17. Specimens of mummy **linen cloth** of the Roman period, ornamented with patterns, designs, etc., in coloured wool.   [Nos 18,199, 12,550, 37,107, 18,200]

Nos. 18–27. A group of fragments of **mummy cloths, grave shirts,** etc., many of them ornamented with figures and designs in purple wool. These belong chiefly to the Coptic period, A.D. 300 to A.D. 700, and come from the necropolis of Akhmim, which marks the site of Panopolis, a city which was famous for its linen industry. [Nos. 16,665, etc.]

Nos. 28–32. Mummy bandages of the Ptolemaïc and Roman periods. No. 28 is ornamented with a figure of the god Anubis; No. 30 has a hieroglyphic inscription; and Nos. 31 and 32 are specimens of linen which were dyed purple by the *Carthamus Tinctorius.* [Nos. 23,232, etc.]

Nos. 33–38. A **cap** made of ancient glazed faïence beads, and five bags made of wool and linen. Coptic period, A.D. 300–700. [Nos. 21,632, etc.]

Nos. 39–51. Specimens of **linen embroidered** with **figures of saints,** religious symbols, birds, etc.; they were originally sewn on mummy shirts of the Coptic period. No. 40 is part of a **band** or **stole,** embroidered with scenes from the life of Christ and various

No. 30,806.

saints. [No. 30,806.] Nos. 48–51 are four squares of linen worked with coloured figures of birds (doves?). In the corners of two are signs of crosses within wreaths ; one has the sign of the cross without a wreath, and the other has the old Egyptian sign for life, ⚥ *ānkh*, within a wreath. These facts show that the Coptic Christians confused the old heathen symbol ⚥ with the Christian cross.

[Nos. 22,867–22,870, etc.]

Nos. 52–55.   Hard wood **carding combs.**   From Akhmim.   [Nos. 18,182, etc.]

No. 22,868.

No. 58.   Carding **comb of ivory,** with annular ornaments.   [No. 26,740.]

Nos. 61–102.   A miscellaneous collection of bone, wood and ivory carding and other **reels, spindles, spindle-whorls,** and other implements used in weaving and carding flax and wool, chiefly from Akhmîm, and belonging to the Coptic period.   On Nos. 73 and 76 portions of the **linen thread** still remain.   [Nos. 6119, 6477, and 6480.]

No. 103.   A group of bronze **needles** and **pins,** Roman period.   [Nos. 12,267, etc.]

No 104. Butt end of a wooden **axe handle**, inscribed with the prenomen of a king **Rā-sekhem-seuatch-taui** (⊙ 𓀀𓏏𓏏), who probably reigned between the XIIIth and XVIIth dynasties, about B C 2000. The greater part of the handle was destroyed by fire.   [No 20,923]

No 105. Wooden *uas* **sceptre** 𓌂.   [No. 35,900]

Nos 106 108. Two wooden **bows**, with pointed ends.   [Nos. 5429 5431]

No 109. Wooden **club**, with a thick, heavy end.   [No 5465.]

Nos 110, 111. Two wooden **staves** for ceremonial use, with forked ends.   [Nos. 17,184, 5481]

No. 112. Portion of a **sceptre**, ornamented with bands of bark coloured red, black, and yellow.   [No 35,903]

No. 113. Portion of a **staff** inscribed with the name of its owner, **Pa-Shu-men** 𓏏𓃀𓇋𓏏𓏏𓐍𓏏, XXIst or XXIInd dynasty.   [No 5489]

Nos 114 116. Three wooden **yokes** for human shoulders.   [Nos 35,929, etc]

Nos 117, 118. Sticks or rules inscribed with the name of their owner, Per-pa-Rā ⊙𓏏𓏏𓐍𓏏.   [Nos 6034, 6035.]

No 119. **Stick** or measure, inscribed with the name and titles of its owner, **Bak-en-Mut** 𓏏𓏏𓐍𓏏; above the inscription are figures of Ptah and Amen   [No 24,388]

No 120. Round stick, with handle in the form of a papyrus bud, inscribed with the name of its owner, **Bak-en-suten-bi** 𓏏𓏏𓐍𓏏.   [No 5490]

On the floor of the case will be found a large, miscellaneous collection of **boomerangs**, staves, wands, and

wooden objects which were used ceremonially   Worthy
of note are two **oars,** the handles of which terminate in
heads of Anubis, from funeral barges (Nos 5505, 5506),
and the wooden **crutch** (No. 3593)

STANDARD-CASES F and G.   On each side of
these cases are exhibited a series of vignettes, and the
hieroglyphic texts of the accompanying chapters from the
Book of the Dead, as they appear in the **Papyrus of
Ani.**   The Papyrus of Ani was found at Thebes ; it
measures 78 feet by 1 ft 3 in., and is the longest known
papyrus of the Theban period , the inscribed portion of it
is complete   It was copied by three or more scribes, and
is composed of several sections which have been neatly
joined together.   The vignettes were drawn before the text
was written   The Papyrus of Ani is undated, and no facts
are given in it concerning the life of Ani, whereby it would
be possible to fix its exact place in the series of the illustrated papyri of the Theban period, to which it belongs
His full titles are, " Veritable* royal scribe, scribe and
accountant of the divine offerings of all the gods, the
governor of the granary of the lords of Abydos, scribe of
the divine offerings of the lords of Thebes "†   That he was
a favourite of his king is proved by the fact that he calls
himself, " beloved of the lord of the South and North," and
he declares that his king " loves him "   The name Ani
is an uncommon one   His wife, whose name
was **Thuthu**   , held the position of priestess
in the temple of Amen-Rā at Thebes.   The papyrus was
written probably between BC 1500 1400, and contains the
following chapters —

  1   Of coming forth by day.
  2   Of coming forth by day, and of living after death

* *I.e.,* Ani actually worked as a scribe, and the title was not
honorary

†

6. Of making the *ushabti* figure work in the under-world
8. Of passing through Amenta, and of coming forth by day.
9. Of passing through the tomb, and coming forth by day.
15A A hymn of praise to Rā when he riseth
15B A hymn of praise to Osiris Unnefer.
15c A hymn of praise to Rā in rising and setting
17. Of coming forth by day, of playing at draughts, of sitting in the Sekh hall, and of coming forth as a living soul.
18 Of the gods of localities. [Two copies of this chapter occur in the papyrus]
22 Of giving a mouth to Osiris Ani.
23 Of opening the mouth of Osiris Ani
24 Of bringing words of power unto Osiris Ani
26. Of giving a heart unto Osiris Ani.
27. Of not letting the heart be taken away from Ani
29 [Another chapter with the same title]
29B Of a heart of carnelian
30B Of not letting the heart of Osiris Ani be driven away
42 [Of repulsing slaughter in Suten-henen.]
43. Of not letting the head be cut off.
44 Of not dying a second time.
45 Of not suffering corruption.
46 Of not perishing, and of becoming alive
48. Of coming forth by day against foes
50 Of not entering in unto the block.
54 Of giving breath in the Underworld
55 Of breathing the air, and of having power over the water
56. [Another chapter with the same title]
57 Of not letting the soul be taken away.
74 Of walking with the legs, and of coming forth upon earth
77. Of changing into a golden hawk.
78. Of changing into a divine hawk.
80 Of changing into the god who giveth light
81A. Of changing into a lotus.

TABLE-CASE H. In the upper portion of this case are exhibited series of small but interesting antiquities which consist of **figures in gold, silver,** electrum, bronze,

---

* A facsimile of the Papyrus of Ani has been published by the Trustees of the British Museum (folio or half bound), price £2 10s., also the Egyptian Text, with interlinear transliteration and translation, a running translation, introduction, etc., half mor., 4to., price £1 10s.

crystal, and other rare stones, **glass vases, bowls,** bottles, etc. which illustrate the finer Egyptian work in these materials. Worthy of special note are :—

Nos. 1—4. Bronze kneeling **figures of kings** making offerings, XXVIth dynasty to the Ptolemaic period. No. 1 is from Tell-Gemayemi, and was presented by the Egypt Exploration Fund.
[Nos. 24,323, 36,297, 23,458, and 36,212.]

No. 5. Portion of a hollow-work amulet (**menát**) in bronze. The goddess represented is Hathor ; in the oval portion is a figure of a cow, which was the sacred animal of this goddess, and above it is the Hathor sistrum. Near the sistrum is the prenomen of Amen-hetep III.

No. 36,212.

in whose tomb the object was found.   [No. 20,760.]

No. 6. Group of **gilded bronze figures of gods.** In the centre is Isis, who is suckling Horus ; on her right stands Mut, and on her left Nephthys. In front are three uræi, the middle one, which represents Uatchet, wearing the crown of Lower Egypt. Ptolemaic period.
[No. 34,954.]

No. 7. Bronze figure of the god Nefer-Atmu, who wears a cluster of papyrus plants on his head. Roman period.   [No. 319.]

No. 8. Silver figure of the god Nefer-Atmu. XXVIth dynasty.   [No. 11,072.]

No 9   Bronze figure of the god Khonsu, wearing the disk and lunar crescent and horns; on the right of his head is the lock of Harpocrates, symbolic of youth. The figure is studded with gold, inlaid.   XXVIth dynasty.

[No. 29,410.]

No. 10.   Bronze figure of the god I-em-ḥetep, the Imouthês of the Greeks, seated and holding an unfolded roll of papyrus on his knees.   Ptolemaïc period.

[No. 27,357]

No. 11   Bronze figure of Amen-Rā, in the form of Amsu or Mın; he is sometimes styled in the funeral text, "the god of the lifted hand."   The god stands on a pedestal, which is inlaid in gold with mythological figures, winged uræi, etc. , beneath his feet are nine bows, signifying the god's sovereignty over the nine great foreign nations. Before him, ınlaid in gold, is the cartouche Ānkh-s-nefer-ab-Rā ⟮ 𓋹𓏤𓊖𓏤𓇳 ⟯.   The figure was dedicated by Aba 𓏏𓄿𓅆, the son of Abet 𓏏𓄿𓊹 ⌒, who was a scribe, and held the ecclesiastical dignity of *am khent* to the queen whose name is mentioned above   On the sides of the lower pedestal are figures of the Nile-god bearing trays of offerings, the god Shu supporting the solar boat, and the symbol of the unity of Egypt.   XXVIth dynasty

[No 42.]

No 12.   Bronze cat with eyes and double collar inlaid in gold.   [No. 22,927]

No. 13   The hawk of Horus, wearing the double crown, in hæmatıte.   [No. 26,251]

No. 14   Bronze human-headed hawk, emblematic of the soul, wearing the solar disk.   [No. 27,365]

No 15.   Lapis-lazuli pendant in the form of a figure of the goddess Isis suckling Horus ; on her throne is cut the emblem of life   [No. 35,089.]

No. 16   Hinged **bronze box**, inlaid in gold with the names and titles of a king of the XXVIth dynasty.   The sides were inlaid with panels of silver.   On the plaque in

the cover the king, inlaid in bright copper, kneels in
adoration before the cow of Hathor. From Thebes.
About B.C. 550.   [No 24,639.]

No. 17. Rare bronze and silver figure of Rā-Heru-
Khuti, *i e*, Rā-Horus of the two horizons ; as typifying the
god of the morning and the evening, the figure is provided
with two hawks' heads.   [No 15,675.]

No. 18. Portion of a hollow bronze cylinder with an
outer covering of gold overwork, representing a procession
of deities.   [No. 27,381.]

No. 19.   Gold figure of the goddess Bast, wearing
uræus   [No. 27,734.]

No. 20.   Gold figure of the goddess Mut, wearing the
double crown. Attached to the ring at the back of the
neck are two links of the chain by which it was worn.
Presented by Mrs. C. Ashley Dodd, 1900. [No 33,888]

No 21.   Gold figure of the god Thoth, holding the
utchat , or " symbolic eye."   Bequeathed by Dr J.
Anthony, 1895.   [No 23,426.]

No. 22. Gold figure of the moon-god Khonsu, hawk-
headed. Presented by Thomas Biddle, Esq , 1882.
                                               [No 38,006.]

No. 23. Electrum figure of the goddess Sati, XIIth
dynasty. From Dahshûr. About B.C. 2500.
                                               [No. 29,201.]

No. 23A. Electrum figure of a goddess, Nekhebet or
Mut(?), XIIth dynasty. From Dahshûr, B C. 2500.
                                               [No 29,202.]

No 24   Gold pendant, in the form of a staff surmounted by the head of the goddess Hathor. XXVIth
dynasty.   [No. 26,977]

No. 25.   Gold figure of the god Ptah   XXVIth
dynasty.   [No 26,976.]

No. 26. Gold figure of the god Rā and the silver
shrine in which it was found ; XXVIth dynasty. From
Tell Defna (Tahpanhes, or Daphnai). Presented by the
Egypt Exploration Fund, 1886.   [No. 38,005.]

No. 27.   Green slate figure of a hippopotamus; this animal was sacred to Hathor.   XXVIth dynasty
[No. 24,386]

No 28.   Lapis-lazuli ram; this animal was sacred to Amen-Rā, the king of the gods.   [No. 24,956]

No. 29.   Bronze ægis of Rā, inlaid with gold, from the bows of a sacred bark; on the front, inlaid in gold, is the cartouche (⊙ ⚱ ☥), the prenomen of Apries, king of Egypt, about B.C. 590.   Presented by Professor Petrie, 1885.   [No. 16,037.]

No. 30.   **Crystal figure** of the Hippopotamus-goddess **Ta-urt** (Thoueris), holding before her the emblem of magical protection ♀.   XIIth dynasty.   From Dahshûr(?).
[No. 24,395.]

No 31.   Carnelian figure of **Apet,** the goddess of Thebes.   From Karnak.   [No. 32,638.]

No. 32.   Bronze shrine inscribed with the cartouches of **Nekau,** a king of the XXVIth dynasty (Pharaoh Necho).
(⊙ ⚱ ☥) (☥ ⚱).   [No. 26,973.]

No. 33.   Bronze figure of Osiris, with elaborate crown.
[No 27,358.]

No. 34.   Bronze figure of the god Osiris, wearing plumes, and holding crook and flail, inlaid in gold; the god is enveloped in feather work, which is formed by the wings of the hawk god Horus.   [No. 24,718.]

No. 35.   Gilded bronze figure of Osiris, with inlaid obsidian eyes.   [No. 11,117]

No. 36.   Black steatite figure of the god Ptaḥ, gilded, with a bearded head of white stone inserted.   The inscription on one side of the throne reads, " Give a royal offering to the royal priest of Khāfrā," ⌐ △ 👄 ⌐ ⊙ 🏺 🔨.
The style of the hieroglyphics is ancient, and the head of the figure undoubtedly belongs to the period of the Old Empire.   This figure therefore dates, in all probability,

D

from the IVth or Vth dynasty, and is unique   From Memphis.   [No 35,088.]

No. 37.   Bronze figure of Ptah, inlaid in gold, with a feather work covering and tunic.   Roman period
[No 27,363.]

No. 38.   Green stone pendant, a hawk wearing the double crown.   [No. 27,724.]

No. 39.   Green stone ram-headed hawk, gilded
[No 27,370]

No. 40.   Electrotype of an **ægis of Bast,** inscribed with the names of a king and queen of the XXIInd dynasty (Uasarken and Teṭā-Bast)   The original is in the Museum of the Louvre.   [No 34,939.]

No. 41.   Fine bronze figure of Osiris, with the eyes, beard, and collar inlaid in gold ; this is the finest figure of the god in the collection.   [No. 35,268.]

No. 42.   Silver figure of the god **Åmen-Rā,** plated with gold   XXIInd dynasty.   [No. 6.]

No. 43.   Bronze **ape,** the companion of the god **Thoth,** inlaid with gold.   [No. 29,414.]

No. 44.   Gilded stone figure of Isis and Horus, on a pedestal, inscribed with the cartouches of **Psammetichus I. ;** it was dedicated on behalf of the royal tutor Pe-nub ⟨hieroglyphs⟩ the son of Nekht   XXVIth dynasty.
[No. 23,050.]

On the other side of this Table-Case will be found a collection of ancient **Egyptian glass ;** the earliest belongs to the XVIIIth dynasty, and the latest to the Roman period. Nos. 45 55 are examples of the beautiful opaque, variegated glass vases and bottles which were in use in the XVIIIth dynasty, No. 50 is inscribed with the **prenomen of Thothmes III.** ⟨hieroglyphs⟩ ; Nos. 57 59 are from the tomb of Åmenḥetep II , No. 59 being a very fine specimen of a variegated glass vessel ; No 60 is a **flat scarab,** for funeral purposes, in opaque blue glass, and No. 61 is an opaque blue

glass head-dress from a statue of the god Bes. [The fine flint object (No. 30,461), inscribed with the names of the royal scribe Tehuti-nefer and of the goddess Serqet, was found with the glass head-dress.] The other glass vessels here exhibited are of the well-known *lacrimarium*, or "**tear-bottle**" type, and belong to the Roman period. Near these are a number of fine specimens of Roman **millefiori**, or "thousand-flowered" glass panels for inlaying. Nos. 62 and 63 are slices of obsidian, and No. 64 is a portion of an **obsidian** figure of the goddess **Ta-urt**.

At the end of this section of the case is a group of interesting objects from tombs of the XVIIIth dynasty. These consist of:—1. A **wig**, probably intended for a lady of high rank; found at Thebes. 2. A **reed box** wherein the wig was found. 3. A glass tube for stibium, or **eye**

Egyptian Wig. No. 2560.   Wig-box. No. 2561.

paint, in the shape of a papyrus column. 4. A wooden **comb**, with double row of teeth. 5. A pair of small bronze **tweezers** for plucking out hair. 6. Bronze **mirror**, with a handle in the form of the head of the goddess Hathor. Behind these is a **stand made of reeds**, whereon are laid offerings of food for the *ka*, or "double," of the deceased

D 2

person, consisting of **two ducks** and **cakes of bread.**
This very interesting object dates from the period of the
XVIIIth dynasty, about B.C 1500

In the middle portion of this case are exhibited specimens of **foods** and **fruits** which were placed in the tombs
for the sustenance of the *ka*, or double, the greater number
belonging to the period of the XVIIIth dynasty. The
fruits consist of dates, *dûm* palm nuts, pomegranates, grapes,
castor-oil berries, etc., and the foods of:—1. A terra-cotta
bowl filled with **dried fish.** 2 A terra-cotta bowl filled with
crushed wheat, or barley, for making into cakes. 3. A
circular reed mat, or plate, with two **bread cakes.** 4.
Specimens of cakes and **pastry,** one in the form of a
crocodile's head, and another in that of a leaf. 5. Several
fragments of bread cakes. In three glass jars are exhibited
specimens of grain, **wheat, barley,** etc., which may be
ancient Egyptian.   It may be noted here that not
all specimens of **"mummy wheat"** are necessarily
ancient, for it has often happened that mummies intended
for exportation to Europe have been packed in modern
grain, which has commonly, but erroneously, been
held to be of ancient origin.   Specimens of wheat,
of the antiquity of which there is no doubt, are
known, and experiments have been carried out with
these at Kew Gardens, with the view of ascertaining
whether ancient Egyptian wheat, say 3000 years old,
would germinate or not; in every case the experiment
made by the officials at Kew Gardens was unsuccess-
ful, and as a matter of fact it is well known to
botanists that the wheat germ dies in a very few years.
The **bread baskets** here exhibited are contemporaneous
with the bread and grain which are in them, and are good
specimens of reed-plaiting.

On the floor of this case are exhibited massive stone
bowls, **mortars, kneading troughs, corn grinders,** etc.,
belonging to the period which lies between the XIIth
dynasty and the period of the Ptolemies The smaller pots,
with square lugs, are chiefly from foundation deposits.
Here may be noted a large red granite corn-grinder (No.
27,516), from Tell Gemayemi, presented by the Egypt
Exploration Fund, and some fine wood and **stone clamps,**

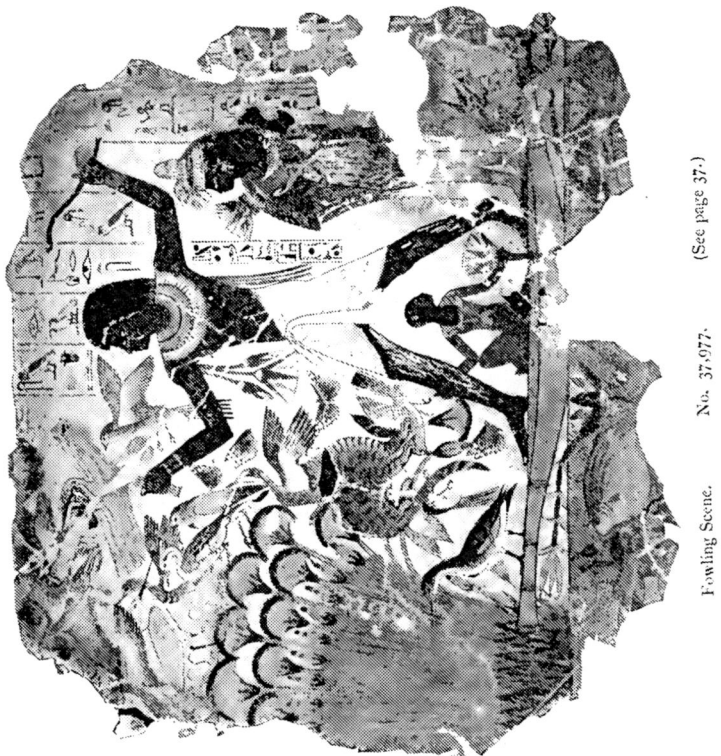

PLATE II.

Fowling Scene.   No. 37,977.   (See page 37.)

for binding together courses of masonry, inscribed with the prenomen of **Seti I.**, B.C. 1370.

STANDARD - CASE I. (Frescoes continued from Case D.)

No. 1. Scene representing **a feast** (continuation of No. 4, Case D). In the upper register are seated a number of gentlemen with their wives, holding flowers, and drinking wine, which is handed to them in cups by a female slave. In the lower register is a group of female musicians, who play on a double flute and clap their hands by way of marking time for two dancing girls who are entertaining the company. The lines of text above probably formed part of a song, and consisted of invocations to various gods to confer happiness upon the deceased and his friends.

[No. 37,984.]

No. 2. Figure of **Ȧmen-ḥetep I.**, King of Egypt, B.C. 1650, holding the crook and wearing the Atef crown.

[No. 37,993.]

No. 3. Figure of **Queen Aāhmes - nefert - ȧri**, the mother of Amen-ḥetep I., holding the flail, her face is painted black, to signify her apotheosis as goddess of the necropolis of Thebes. She wears the Hathor crown.

[No. 37,994.]

No. 4. Figure of the god **Osiris - Khent - Ȧmenti.** Nos. 2-4 are from the same tomb, and belong to the same period.

[No. 37,995.]

No. 5. **Fowling Scene** from the wall of a tomb. The deceased, accompanied by his wife and daughter, stands in a reed canoe in a marsh filled with large papyrus reeds, and is occupied in knocking down birds with a stick, which is made in the form of a snake. In front of him is his **hunting cat,** which has seized three birds, one with his hind claws, one with his fore claws, and one by the wings with his mouth. Numerous butterflies are represented, and the lake is well stocked with fish. The line of hieroglyphics at the back of the deceased indicates that the scene is supposed to represent the state of felicity which he will enjoy in the next world. **(Plate II.)**   [No. 37,977.]

No 6.   Scene representing the driving of a large **herd of cattle** for stocktaking purposes by the overseer or bailiff of a farm belonging to the deceased.   In the upper register we see the cattle being led before the scribe by hinds, one of whom kneels before him and kisses his feet.   In the lower register the cattle are divided into groups of five, and the text states that the scribe is making a detailed list of them.   The man with outstretched hand and arm is addressing a fellow hind who is talking to the scribe, and exhorting him to put his words clearly and quickly before the scribe.   (Plate III.)   [No. 37,976.]

No. 7.   **Farm scene** from the same tomb as No. 6, connected with the management of the poultry yard of the deceased.   In the upper register the seated scribe is preparing to make a **list of the geese**, which are being marshalled before him.   Below we see a group of goose herds with their flock, who are making obeisance before him, whilst one of their number places the birds in baskets.   The scribe has risen and is engaged in unrolling a new papyrus, whereon to inscribe his list.   The horizontal line of hieroglyphics above the geese contains an exhortation of one goose herd to another to "make haste," so that he may bring his flock before the scribe.   In front of the scribe is a red leather sack, or bag, in which he kept his clothes, etc, and round it is rolled the mat on which he sat.   **(Plate IV.)**   [No. 37,978.]

No. 8.   Procession of servants returning from a **hunting expedition** in search of food (?) ; one carries an antelope, and another two hares, and another bundles of corn.
                                             [No. 37,980.]

TABLE-CASE J.   In this case is exhibited a series of pieces of **linen** ornamented with patterns and designs, woven in coloured threads or worked in wools, which were formerly attached to **mummy-shirts** and **grave-clothes**.   In the dynastic period the bandages and swathings of the dead were not ornamented with embroidery or other needle work, and it was not until the Ptolemaïc period that the outer coverings of mummies were decorated with figures of gods and hieroglyphics painted in bright colours.   In the 3rd or 4th century after Christ it became the fashion

PLATE III.

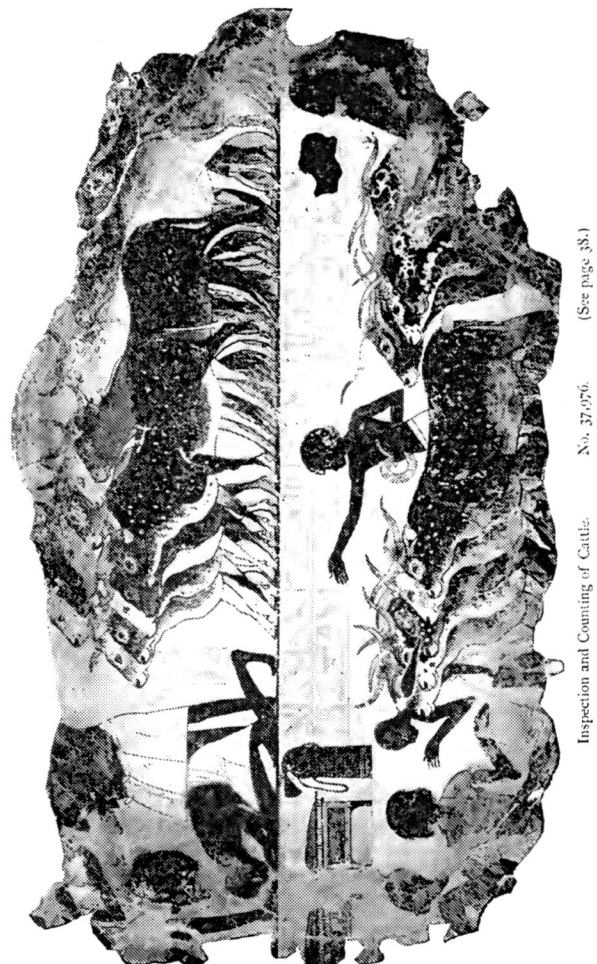

(See page 38.)

No. 37,976.

Inspection and Counting of Cattle.

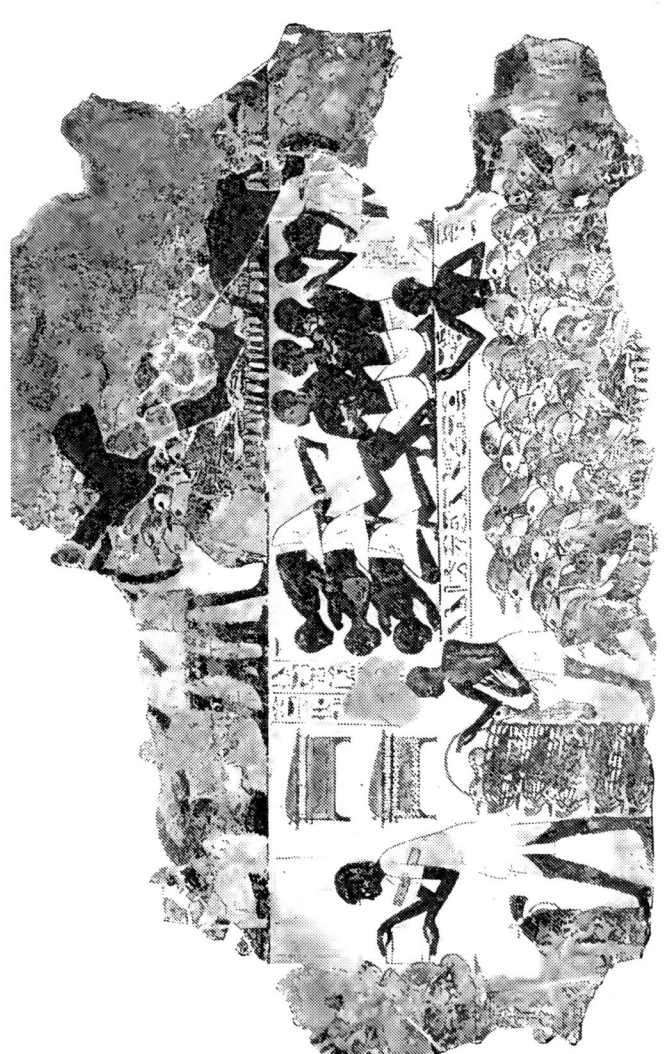

Inspection and Counting of Geese.   No. 37,978.   (See page 38.)

to sew on to mummy shirts and shrouds squares or disks of coloured thread or wool work, and at a later period, squares of silk. The home of this industry was Akhmim, or Panopolis, in Upper Egypt, a city which, according to Strabo, was famous for its stone-workers and linen-weavers The specimens of linen work arranged in this case are very fine, and illustrate the various developments of the fabric and its ornamentation between about A D. 300 and A D. 900 The most interesting pieces are :—

No 1 Piece of linen with monochrome design in blue : subject, a frieze filled with figures apparently intended for Greek deities, among whom are Erôs and Apollo
[No. 21,789]

No. 2 Linen fragment, with fine fringe, ornamented with figures of animals, stag, dog, lion, etc, and a human figure dancing and holding a cornu-copiæ, or horn of plenty. [No. 21,790]

No 4. Linen square with monochrome design ; subject, Adam and Eve [No 21,791.]

No. 5 Linen fragment with a fringed square, having a geometrical and floreated design, and a border formed of figures of birds and plants within scrolls. [No. 21,795.]

No. 6. Fragment with a figure of a lion worked in blue, red, and yellow wools. [No. 21,797.]

No 9. Fragment with a red band, ornamented with figures of lions and plants [No. 18,219]

No. 10. Square, ornamented with figures of four animals and five medallions , the largest, that in the centre, contains the figure of a horseman, and each of the corner medallions is filled with the figure of a man kneeling. [No 21,802]

No 11. Linen square, ornamented with a central design of a figure of a man carrying a palm branch, and wearing a cloak and high boots, within a border of medallions, each of which contains the figure of an animal [No 17,171]

No 12. Linen square with design similar to that of No. 10, but ornamented with the figure of a basket of flowers. [No 17,172]

No. 13. Linen square, ornamented with a border of flowers in green and red upon a yellow ground; in the centre is a figure of a youth, armed with shield and sword, and wearing a flying cloak, worked in dark coloured thread   [No. 17,176.]

No. 14. Circular piece of linen, worked with the figure of a cross lying upon a crown of flowers.   [No. 17,174.]

No. 15. Linen fragment, ornamented with scenes from the lives of the saints, elaborately worked, in the centre is God the Father.   [No. 17,175.]

Nos. 11-15 were presented by the Rev. W. MacGregor, M.A., 1886.

Nos. 16, 17. Circular linen ornaments, worked with figures of birds and flowers   [Nos. 18,218, 18,231.]

No. 18. Linen, with circular ornament · **St. George slaying the dragon.** In the field are angelic ministrants.
    [No. 18,230.]

No. 19. Linen square, with design generally similar to those of Nos. 10 and 12, but with baskets of fruit in the place of animals.   [No. 21,796.]

No. 20. Linen mummy-shirt, with square pectoral of design similar to that of No. 11; in the centre is a male figure dancing, surrounded by a border of medallions containing flowers.   [No. 21,803.]

Nos. 21–24. Linen fragments with elaborate designs, worked in colours, of God the Father among the Seraphim, etc.   [Nos. 20,431, etc.]

No. 25. Fragment of fine **yellow silk** mounted upon linen cloth, with a square of silk worked in red, blue, green, and yellow, with two figures of Saint George slaying the dragon.   [No. 17,173.]

Presented by the Rev. W. MacGregor, M.A., 1886.

Nos. 26, 27. Two pieces of **yellow silk**, ornamented with arabesque designs and Arabic inscriptions in the Kûfi character, A.D. 900.   [Nos. 24,909, 24,910.]

TABLE-CASE K. In this case is exhibited a very interesting collection of workmen's tools and implements of various periods, and ancient models of the same. These last are chiefly specimens placed with samples of materials used in construction, which were deposited in the foundations of new buildings

No. 1. Iron **sickle** blade. [No 36,797]

No. 2 Bronze **sickle** blade, serrated. Bought at Luxor. Presented by Sir John Evans, K.C.B., 1899 [No 30,494]

No. 3 Iron sickle blade, much oxidized. Found by Belzoni under a sphinx at Karnak. Before the XIXth dynasty (?) [No. 5410]

No 4 Iron sickle, serrated, mounted in a wooden handle, Roman period. Presented by Sir J. G Wilkinson, 1834 [No 5412.]

Nos. 5, 6. Iron **chisels**, No. 5, with a ring for strengthening the handle [Nos. 23,064, 30,089]

Nos 7-13. Bronze chisels or axe-heads, of various periods. [Nos 36,727, etc]

Nos. 14-20 Bronze **spatulæ**, of various periods [Nos 20,900, etc]

No. 21. Bronze **knife**, with a wooden handle [No 6052]

No. 24. Iron knife, with a **horn hilt**, in leather scabbard Byzantine period [No 26,778]

Iron Sickle.
No 5412.

No 29 Fragment of **iron plate**, found near the mouth of one of the air passages of the **Great Pyramid** at Gizeh IVth dynasty There is no doubt that this object is contemporaneous with the building of the pyramid Presented by Col. Howard Vyse, 1838. [No 2433.]

No. 30. Bronze **saw.** [No. 30,245.]

No. 31   Iron knife.   [No. 26,775]

No. 32   Portion of a bronze trap, with lead counter-poise   From Zakâzik.   Ptolemaic period   Presented by G. W. Fraser, Esq, 1893   [No. 24,899]

No. 33.   Bronze knife-saw, with a curved wooden handle.   [No 6046.]

Nos. 34, 35.   Models of bronze knives, inscribed with the name and titles of Thothmes III.   [Nos. 6064, 6065.]

No 36   Wooden model of a knife, inscribed with the name and titles of Thothmes III.   [No. 17,079]

No 39   Stone model of a knife, inscribed with the name of the "Sem" priest, the "great wielder of the hammer, Ptah-mes."   [No. 5472.]

Nos. 40-52.   Bronze and iron knife blades   No 46 is set in an agate handle.   [Nos. 15,786, etc]

Nos. 53, 54.   Bronze fish-hooks or model harpoons.
                                        [Nos. 20,898, 17,109.]

Nos. 55, 56.   Bronze and iron spatulæ.
                                        [Nos. 5599, 20,719]

No 57   Bronze knife, with a handle in the form of a goose's head and neck, and incised floral decorations on the blade.   [No. 36,653]

No 58.   Bronze knife of unusual shape.
                                              [No 12,277]

Nos 62-85.   Bronze sticks for the application of kohl or stibium to the eyes, pins, borers, etc., of various periods.
                                        [Nos. 36,732, 36,743, etc.]

Nos. 86-92.   Bronze ornaments of a late period, with figures of cats, serpents, etc   [No. 6209, etc.]

No. 93   Portion of a stone instrument, perhaps a cubit measure, inscribed with a dedication, lists of the gods of nomes, and subdivisions of the cubit.
                                              [No. 36,656.]

No 94. Wooden **measure** of two cubits (?), with subdividing lines. [No. 6025]

No. 95. Iron **strigil**, or **skin-scraper.** Roman period. [No 18,181]

Nos 96–108. Fragments of iron tools and weapons From Tanis. Presented by the Egypt Exploration Fund, 1885. [Nos. 37,135, etc.]

No. 109. Stone **drill-holder** (?). [No. 18,335.]

Nos. 110, 111. Limestone **chisels.** From Beni Hasan. XIIth dynasty. Presented by the Egypt Exploration Fund [Nos. 23,149, 23,150.]

No. 112 Green slate or schist **polisher,** made by or for a person called Khensu, in the reign of Thothmes I,

[No. 30,091.]

No. 113. Green slate **hone,** perforated for suspension. [No. 36,728.]

Nos 114, 115. Emery hones, perforated for suspension. From Drah abu'l Nekka. [Nos. 15,770, 15,771.]

No. 116. Stone **borer,** for working stone vases. IIIrd or IVth dynasty (?) From Shêkh Sa'id. Presented by N. de Garis Davies, Esq., 1902 [No. 36,266]

Nos 117–125. A group of fragments of miscellaneous bronze ornaments [Nos. 36,756, etc]

No 126. Bronze **heart** at the end of a chain. [No. 25,297.]

No. 127. Bronze **mortar rake.** Presented by Prof. Petrie. [No. 16,036.]

Nos. 128–148. Miscellaneous bronze **nails,** etc. [No. 36,654, etc]

No 149 **Foundation deposit,** consisting of a series of samples of building material, precious metals, porcelain ; many of the plaques are inscribed with the names of **Psammetichus I.,** king of Egypt, about B.C. 650. From Tell Defenneh (Tell Dafna), the ancient Daphnæ, or Tahpanhes. [No. 23,556.]

No. 150. Set of foundation deposits, including models of tools. From the N.W. corner of a large building at Tell Gemayemi, in the Delta. Ptolemaic period.

[No. 23,452.]

No. 151. Set of foundation deposits, many of which are inscribed with the name and titles of Amasis II. king of Egypt, about B C. 550. From Tell Nebesha.

[No. 23,503.]

Nos 149–151 were presented by the Egypt Exploration Fund, 1886 and 1887.

Nos. 152–156. Stone **polishers.**   [Nos 21,907, etc.]

Nos. 157, 158. Limestone and crystal **burnishers, set** in bronze.   [Nos 22,721, 22,722.]

Nos. 161–179. A set of bronze **models of tools,** implements, paint palettes, etc ; they were originally gilded. They formed part of the tomb furniture of a high official called Átenâ $\left\lceil \right.$ 🐟 $\left\lceil \right.$, who held the offices of *smer uāt* and *kher heb,* and was " the loyal servant of the great god," *i.e.,* Osiris.   VIth dynasty.   [Nos. 6075, etc.]

No 180. Bronze plate perforated with two holes, and inscribed " Captain of the boat of Khensu." [No. 6211.]

Nos. 181, 182 Two **bronze plaques,** inscribed with the names and titles of **Tirhakah,** king of Egypt, about B.C. 670   [Nos. 5310, 5311.]

Nos. 183–194. Set of models of tools, probably from a foundation deposit.   [Nos 15,686, etc.]

No. 195. A set of bronze models of articles of **funeral furniture,** including a pair of grain bags, with yoke, and two hoes , they are inscribed with the name of Heq-reshu, an official. XVIIIth dynasty   From Abydos.

[No. 32,693]

Nos 198-209   A group of bronze and silver **tweezers, scrapers,** etc   [Nos 20,718, etc.]

No 210. Bronze **strainer.**   [No. 20,896.]

Nos. 211-213. Three pointed bronze **ferrules.**

[No. 12,535.]

Nos. 214-229. A collection of bronze **chisels** set in wooden handles; some of these are inscribed with the names and titles of **Thothmes III.**, and formed part of his funeral furniture. [Nos. 6055, etc.]

Nos. 230-248. A collection of copper, bronze, and iron **chisels**, of various periods. No. 234 is a very fine specimen. [Nos. 23,907, 36,735, etc.]

Nos. 249-254. A fine group of heavy, wooden, stone-mason's **mallets**, which were left accidentally by the workmen when excavating the tombs. XVIIIth and XIXth dynasties. From Thebes.
[Nos. 6028, etc.]

No. 255. Bronze model of **a hoe.**
[No. 29,431.]

No. 256. Wooden stick for working **a drill.**
[No. 6040.]

Wooden Mallet. No. 6028.

Nos. 257, 258. Wooden models of the sepulchral tool which was used in the mystic ceremony of "opening the mouth" of the mummy, and was called **Ur-hekau** 〰 𓎸 ⌟. No. 257 was made for prince **Nehi**, and No. 258 for Queen **Hātshepset**, the beloved of Åmen.
[Nos. 15,779, 26,278.]

No. 259. Model of an **adze**, inscribed with the name of Queen **Hātshepset**, the beloved of Åmen.
[No. 26,279.]

Nos. 260, 261. Models of **adzes**, inscribed with the names of **Thothmes III.**, and forming part of his funeral furniture. [Nos. 6060, 6061.]

No. 262. **Adze**, with a wooden handle. [No. 6048.]

No. 263. Massive adze, with a bronze blade, which was fastened on by means of leather thongs. From the tomb of Ani. XVIIIth dynasty. [No. 22,834.]

No. 264. Wooden **drill socket.** [No. 6041.]

No. 265. Wooden **pulley.** [No. 37,094.]

TABLE-CASE L. This case contains a miscellaneous collection of antiquities of the later **Pre-dynastic** and **Archaic Periods**, which illustrate the beginnings of Egyptian art. The period to which they may be assigned lies roughly between B.C. 5000 and B.C. 3800. A large number of the objects in this case were presented by the Egypt Exploration Fund.

Green slate objects, which were apparently used as amulets and for ceremonial purposes :—

Nos. 1 3.   Three **tortoises** or turtles, perforated for suspension.   No 3 has inlaid bone eyes

[Nos. 36,367, 23,061, 37,913.]

No 4.   **Cuttle-fish**, perforated for suspension.

[No 24,319.]

No 5   Horned animal, antelope ?   [No. 35,049.]

No. 6.   Object which was probably carried in processions, or used in ceremonials, of the class of which specimen casts are exhibited on the Landing of the North-west Staircase.   The offering appears to have been laid in the circular hollow in the centre, which has been thought by some to be a vase for grinding paint   Above is the figure of a victim, and below are two ostriches dancing.

[No. 32,074.]

Nos. 7, 8.   Rectangular slabs for grinding paint

[Nos. 37,359, 37,273.]

No 9   **Bat** with outstretched wings, perforated for suspension.   From Gebelên.   [No. 21,901.]

No 10   **Bear**, with inlaid bone eyes, perforated.

[No. 29,416.]

No 11.   Horned object of unknown use.

[No. 36,366.]

Nos. 12 -15.   Diamond-shaped objects of unknown use.

[Nos. 32,500, 32,501, 32,502, 21,899.]

Nos 16-20   Small objects (amulets ?) of irregular shape   [Nos 26,730, 21,903, 23,421, 20,911, 21,902.]

No 21   **Ram**, with inlaid bone eyes, perforated From Gebelên.   [No. 20,910.]

No. 22. **Ram,** lying down, with head turned back, and inlaid eyes ; the horns are carefully worked.

[No. 36,368.]

No. 23 Flat object for grinding paint. From Gebelên.

[No. 21,900.]

No. 24 Object used for ceremonial purposes, perforated for suspension, and sculptured in relief with the hieroglyphic ⟨hieroglyph⟩. From Al-'Amrah near Abydos. This is probably the earliest written Egyptian symbol known.

[No. 35,501.]

Nos. 25, 26. Oval objects, one end of each of which terminates in two birds' heads.   [Nos 32,503, 23,060.]

No. 27. Stone for rubbing down the insides of stone vases.   [No 37,278]

Nos. 28–31. Variegated granite slabs for grinding paint.   [Nos. 29,673, 15,776, 36,372, 36,373.]

No. 32. Serpentine stone slab for grinding paint.

[No. 26,672]

No. 33. Fragment of black and white quartzite stone, carefully worked with a moulding and polished.

[No. 34,863.]

Nos 34–36. Red stone and alabaster elliptically-shaped **mace-heads.** Predynastic period

[Nos. 30,406, 26,957, 26,958.]

Nos. 37–42. A group of **ivory figures** of women or **dolls.** Nos. 37 and 38 are shaved or bald Nos. 39 and 40 have wigs, the latter having inlaid lapis-lazuli eyes. No. 41 has the hair arranged within a band, wears a long close-fitting dress, and carries a child on her left shoulder. No. 42 is that of a steatopygous woman, and the eyes were inlaid.   This group of figures is of great interest and gives contemporaneous representations of the personal characteristics of the predynastic Egyptians.

[Nos. 32,139-32,144]

Nos. 43–47. Five **spindle whorls** made of limestone and breccia. No. 47 is unfinished.

[Nos. 37,271, 37,272, 30,392, 30,393, 30,395.]

No. 48.   Green felspar circular perforated object.
[No. 32,253.]

No. 49.   Variegated green stone **mace-head** or celt.
[No. 32,118.]

Nos. 50, 51.   Two massive red breccia **axe-heads**, carried, probably, on festival or ceremonial occasions.
[Nos. 30,746, 30,747.]

Nos. 52–54.   Red breccia **sling-stones**.
[Nos. 32,119, 32,120, 32,121.]

No. 55.   Red breccia **mace-head**, conical, and perforated to receive a handle.   Archaic period.   By the side is exhibited a cast (No. 56) of the famous mace-head of **Sargon of Agade**, in Babylonia, B.C. 3800, for purposes of comparison.   This and other instances of similarity appear to prove an early connexion between Egypt and Babylonia.
[No. 32,089.]

No. 57.   Limestone **spiked mace-head**, of similar shape, augmented in relief with a representation of a snake coiled round it, figures of hawks (?), etc.   Early archaic period, a unique object.   [No. 26,247.]

Nos. 58–62.   A group of limestone mace-heads, conical in shape   [Nos. 32,090, 32,091, 21,992, 21,991, 30,394.]

Nos. 63–84.   A fine collection of granite and breccia objects; use unknown.   No. 63 is unfinished.
[Nos. 30,390, 30,391, etc.]

No. 85.   Red breccia flat **axe-head**, perforated for attachment to a stick by means of a leather thong.
[No. 32,092.]

No. 86.   Red breccia **cone**.   [No. 32,122.]

No. 87.   Black granite **cube**.   [No. 15,772.]

No. 88.   Green felspar **cone**, perforated.
[No. 37,464.]

No. 89.   Portion of a green slate object, employed for ceremonial purposes, sculptured in relief with figures of a prisoner of war being cast out into the desert to be devoured by lions and vultures.   His hands are tied behind his back, and a weight is suspended from his neck; the officer who is thrusting him out wears a long fringed tunic, ornamented with a pattern formed of ovals Other prisoners are lying round about and are being devoured On the reverse is a portion of a scene in which two giraffes are eating the leaves of a palm tree.   [No. 20,791.]

No 90. Two pieces of a green slate object, of the same class as those of which casts are exhibited on the Landing of the North-west staircase ; to these are added the cast of a third fragment of the same object, which is preserved in the Louvre at Paris The scene represented is a desert hunt, *i e.*, the chase of ostriches, jackals, hares, antelopes, and lions, by warriors who are armed with double-headed stone axes, maces, celts in wooden hafts (or boomerangs ?), bows and arrows tipped with square flints, and spears having metal heads The warriors wear feathers in their hair and jackals' tails pendent from their waist belts A few are engaged in lassoing a gazelle, and the leaders of each row of men bear a standard surmounted by a hawk. This fact, and other considerations, suggest that the men here represented belonged to the **Heru-shemsu,** or "followers of Horus," who are so often mentioned in hieroglyphic texts as the legendary conquerors of Egypt. who preceded the kings of the 1st dynasty, and the emblem of whose chief god was a hawk At one end are two archaic hieroglyphics, the exact meaning of which is uncertain. This and the preceding object date from the earliest archaic period, and were made before the time of the 1st dynasty, that is to say, before B.C 4400.   [No. 20,790.]

Nos 91–170 A collection of miscellaneous objects from royal and private tombs of the first three dynasties, chiefly from Abydos and the neighbourhood.

No 91. Fragment of a clay **jar-sealing**, with the name of **Ka** ⌊⌉, a predynastic king (?)   [No 35,509]

No. 92. Part of a clay **jar-sealing**, with the name of **Re,** ⌇⌇⌇, a predynastic king (?).   [No. 35,510.]

No. 93. Fragment of an alabaster vase, with the Horus name of **Nār-mer,** one of the earliest known kings of Egypt, in relief.   [No. 32,640.]

No. 94   Slate **slab** for grinding **eye-paint** (antimony, or *kohl*)   [No. 35,511.]

No. 95   Ivory box-lid, inscribed with the name of the royal personage **Nit-hetep**   Following this name are the ⏝ 𓏤 ⏝, which have been thought by some to mean "**King Sma,**" but it is possible that they only form a title of Nit-hetep.   [No 35,512]

No. 96   Part of an ivory box, inscribed with the name of **Aha** 🦅 , one of the earliest kings of Egypt, and one who   has been identified with the legendary **Mena,** or 𓂧𓄿   Menes, whom the later Egyptians believed to have 𓎛 founded the monarchy   Close by the king's name are the signs ✳️ ♉ **Bener-ab,** *i e*, "gracious of heart," which have been supposed to form a proper name of a princess, but which more probably form an epithet of the king.   [No 35,513]

Nos 97, 98.   Portions of **ivory plaques**, with incised figures of prisoners.   [Nos 35,514, 35,515.]

Nos. 99, 100   Two rectangular **ivory labels**, inscribed with hieroglyphic characters.   [Nos 35,516, 35,517.]

No 101   Fragments of an **ebony tablet**, inscribed with the name of king **Aha** and archaic hieroglyphics
                                                              [No 35,518]

No. 102   Fragments of similar tablet with the name Aha (?).   [No 35,519]

No 103   Fragments of a red marble dish from the tomb of **Tcha** ⟍, an early king of the Ist dynasty.
                                                              [No 32,643]

No 104   Small alabaster vase from the tomb of **Tcha,** containing traces of red paint   [No. 32,644]

No 105.   Fragment of ivory, stained blue, and inscribed with the name of **Tcha.**   [No. 32, 641]

Nos. 106, 107. **Beads** of ivory and lapis-lazuli in the form of hawk standards. [Nos. 35,527, 35,528]

No. 108. Ivory **hand and arm** from a doll (?). [No. 35,531]

No. 109. Semicircular object of gold. Use unknown. [No. 35,526.]

No. 110. Carved ivory **lion** of archaic style. [No. 35,529.]

No. 111 **Ebony plaque,** inscribed with the name of **Khent** (or **Tcher** (?)) ⌷⌷⌷ (or ⌷⌷), an early king of the Ist dynasty The reading of the archaic sign which stands for his name is doubtful. [No. 35,524]

No. 112. Wooden plaque, inscribed with an unknown sign. [No. 35,525.]

No. 113. A set of ivory implements, **awls, pins,** etc. [Nos. 35,534, etc.]

No. 114. Foot from an **ivory casket,** in the shape of a bull's leg [No 35,530]

No. 115. Clay **jar-sealing,** with the name of king **Khent** [No. 35,607.]

No. 116. Two oval clay objects of unknown use. [Nos. 35,532, 35,533.]

Nos 106–116 are from the tomb of **Khent** at Abydos.

Nos. 117–122. Ivory fragments with incised fluted patterns [Nos 32,652, 32,653, etc.]

No. 123 Fragment of the ivory lid of a box, inscribed with the legend "golden seal of judgment" ⌷⌷ Ǫ, and the name of **Ten,** whose personal name was **Semti,** and who is to be identified with the **Ḥesepti** of the King Lists and of the Book of the Dead. [No. 35,552.]

No. 124 Ebony tablet, inscribed with the names of king **Ten** and of **Ḥemaka,** the "treasurer of Lower Egypt" The tablet was probably made to record the events of a year of the king's reign, *e.g*, a ceremonial dance before Osiris, a festival of the god Seker, a palace ceremony, etc. [No. 32,650]

No. 125   Gold button.   [No. 35,553.]

No. 126   Small copper chisel   [No. 35,554.]

Nos. 128, 129.   Fragments of alabaster vases, one
burnt.   [Nos 37,417, 37,418]

Nos. 117–129 are from the tomb of Semti-Ten

No 130   Fragment of a felspar vase, inscribed with
the personal name of king Semti, and the Horus name of
king Ātch-ab ⋈ ☥, whose personal name was Mer-p-ba,
the Mer-ba-pen of the King Lists   [No. 32,659]

Nos 131, 132.   Fragments of crystal vases, inscribed
with the name Mer-p-ba   [Nos 32,665, 32,666]

No 133.   Clay jar-sealing, inscribed with the name of
Mer-p-ba Ātchab   [No 32,660]

Nos 134–136   Fragments of ivory, ornamented for
inlaying   [Nos 32,661–32,663]

No. 137   Fragments of an alabaster vessel, inscribed
with the name of Ātchab.   [No 32,667]

Nos 130–137 are from the tomb of Mer-p-ba

No. 138   Jar-sealing, inscribed with the name of
Semerkhā, a king of the Ist dynasty, whose personal
name was Hu (or Nekht), he is the Semempses of
Manetho   [No 32,670]

No 139   Clay sealing, inscribed with the name of
Semerkhā.   [No. 32,669]

No. 140.   Ivory tablet of king Hu Semerkhā, recording the celebration of the festivals of Seker and Thoth
in a certain year of his reign.   [No 32,668]

No. 141   Two fragments of stone bowls, inscribed with
the name and titles of a official of Qa,* the last king of
the Ist dynasty, whose Horus name was Sen 𝍖 , the

* A cast of a stone with the name of this king upon it will be
found in Wall-Cases 7–12, on the landing of the North-west Staircase

Qebḥ 〖 of the King Lists. The later reading, Qebh, is due to a confusion in the hieratic signs for Qebḥ and Sen. [Nos. 32,672, 32,673.]

No. 142. Clay jar-sealing with a royal inscription of the Ist dynasty. [No. 32,646.]

No. 143 Six fragments of blue **glazed faïence** for inlaying. [Nos. 35,560–35,565.

No. 144. Copper axe-head, with a perforation through which the thong passed that fastened it to a handle.
[No. 35,574.]

Nos. 145–158. A set of copper **models of weapons,** tools, implements, etc. Some are of unusual form. No. 153 is a model of an axe-head. [Nos. 35,575–35,588.]

No. 159. Variegated black and white flat **marble vase,** with a lid made of a thin plate of beaten gold, fastened round the neck of the vase with gold wire, and secured by a seal. [No. 35,567.]

No. 160. Model of a vase in limestone, made in the shape of a mace-head, with a similar gold cover.
[No. 35,568.]

No. 161. Flat vase of dolomite marble, with two handles for suspension. [No. 35,566.]

Nos. 143–161 are from the tomb of king **Khāsekhemui-Besh** ⌇, who is probably to be identified with the **Betchau** (Manetho's Boethos) of the King Lists, the first king of the IInd dynasty.

No. 162. Fragment of a stone vase, inscribed with the name of **Ḥetep-sekhemui** ⌇, a king of the IInd dynasty. [No. 35,559.]

No. 163. Three fragments of a green slate bowl inscribed with the names of the kings **Rā-neb** ⌇ and **En-neter** ⌇, kings of the IInd dynasty.
[Nos. 35,556–35,558.]

No. 164. **Jar-sealing** inscribed with **Se-Sekhem-ab** , the Horus name of **Per-àb-sen,** a king of the IInd dynasty. [No. 35,596.]

No. 165. Fragment of a crystalline stone vase inscribed with the name and titles of king **Per-ab-sen** 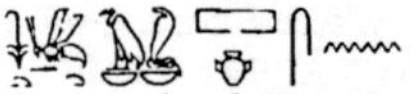, a king of the IInd dynasty. From the tomb of Per-àb-sen. [No. 32,647.]

No. 166. Fragment of a stone vessel inscribed with the name of **Mer-Nit,** a royal personage (?). Ist or IInd dynasty. [No. 32,465.]

No. 167. Fragment of a serpentine stone jar, with ivory handle, and ornamentation in the form of rope-work. [No. 32,648.]

No. 168. Fragment of ivory. [No. 32,649.]

Nos. 166–168 are from the tomb of Mer-Nit.

No. 169. Fragment of a slate vase inscribed with the name of **Tcheser** , a king of the IIIrd dynasty. [No. 32,658.]

No. 170. Fragment of the neck of an earthenware wine jar. From the tomb of **Ḥen-nekht,** or **Sa-nekht,** a king of the IIIrd dynasty, at Bêt Khallâf, near Girga. [No. 37,419.]

Nos. 171–223 form a miscellaneous collection of antiquities belonging to the archaic period, a number of which were presented by the Egyptian Exploration Fund in 1903, and come from the Temple of Osiris at Abydos.

Nos. 171–172. Small red breccia lions of archaic style. [Nos. 26,360, 32,488.]

No. 173. Limestone steatopygous female figure; head broken off, and arms folded. [No. 32,126.]

No. 174. Limestone figure of a woman, with the hair bound in a fillet, and the arms folded. [No. 32,125.]

No. 175. Figure of similar shape in lead. Rough workmanship. [No. 32,138.]

Nos. 176–179.   Squatting figures of apes in limestone and arragonite.   [Nos 32,128–32,131.]

Nos. 180–186.   Glazed faience figures of dog-headed apes, *i.e.*, animals sacred to Thoth.

[Nos. 37,280, 37,281, etc.]

No 187.   Stone figure of a hawk from a standard.

[No. 38,049.]

No. 188.   Hawk, from a standard   The upper part of the bird's body is made of black stone, and the lower part of white   The eyes are inlaid with bone.   [No. 30,742]

No. 189.   Yellow stone hawk ; the eyes are wanting.

[No. 32,135.]

No. 190.   Stone frog.   [No. 32,132.]

No. 191.   Ivory fish, with inlaid eyes made of blue beads   [No. 32,137.]

No. 192.   Glazed faience pig.   [No 38,018.]

No. 193.   Head of an ox in stone.   [No. 32,134.]

No. 194.   Head of a dog-headed ape, with inlaid ivory eyes.   [No. 32,133]

No. 195.   Red terra-cotta frog.   [No. 38,044.]

No. 196.   Red terra-cotta head of a man.   The head-dress resembles that of the early Sumerian inhabitants of Babylonia.   [No 38,043.]

No. 197.   Upper portion of an ivory **figure of a king** wearing the crown of Upper Egypt, and dressed in a heavy cloak ornamented with various designs and patterns, among which is the *mæander*.   The person represented is an old man, with well marked features, and the head bowed ; his cloak is caught up on his right arm, and he is apparently walking.   The workmanship of the object is remarkably fine and delicate, and the figure is, no doubt, an accurate portrait of the king represented.   It is the most important object of archaic Egyptian art hitherto discovered.   1st dynasty.   [No. 37,976.]

No. 198.   Fragment of a large faience vase inscribed with the Horus name of king **Āḥa**, in inlaid yellow glaze. The name as here written shows the hawk grasping the

shield and mace ⌒⌒ which form the hieroglyphic *âha,*
i.e., "fighter," and well illustrates the archaic method of
writing.   [No. 38,010.]

No. 199.   Flat, green felspar vase, with handles over-
laid with gold.   [No. 36,356.]

No. 200.   Flat, dark green marble vase, of similar
shape.   [No. 4711.]

No. 201.   Black stone vase, with two suspension
handles, made in the form of a hawk grasping its quarry.
Head wanting.   [No. 32,250.]

No. 202.   Black stone model of a vase, with perforated,
wavy handles.   [No. 36,336.]

No. 203.   Black and blue glazed vase, which probably
came from the temple deposit of Âha.   [No. 38,013.]

No. 204.   Fragment of a blue glazed faience fluted tile.
                                                      [No. 37,282.]

No. 205.   Fragment of a blue glazed faience flower.
                                                      [No 38,012.]

No. 206.   Plaque for inlaying, with the figure of a
palm tree.   [No. 38,011.]

No. 207.   Glazed *faience* object of unknown use.
                                                      [No. 38,017.]

Nos 208, 209   Rectangular blue glazed porcelain tiles,
similar to those found in the pyramid of Tcheser, a king of
the IIIrd dynasty, at Ṣaḳḳâra. (See Table-Case K.   Fourth
Egyptian Room.)   [Nos 38,024, 38,025.]

No. 210.   Blue glazed porcelain ornament.
                                                      [No. 38,014.]

No 211.   Model vase stand, in blue glazed porcelain.
                                                      [No. 38,016.]

No 212.   Model vase, in blue glazed porcelain, on
stand.   [No 38,015.]

No 213.   A group of blue glazed porcelain beads of
various shapes.   [No. 30,798.]

No. 214.   Necklace of light blue and black porcelain
beads.   [No. 37,283.]

No. 215.   A collection of unpierced round and conical stone beads   They were found placed in rows on a layer of clay, which was intended to serve as a necklace or breastplate for a mummy.   [Nos. 30,798, etc.]

No. 216.   Three unpierced marble and chalcedony beads of similar shape.   [No. 32,702.]

No. 217.   Two slate rings.   [Nos. 38,051, 38,052.]

No. 218.   Copper axe-head, unperforated.
[No. 37,276]
No 219   Copper chisel   [No. 37,277]

No. 220.   Ornamental ivory object in the form of a victim bound for sacrifice.   [No. 38,050.]

Nos. 221, 222.   Two vases of polished black ware.   Ist dynasty.   [Nos. 38,046, 38,047.]

No. 223.   Black and white flat diorite bowl.
[No 38,054.]

No. 224.   Diorite cup.   IVth dynasty (?).
[No 30,798.]

No. 225.   Collection of baked clay objects of unknown use ; they are probably models of offerings.   IVth dynasty
[Nos. 38,055, etc.]

No 226.   Jar-sealing, with the name of **Ka-Sekhemui** ⨆ 𓎼𓎼, a king of the IInd dynasty.   [No. 38,053.]

No. 227.   Jar-sealing, with the name of **Men-kau-Rā** ⊙ 𓌳 𓎟, a king of the IVth dynasty.   [No. 38,064.]

No. 228.   Jar-sealing, with the name of **Nefer-àri-ka-Rā** ⊙ 𓄤 𓂝 ⨆, a king of the Vth dynasty.   [No. 38,070.]

No. 229.   A glazed porcelain plaque, commemorating a *Set* festival of **Pepi I. Meri-Rā**, a king of the VIth dynasty.   [No. 38,075.]

No 230.   Electrotype of a gold bar inscribed with the name of king **Āḥa**.   Presented by Mr. Augustus Ready.
[No. 38,159.]

TABLE-CASE M. In this case is exhibited a fine collection of **flint weapons and implements**, which belong chiefly to the late **Palæolithic** or early **Neolithic** period; some date from the time of the first four dynasties, at which epoch the use of the metals had long been established in Egypt. The greater number of the finer

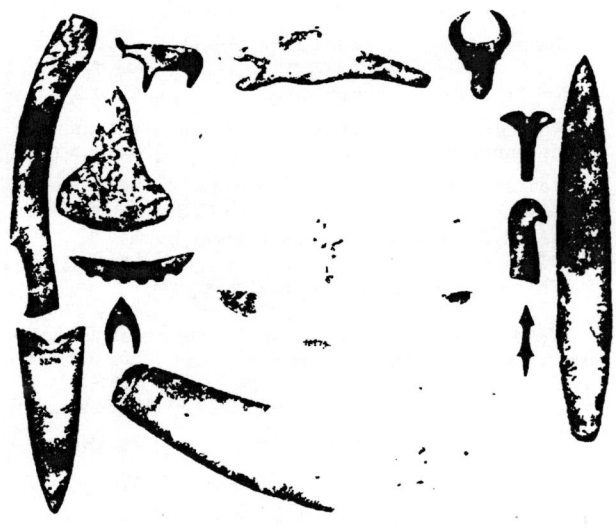

Miscellaneous Flint Weapons and Implements

flint objects were found with the bodies and pottery of the predynastic Egyptians, who were buried in and near Gebelên, Nakâda, and Abydos (Al-'Amrah) [see Guide to the First and Second Egyptian Rooms, p. 20 ff.], and belong to the late Neolithic period.   Worthy of note in this case are :—

Nos. 1–3.   Three **flint borers** for piercing skins. Palæolithic period   [Nos. 30,220, 30,408, etc.]

No. 6.   Flint knife with a gold handle. The gold handle is probably modern. Predynastic period
[No. 30,409]

Nos. 15-29.   A group of fine **flint knives**, some being symmetrically chipped and having serrated edges. Predynastic period.

Nos. 30-36.   A group of heavy, comparatively coarsely-chipped, **flint knives.** Early dynastic period.

Nos. 37-45.   A group of fluted, veined, flint and **chert knives**, with serrated edges , No. 44 is one of the finest examples of the class known, and the working of this type is far superior to that of any other Neolithic flint work known. Predynastic period.

Nos. 47-58.   A group of flint **spear-heads,** the blade edges of which are finely serrated. Predynastic period.

Nos. 59-83.   A group of heavy, coarsely-chipped, flint **butchers' knives**, with hilts fashioned to fit the hand. Early dynastic period.

No. 84.   Flint object $\big\rangle$, the use of which is unknown ; it probably represents a feather.   [No. 32,097.]

No. 85.   Model of a horned animal (ox or ram ?) in flint.   [No. 30,411.]

No. 86.   Model of a human head with a cow's horns, intended to represent the head of the goddess **Hathor.**
[No. 32,124.]

No. 88.   Curved **saw-blade** in flint.   [No. 30,412]

No. 89.   Double **arrow-head**, barbed, in flint.
[No. 32,117.]

No. 90.   Heavy flint knife, of unusual shape, with handle.   [No 30,121.]

No. 883.   Model of an animal in flint.   [No. 37,269.]

Nos. 884, 885.   Flint **scrapers**, with serrated edges
[Nos. 37,264, 37,265.]

No. 886.   Flint **celt,** with polished end.   [No. 37,268.]

No. 887   Flint **core**, from which flakes have been chipped off   [No 37,270]

No 888   Flint **amulet** (?), probably of the type which was later known as the *Pesh-ken*, and was used in ceremonies connected with the dead   [No 37,279]

Nos 889, 890.   Flint flake, and a half-moon shaped object.   [Nos. 37,267, 37,266.]

Nos. 883- 890 were presented by the Egypt Exploration Fund.

Nos 91 733.   A large collection of flint **arrow-heads** of miscellaneous types of the predynastic period   The various types have been grouped together as far as possible. The finest specimens are illustrated on page 58.

Nos 734-755   A group of miscellaneous flint and diorite objects, including cores, celts, chisels, etc   Nos 750-753 are highly polished.   Predynastic and early dynastic periods

Nos 756-762.   Flint knives, celt, etc., from Wâdî Shêkh in the Libyan Desert, to the west of Maghagha   Predynastic period.   Presented by W. H. Seton-Karr, Esq, 1901.

Nos 775-789   A group of fine flint weapons, with a curved V-shaped blade; the pointed end was fixed in a haft, and many of the examples have the blades finely serrated.   Predynastic period.

Nos 790-791.   Flint scrapers.

Nos 805-812   Flint flakes and scrapers, serrated

Nos 816-827.   Flint scrapers, rectangular, and finely chipped.

Nos 834-837.   Straight-topped arrow-heads, some ornamented with gold   Early dynastic period

Nos. 838-882.   Flint arrow-heads and chips from the Western Desert

WALL-CASES 93-96.—Mummied animals.

Nos 1-3. **Apis Bulls.**   The heads and the fore quarters only are mummified.   The best specimen is No. 3, for we see on the forehead a representation of the white triangular blaze which was one of the principal characteristics of the Apis Bull, and an attempt has been made to paint on the mummy cloth the brown colour of the head of the animal and the dark limpid colour of the eye. [Nos. 6771–6773.]

No. 4. Skull of an **Apis Bull**. [No. 6774.]

The cult of the **Bull** in Egypt was of very ancient origin, and this animal was regarded as the symbol of strength, and

No. 6771. Mummy of an Apis Bull.

kings were proud to call themselves " mighty bull," and the god Osiris was called " Bull of Amentet " (i.e., the Underworld). The principal forms of bull-worship obtained at Memphis and Heliopolis; in the former city the Bull was called **Ḥāp** 𓎛𓂝𓊪, i.e., **Apis,** * and was regarded

* According to Diodorus Siculus the Egyptians honoured Apis and Mnevis by the command of Osiris, "both for their usefulness " in husbandry, and likewise to keep up an honourable and lasting " memory of those that first found out bread-corn and other fruits of " the earth."

as an incarnation of Ptah-Seker-Asar, the Memphite god of the dead At Heliopolis the Bull was called **Mnevis**, and was held to be an incarnation of the Sun-god Rā. According to Herodotus (iii 28), "this Apis, or Epaphus, is " the calf of a cow which is never afterwards able to bear " young. The Egyptians say that holy fire comes down " from heaven upon the cow, which thereupon conceives " Apis. The calf which is so called is black, and has the " following marks —Upon the forehead is a white triangle, " upon the back the figure of an eagle, in the tail double " hairs, and under his tongue a beetle." The bronze figures of the god Apis which are common in collections prove that the above description is substantially correct, for " figure of an eagle " we should, however, read, " figure of a " vulture." From the XVIIIth dynasty onwards the mummied Apis bulls were buried in a large tomb at Sakkâra, now commonly known as the **Serapeum**, with great pomp and ceremony, and vast sums of money were often spent by the devotees of the god upon the funeral ceremonies of the bulls, and the sumptuous entertainments which followed them Each bull was laid in a massive granite sarcophagus, and to commemorate him was set up a funeral stele on which were inscribed the dates of his birth and death These records of the lives of the Apis bulls are often of the greatest use for purposes of chronology A new element was introduced into the Apis worship by Ptolemy Soter, who, about B C. 300, identified Osiris-Apis, i e, **Serapis**, with a form of the Greek god of the Underworld, **Hades**. From this time onwards the deity Serapis was always represented with the head of the Greek god Hades [See Standard-Case H, No 37,448]

Nos 5, 6. Skulls of the Barbary **Sheep** (*Ovis tragelaphus*).   [Nos. 35,863, 6779]

No. 7 Mummy of a **ram**, the animal sacred to Amen-Rā From Thebes.   [No 6781.]

Nos 8–10 Three mummies of the **Cynocephalus** or dog-headed **Ape**, an animal which was associated with the Moon, and was the companion of Thoth, and which, under certain circumstances, was the representative of this god. This animal was sacred to Khonsu as the god of the Moon.

The sun at his rising was supposed to be hymned by a
company of seven of these apes, which, as soon as the
disk was above the horizon, turned into the spirits of the
dawn. The dog-headed ape was, and still is, a native of
the Súdán, and is often associated with the god Bes, who,
according to some, is of Nubian or Sudanese origin.
[Nos. 35,856, 6736, 35,857.]

No. 6758.　　No. 6752.　　No. 36,847.　　No. 37,348.　　No. 6750.
Mummied Cats.

No. 11. Mummy of a **gazelle** with a painted linen
face. From Kom Ombo. Presented by J. A. Home, Esq.,
1868. For an example of a gazelle, with the sheaths
on the horns, see No. 45. [No. 35,855.]

Nos. 12 15. A group of **mummied cats**, with eyes formed of pads of linen painted and sewn on to the outer wrapping. Nos. 13 15 are specially interesting on account of the careful bandaging in linen of two colours, arranged in a symmetrical diamond pattern. XXth dynasty, or later (B.C. 1000 ?)   [Nos. 6751 6753, 6756.]

On the **second shelf** is arranged a fine representative series of bronze and wooden figures of **cats**, and cases for mummied cats ; among these may be specially mentioned :—

No 16. Wooden, mummied cat case, which was originally covered with plaster and painted linen. The irides of the eyes are formed of slices of crystal laid upon a gilded surface, and the closed pupils are made of black obsidian ; the eyelids are of bronze. From Memphis.
[No 6761.]

No. 17. Massive wooden case in the form of a seated cat ; the head is painted green and the body white.
[No 22,752.]

No 18. Solid wooden figure of a seated cat. Presented by Major (now Colonel) Arthur Bagnold, R.E., 1887. From Sakkâra.   [No. 20,725.]

No. 19. Bronze case for holding a mummied cat.
[No 35,854.]

No. 20 Bronze case for a mummied cat, ornamented with the figure of a scarab and a necklace carefully engraved ; an attempt has been made to represent the appearance of a cat's fur. From Abûsir.   [No 6768.]

No. 21. Wooden case for holding a mummied cat, with eyes made of white obsidian inlaid   [No. 6769.]

No 22. Fine bronze figure of the cat-headed goddess **Bast**, with eyes inlaid in gold, arrayed in a long, sleeveless garment, the pattern of which is carefully engraved. In her right hand she holds a Hathor-headed sistrum, with the figure of a cat in the upper portion ; in her left she holds an ægis of Bast, wearing the solar disk. (For a large model of such an ægis, see Table-Case H, No. 34,939.) The goddess stands upon a bronze pedestal fashioned in the shape of the hieroglyphic ⌠, which is the symbol of her name , at her feet are four seated cats On the edge of the pedestal is a dedication to Bast on behalf of . . . ., the son of Nefer-renpit. Presented by the Committee of the Egypt Exploration Fund, 1894. XXIInd dynasty   [No. 25,565]

No. 23 Bronze case for holding a mummied kitten, with a pedestal in the shape of ⌠, the symbol of Bast
[No. 6764]

No 24 Bronze case for holding a cat-fœtus, surmounted by the figure of a cat   [No. 6767]

No 25. Bronze case for holding the mummy of a **kitten**, surmounted by figures of two cats, one seated and one lying down Presented by Sir John Evans, K C.B.
[No 22,540]

Nos 24 and 25 are rectangular in shape.

No 26. Solid wooden figure of a cat, plastered and gilded, seated upon a wooden pedestal made in the form of the hieroglyphic symbol for the cat-goddess Bast
[No. 6759]

No. 27. Bronze head from a wooden mummied cat-case.   [No 36,173]

Nos. 28, 29. Mummies of two cats, which have been unrolled ; the fur of No 28 is well preserved.
[Nos. 6748, 6746]

Nos 30-40 Eleven miscellaneous mummied cats, some of which are swathed in the same style as Nos 12-15 ; No 33 dates from the Roman period, and came from Abydos. Presented by the Egypt Exploration Fund.
[Nos 6749, 6750, etc]

No 41 Mummy of a **dog**, neatly swathed. Roman period Presented by Joseph Hull, Esq , 1879
[No 35,849]

Nos 42, 43 Two mummied **jackals**, neatly swathed. No. 43 is carefully painted The jackal was sacred to Anpu 𓇋𓈖𓊪𓃢 (**Anubis**), the god of the tomb, who is

F

always depicted with the head of this animal. At all
periods the jackal was regarded as the guardian of the
tombs, and the protector of the dead, on account of its
habit of prowling at night in and about the cemeteries of
the desert. Another jackal-headed deity, the counterpart
of Anubis, was **Ap-uat** ⟨hieroglyphs⟩, *i.e.*, 'the opener
of the ways [of the Underworld]" In the Roman period
some confusion existed between the jackal and the dog,
which was not originally a sacred animal, but which had
by that time also become sacred to Anubis   Under
the early dynasties the dog was highly valued for purposes of the chase, and distinctive breeds were carefully
maintained, but there is no evidence that this animal was
regarded with veneration until the time of the Romans.

[Nos. 35,847, 35,848.]

No 44 Mummy of a **lamb**, sacred to Amen-Rā,
the great god of Thebes, from the XIIth dynasty to the
Ptolemaic period. From Thebes.   [No. 37,158.]

No. 45 [See No. 11.]

No 46 Head of a mummied **ram**, of unusually large
size, with spiral horns projecting from the head horizontally,
this species of sheep was originally sacred to **Khnemu**
⟨hieroglyphs⟩ **(Khnoumis)**, the god of Elephantine, but in
the late period was confused with the **ram of Amen**
(Ammon), the horns of which were of the usual type.
It has been suggested that the ram of Khnemu was
originally the *kudu*, an animal now chiefly found in South
Africa, or was closely related to it.   [No. 6777.]

On the **floor** of these cases are :—

No 47 Mummy of a full-grown female **crocodile**,
measuring 12 ft 3 in ; arranged in rows along its back
are a number of very small crocodiles, which are probably
its young   Presented by the Egyptian Government, 1895.
From Kom Ombo   [No 38,562]

The **crocodile** was worshipped in Egypt from the
earliest times as the representative on earth of the Nile-
god **Sebek** ⟨hieroglyphs⟩, the **Souchos** of the Greeks , his

worship was very general under the XIIth and XIIIth dynasties, and during the Ptolemaic period, his principal shrines were at Crocodilopolis (Manfalût) and Ma'abda in Upper Egypt, and in the district of the Fayyûm, which was specially favoured by Amen-em-hāt III. (the king Moeris of Herodotus) and his immediate successors. In the Ptolemaic period the god was worshipped in the Fayyûm under the name of **Soknopaios**. Under the New Empire Sebek became identified with the Sun-god Rā, and was adored as **Sebek-Rā.**

No 48 Portions of the skin of a crocodile which were used as armour From Manfalût. Presented by Mrs Andrews, 1846   ·   [No 5473.]

WALL-CASES 133–136 Here are exhibited collections of **mummied birds, snakes, fish,** and **crocodiles,** and a series of cases in wood and bronze to hold hawks, snakes, scorpions, etc On the **upper shelf** are specimens of the ibis mummified, Nos 1 and 2 contain both birds and eggs, and No. 3 is remarkable for the neat and careful bandaging On the **lower shelf** are examples of mummified fish and snakes, carefully bandaged in cloth of two colours (Nos 4 and 5), and among the other objects may be noted —

No. 6 Bronze **snake case,** surmounted by a figure of a snake with human head, bearded, held erect, and surmounted by the crowns of the South and North.

[No 36,151.]

No 7. Bronze snake case, with a model of a snake lying in folds upon it.   [No. 12,704]

No. 8 Wooden case containing a **mummied lizard;** on the top of the case is a wooden figure of a lizard.

[No. 36,158.]

No. 9 Wooden case containing a mummied lizard, with a sliding lid working in grooves   [No 24,657.]

No. 10 Wooden case containing a mummied snake

[No 23,077]

Nos 11, 12. Bronze cases for **mummied ichneumons;** above each is a figure of the creature.

[Nos. 6770, 36,157]

F 2

No. 13.   Bronze case for mummied ichneumons ; on it are three figures of the creature.   [No. 26,258.]

No. 14.   Portion of bronze case with a figure of the **goddess Selq,** in the form of a woman-headed scorpion ; the case was dedicated to Isis.   [No. 11,629.]

No. 15.   Bronze figure of Selq, in the form of a woman-headed scorpion.   [No. 18,667.]

No. 16.   Wooden case for holding a **mummied beetle.**
[No. 36,155.]

No. 17.   Stone case for holding a mummied beetle.
[No. 36,149.]

No. 18.   Bronze case for **mummied hawks,** in the form of a pylon, surmounted by figures of four hawks wearing the crowns of the South and North.
[No. 37,916.]

Nos. 19, 20.   Two shells of **ostrich eggs.**
[Nos. 22,554, 22,555.]
[For the shell of **a predynastic ostrich egg,** see on the Landing of the North-west Staircase, Wall-Case 4, No.36,377.]

No. 37,916.

No. 21.   Mummied hawk, with bronze head.
[No. 27,338.]

No. 22.   Two mummied hawks bandaged together.
[No. 15,980.]

No. 23.   Wooden case for holding a **mummied fish,** with inlaid eyes.   [No. 36,169.]

No. 24.   Wooden case for a similar fish.
[No. 12,258.]

No. 25.   Part of a wooden case containing a **mummied ibis.**   [No. 36,148.]

No. 26. Mummied fish. [No. 24,647]

No. 27 Wooden case, in the form of a fish, containing a mummied fish. [No. 20,764.]

On the floor of the case, in stands, are a number of terra-cotta jars, containing examples of the mummied ibis, the saucer-shaped lids of which were fastened on with plaster [No. 36,239, etc.] Here, too, are a number of small mummied **crocodiles**, a few of which [*e.g.*, Nos. 6848, 6837] have been unrolled, and other **birds and reptiles.** Nos 6786, 6798, etc., were presented by Sir J. G. Wilkinson, in 1834, No. 35,738 by Mr J. Doubleday, in 1839; No 6835 by the Rev J Vere Monroe, Nos. 6851, 35,728, etc., by W. Boyne, Esq., in 1846; Nos 5387, 5388 by Mrs Andrews; No 35,750 by Sir W Pearson, in 1874, and Nos 27,399, 27,397 by Somers Clarke, Esq, in 1897.

WALL-CASES 97, 98. On the shelves in these cases is exhibited a fine and comprehensive collection of stone, wooden, and ivory **Pillows** or **Head-rests,** which were placed under the heads of mummies in the tombs, many of them were probably used by their owners during their lifetime The examples here displayed belong to all periods of Egyptian history, from the IVth dynasty to the Ptolemaic period. The peculiar form of the pillows or head-rests is characteristically African, and pillows of similar shapes are in use among the Negro and other tribes of Central and South Africa at the present day The pillow was always regarded as an object of sacred significance, and small model pillows, made of hæmatite, etc, were often worn by the living, and were placed upon their mummies after death. The CLXVIth Chapter of the Book of the Dead has for its vignette a head-rest, from which we see that it was customary to lay a small cushion on the concave upper portion; and in the text it is said, "They lift up thy head in the "horizon, thou art raised up, and dost triumph by reason "of what hath been done for thee . . . . . Thy head shall not "be carried away from thee after [the slaughter], thy head "shall never, never be carried away from thee." Among the head-rests here exhibited the following are of special interest :—

No 49   Head-rest of sycamore wood, ornamented with an ebony band and two ivory studs.   Ancient Empire.
[No. 2541.]

No. 50.   Head-rest roughly shaped out of a block of wood.   [No. 29,565.]

Nos. 51, 52.   Head-rests of wood, having a support in the form of a pillar   Nos. 50 52 are of the Vth dynasty, about B.C 3500, and were found at Dashasha, in Upper Egypt.   Presented by the Egypt Exploration Fund.   [Nos. 29,566, 29,567.]

No. 53   Head-rest on a support, with a pylon-shaped opening in it.   [No. 35,803]

No. 54.   Portion of a head-rest **found in the Great Pyramid**.   IVth dynasty.   Presented by Colonel Howard Vyse and J. Perring, Esq., 1840.   [No. 2555]

No. 55   Base of a wooden head-rest, ornamented with small ivory studs , it was made for **Rerâ** ⬭⎸⧖, a royal kinsman, who was an official of the court of the "great royal wife, who was united to the beauty of the Crown of the South," **Sebek-em-sa-f** ⬭ 𓅓 𓊏 𓈖.   XIVth dynasty, B C. 1900.   [No. 23,068.]

No. 56   Head-rest, in the form of a folding chair, XVIIIth dynasty.   From Thebes.   Presented by Sir J. G. Wilkinson.   [No. 2556]

No. 57   **Head-rest, in the form of a folding chair**, the legs of which terminate in the heads of geese ; the ends of the concave portion are ornamented with heads of the god Bes in relief.   XVIIIth dynasty.   From Thebes.
[No. 18,156.]

No. 58.   **Head-rest, in the form of a hare**, the ears of which are extended to form the support of the head.   XVIIIth dynasty.   [No. 20,753.]

Nos 59, 60.   Head-rests, of unusual form, with widely extended legs.   From Thebes.   XVIIIth dynasty
[Nos. 18,152, 18,153]

Nos. 61-63. Head-rests, with a number of small rounded supports. New Empire From Akhmim.
[Nos. 2542, 2543, 18,155]

No 64 Head-rest, in hard wood, with carefully carved base and support [No. 32,601]

No. 65 Massive, solid wood head-rest, ornamented with figures of apes and of the god **Bes,** and inscribed with a text in which **Bes, Ta-urt,** and other gods promise life and health to the man for whom the object was made XIIth dynasty. [No 35,807.]

Presented by the Trustees of the Christy Collection, 1866.

Ivory Pillow of Kua-tep. No 30,727.

No 66 Head-rest, ornamented with grotesque figures of the god Bes in outline [No 35,799.]

No. 67. Head-rest made for **Aāua** ⌢ 𓏏 𓅯 𓎡 , the daughter of Heru, a priest of Menthu, lord of Thebes, and of the lady Nes-Mut ⌢ 𓏏 𓅯 𓎡 . The concave portion is ornamented with lotus flowers and a figure of the Utchat 𓂀 , and the base is inscribed in ink with the LVth, LXIst, and LXIInd Chapters of the Book of the Dead. XXIInd dynasty, or later. [No 35,804.]

No. 68.   Head-rest made for **Heru-á** , a priest (?) of Amen.   New Empire.   [No. 2530.]

No. 69.   **Ivory head-rest,** with the supports made in the form of the *thet*, or "buckle" of Isis.   A very rare object.   It was made for **Ḳua-ṭep**, whose massive coffin is exhibited on the landing of the North-west Staircase [No. 30,839].   XIth or XIIth dynasty.   From Al-Barsha.   [No. 30,727.]

No. 70.   Head-rest, made of a hard light-coloured wood and ebony, inlaid with ivory plaques and rosettes.

No. 26,256.

Two of the plaques are in the form of lotus flowers, and the others are ornamented with lotus flowers and buds, lions, and four figures, two seated and two standing, of a personage, who holds lotus and papyrus flowers in his hand. The head-dress and ear-rings suggest that the object is of Ethiopian [Nubian] origin.   XXVth or XXVIth dynasty.
                                [No. 26,256.]

Nos. 71-77. Stone and wooden head-rests, with supports in the form of pillars with square capitals, chiefly of the Ancient Empire. No. 71 is inscribed in hieratic, and belongs to the XIIth dynasty , No 72 has two fluted supports . No. 74 was made for the scribe **Mershi** , and the form of the hieroglyphics and the name show that this object was made under the IVth dynasty, about B C 3700.

[Nos 21,886, 17,102, 32,603, 32,602, 2524, 2527, 2528.]

No. 78 Head-rest, with a support turned on a lathe , the whole object has been covered with bitumen Roman period. Presented by Sir J. G. Wilkinson [No 2538.]

WALL-CASES 99-114.   Upper   Shelf. On this shelf, and in the back of the case, are exhibited a large and miscellaneous collection of painted wooden **sepulchral tablets**, and an important group of models of **funeral boats.** The stelæ are of a comparatively late date, *i e* , from about B.C 1300 onwards, and the greater number belong to the period which lies between the XXVIth and XXXth dynasties. Being imitations of the fine stone stelæ of the earlier period of Egyptian history, they have rounded tops, which were intended to represent the vault of heaven, and have figures of the gods of the dead painted upon them, with dedicatory inscriptions beneath them after the manner of the costly stone stelæ. When of a large size, wooden stelæ were mounted on bases, and placed either at the head or foot of the coffin , and when small they were placed inside it At the top of the stele we usually find the winged sun, the emblem of the god Horus of Behutet, *i e.*, the sky-god. Beneath this comes a representation of the deceased, who is seen making offerings either to Râ. or Osiris, or to the principal gods of the company of Osiris, or to the four children of Horus , he is often accompanied by his wife. and sometimes by his sons and daughters also The texts beneath these scenes are of two kinds, that is, they are either hymns to Râ, in which the deceased asks the god for permission to enter the Boat of Millions of Years, and to travel with him, or prayers to Osiris

Anubis, etc., that the customary general offerings may be made to the *ka* ⎍ or "double" of the deceased at the appointed seasons for ever. In the case of tombs which were visited by the relatives and friends of the dead, these were expected to repeat the prayers which were inscribed on the stelæ, for it was a matter of common belief that the repetition of such funeral prayers would bring an abundance of sustenance to the deceased in the next world. The elaborately painted pictures of offerings representing oxen, feathered fowl of various kinds, vegetables, fruit, flowers, wine, milk, incense, linen garments, unguents, etc., were believed to turn into food, etc., for the *ka*, or double, as soon as the proper words of power were uttered, either by the deceased in the Underworld or by his friends and relatives upon earth.

No. 79. Wooden stele, with a painted figure of the lady **Nes-Hathor** ⌐ 𓅓, worshipping Rā-Harmachis. XIXth dynasty.   [No. 22,917.]

No. 80. Wooden stele, with a figure of the lady **Tchet-Bast** ⌐ 𓏏 ⌐, worshipping Rā-Harmachis and Osiris; the deceased was a temple woman of Amen   XXIInd dynasty.
                                                              [No. 8452.]

No. 81. Wooden stele, with a figure of the lady **Nehems-Bast** 𓈖 𓏏 ⌐, the wife of **Petā-Āmen-[neb]-taui** ◻ 𓍯 ═══, who had predeceased her, worshipping Rā-Harmachis.   XXIInd dynasty.   [No. 22,916]

No. 82. Wooden stele, with a figure of **Nekht-f-Mut** 𓈖 𓆈 𓀭, a "divine father" of Amen, the son of **Utchat-Āmen-mes** 𓂀 𓏏 𓀭, worshipping Rā-Harmachis; he is accompanied by his daughter, "the lady of the house," **Shepu-en-Āst** ◻ ||| 𓂋 ⌐. XIXth dynasty.   [No. 37,899.]

No. 83. Wooden stele, with a figure of the priestess of Àmen Sheps-en-Àāḥ 𓀀 ~~~ [▭ 𓏞 ⌒ 𓀀, worshipping Rā-Harmachis. XIXth dynasty. [No. 25,262]

No. 84. Wooden stele, with a figure of Pa-ṭā-Àmen 𓀀 𓏞 𓏞, a priest of Àmen, and the overseer of the artificers of the temple of Àmen, offering incense to Osiris. XXth dynasty. [No. 8484]

No. 85. Painted stone stele, with the figure of an unnamed priest adoring Osiris, Isis, Nephthys, Mestha, and Tuamutef. Ptolemaic period. [No. 8490]

No. 86. Painted stone stele, with a figure of the lady Ta-sheret-en-Meḥet ⌒ 𓏞 𓏞 ~~~ 𓏞 ⌒ 𓏞 adoring Rā-Harmachis, Isis, and Nephthys. Persian period. From Abydos. [No. 29,422.]

No. 87. Wooden stele, with a figure of the lady Ḥetep-Amen ▭ 𓏞 𓏞, the daughter of the priest of Menthu, Māpu 𓏞 ▭ 𓏞 and of Nares 𓏞 ⌒ [𓏞, addressing Rā-Harmachis and Osiris. From the feet of the former god springs a bearded serpent; the deceased is represented coming from the east 𓏞 to the west 𓏞, where the Underworld was supposed to be situated. XXth dynasty [No. 8453.]

No. 88. Wooden stele, with a figure of the priest Tcheṭ-Menthu-àuf-ānkh 𓏞 𓏞 𓏞 𓏞 𓏞 𓏞, the son of Nini ~~~ ~~~ 𓏞 𓏞, adoring Rā-Harmachis, Isis, and the four children of Horus. XXIInd dynasty. [No. 8460.]

No. 89. Wooden stele, with a figure of the lady Her-àri-su 𓏞 𓏞 ⌒ | | | 𓏞, adoring Osiris and four solar gods. Late Ptolemaic period. [No. 8472.]

No. 90   Wooden stele, with a figure of the priest **Nes-p-sekher** [hieroglyphs], the son of **Tchet-Tehuti-auf-ānkh** [hieroglyphs], and **Set-ȧri-bȧ-ur** [hieroglyphs], adoring Rā-Harmachis and Atmu, *i.e.*, the morning and evening sun. The deceased and his father held the same offices of keeper of the beer cellar and poulterer, and each was the chief cook in the temple of Amen From Akhmim. XXth dynasty. [No. 36,504.]

No. 91   Painted stone stele, in the form of a pylon, made for the judge of appeal [hieroglyphs] **Pen-nubu** [hieroglyphs]; within the shrine is a seated figure of the god Ptah of the " Beautiful Face." XXIst dynasty. [No. 8497.]

No. 92.   Painted stone stele, with a figure of **Āa-pehti** [hieroglyphs] adoring the god **Seti-thiāa-pehti,** [hieroglyphs]. This is one of the very few examples of adoration being paid to the god Set on a stele of this kind.   XIXth dynasty.   [No. 35,630.]

No. 93.   Stone stele with a figure of the lady **I-em-ta-pet** [hieroglyphs], adoring the goddess **Mer-seker** [hieroglyphs] *i.e.*, " Lover of silence," the tutelary deity of the necropolis on the western bank at Thebes. XIXth dynasty   [No. 8501.]

No. 94.   Painted stone stele, with a figure of a man, whose name is illegible, adoring Rā-Harmachis, Mer-seker, and another.   XVIIIth dynasty.   [No. 8493]
Presented by the late Sir J. G. Wilkinson.

No. 95.   Wooden stele, with a figure of the " divine father," **Petāās** [hieroglyphs], surnamed **I-em-hetep** [hieroglyphs] [hieroglyphs], the son of **Pekhar-en-Khensu** [hieroglyphs], adoring Rā-Harmachis and Atmu, the sun god of the morning and evening. XXIst dynasty. [No. 8456.]

No. 96. Wooden stele, with a figure of a deceased person, whose name is illegible, adoring the god Osiris and a number of the gods of his company. Ptolemaic period.

[No. 8469.]

No. 97. Wooden stele, with a figure of **Maat-Ḥeru-Ru** � 𓃾 ⌒ 𓅬 adoring Rā-Harmachis, Isis, and other deities. Ptolemaïc period. [No. 8478.]

No. 98. Portion of a wooden stele, with a figure of **Ȧst-[em]-Khebit** 𓇋𓏏𓈖, a sistrum bearer of Amen, the daughter of a lady who held the same office, adoring Rā-Harmachis, Khepera, Shu and other gods. On the back is a scene in which light is represented falling from the sun on the horizon, with the signs for the East and West, 𓀀 𓀁, on either side. Ptolemaïc period.

[No. 8481.]

No. 99. Wooden stele, with the figure of the lady **Ta-khenen-nu** ☐ 𓃾 𓈖 𓅬, the daughter of **Bakren** 𓅬 𓈖 𓎟 and **Ta-bak-en-Khensu** ☐ 𓅆 𓅂 ⌒ 𓈖 𓏏 𓎛, adoring Osiris, Isis, Nephthys, and the four children of Horus. XXIVth dynasty. [No. 21,637.]

No. 100. Wooden stele of the sistrum bearer **Ta-heb** ☐ 𓃾 𓊵 𓄿 𓎛, the son of **Pe-ṭā-Ȧmen-neb-nest-taui.** In the rounded portion of the tablet are :—The winged disk, with pendent uræi, and the two jackals Ȧnpu and Ȧp-uat 𓃀 ☐ 𓃭 𓎛 𓏤𓏤𓏤. In the first register the soul of the deceased, in the form of a human-headed hawk 𓅐, is making offerings to Rā, Kheperá, Shu, and five other gods, and in the second the deceased is standing in adoration before Osiris, Horus, and five other gods. On the back of the tablet is a scene similar to that already described under No. 98. XXIInd dynasty. [No. 8465.]

No 101. Wooden stele, with a figure of the sistrum-bearer of Bast, **Neḥem-s-Rā-taui** ⟨hieroglyphs⟩, adoring Osiris and five of the gods of his company. XXIInd dynasty.   [No. 8477.]

No. 102. Wooden stele, with a small painted tablet enclosed within a double pylon, in relief, in which the priest **User-ā-harua** ⟨hieroglyphs⟩, the son of **Peṭā-Àst**, is represented adoring Rā-Harmachis and Maāt. XXth dynasty.   [No 8482.]

No. 103. Wooden stele of **Tcha-set-hem** ⟨hieroglyphs⟩. Above the text the mummy of the deceased, with the soul hovering over it, is seen lying upon its bier, in the presence of Isis, Nephthys, and the four children of Horus ; below it are the magical symbols *tet* and *thet* ⟨hieroglyphs⟩, the emblems of the East and West, and the gods Khnemu, Thoth, Shu, and Tefnut holding knives   Ptolemaic period
                                                             [No. 8486]

No. 104. Wooden stele of **Basa-en-Mut** ⟨hieroglyphs⟩, a priest of Menthu, lord of Thebes, the son of **Nes-pa-sefi** ⟨hieroglyphs⟩ and **Shepset-aru-ru** ⟨hieroglyphs⟩. The upper portion contains figures of the deceased adoring Temu and Rā-Harmachis, and beneath are two hymns to these gods. XXIInd dynasty.
                                                             [No. 22,915.]

No. 105. Wooden stele of **Pe-kha-Khensu** ⟨hieroglyphs⟩. a scribe in the service of the goddess Serk (Selk) ⟨hieroglyphs⟩ ⟨hieroglyphs⟩, the son of the priest of Amen, **Pe-ṭā-Àmen-neb-nest-taui** ⟨hieroglyphs⟩, and of the sistrum bearer of Amen-Rā ⟨hieroglyphs⟩, **Neḥem-s-Rā-**

taui. In the upper register the soul of the deceased is seen adoring Rā and his company, who are seated in the Boat of Millions of Years, and below the deceased worships Osiris, Isis, Nephthys, Horus, the avenger of his father, and Hathor. XXIInd dynasty. [No. 8467.]

No. 106 Wooden stele of **Neḥem-s-Rā-taui** ⌣ ☒ ☒ ı ═ ☖⌇. In the upper portion are the two jackal-dogs of the South and North ; a figure of the deceased adoring the dead sun-god **Af**, who stands in his boat within a shrine formed by the Serpent-god **Meḥen**, and is piloted by Harpocrates , and two scenes in which the deceased is adoring Osiris at morning and evening. This stele was originally prepared for a man, the name of the deceased lady being added later. XXIInd dynasty. [No. 8470]

No. 107. Wooden stele of **Seḥetep-Khensu** ⌇ ⎯☉⎯ ☉ ⌇⌇, a priest of Horus. In the upper portion the deceased, who is introduced by Anubis, is seen adoring Osiris, Isis, and Nephthys, and in the prayer below it is stated that he was attached to the service of all the gods and goddesses ⌇⌇⌇ ⌇⌇⌇ of Edfu. Ptolemaic period.

[No. 32,199.]

No. 108 Wooden stele of a priest, who is represented in the act of adoring the dead sun-god **Af**, who is seated in his boat, and a company of nine gods, with Rā at their head, and Osiris and five of the gods of his company. Late Saïte period, about B.C. 400 [No. 8466]

No. 109. Wooden stele of **Sheps-her-ȧb-Ȧset** ⌇⌇ ⎯☐⎯ ♀ ı ⌇⌇⌇⌇, commander of the crew of the boat of Ȧmen, with figures of the deceased adoring Rā-Harmachis and Ȧtmu. XXIInd dynasty, or later. [No. 8457.]

No. 110. Wooden stele of **Ānkh-f-en-Khensu** ♀ ☉ ☒ ⌇⌇⌇⌇, the son of **Bes-Mut** ⌇⌇⌇⌇, and Ḥetep-

Åmen ⌒▱◖⌐, with figures of the deceased adoring Rā-Harmachis and Atmu Bes-Mut was a priest of Amen-Rā and of ◰◖⌐ꬶ◖◠◖⌐ XXVIIth dynasty.

[No 22,919]

⌐·No. 111. Wooden stele of **Uah-ab-Rā** ⵀⵁⵔⵙ, spaces are left blank for the names of his father and mother. In the upper part of the stele, below the winged disk and jackals, the deceased is seen adoring the dead sun-god Af (Hefu ⵀⵁ◠◠◠) and Osiris and his company of gods XXVIth dynasty.   [No 8464.]

No 112. Wooden stele with a figure of **Pef en-Bastet** ◰◖◠◠◖◰◖, adoring Osiris and some of the gods of his company. XXXth dynasty.   [No. 8480]

No. 113. Wooden stele of the divine scribe and governor **Heru-à** ◖◈◖◖◖, who stands in adoration before Rā-Harmachis and Temu ; each god stands in a shrine. The text below consists of two hymns, one to the rising and one to the setting sun XXIInd dynasty.

[No 8455.]

No. 114 Wooden stele, with a figure of **Emmā-Bastet** ◰◖◠◖, daughter of **Tchet-hrā** ◖◈◖, and **Ta-uaru** ◰◖◈◖◖, adoring the deities of the sunrise and sunset. XXXth dynasty.   [No 35,897.)

No. 115. Wooden stele, with a figure of **Pa-nes** ◈◖◖, " president of the secrets of the seat of Maāt," *i.e.*, a high judicial official, adoring Osiris, Isis, Nephthys, and a child of Horus, his father **Heru** ◖◈ held the same office The figures are white, painted with red lines and gold, upon a blue ground ; the use of gold on wooden sepulchral stelæ is most unusual. XXIInd dynasty.

[No 8504]

No 116. Wooden stele with a figure of **Pa-shere-Aset** 𓄿 𓏭 𓊹 adoring Rā-Harmachis, Isis, and the four children of Horus, each of whom holds a palm branch instead of the ordinary sceptre 𓋾. Early Ptolemaïc period.

[No. 8459.]

No. 117. Wooden stele of **Ári-nekht-tcha** 𓄿 𓏭, son of **Menth-ári-ṭās** 𓈖 𓁹 𓊹 and 𓁷 𓈖 𓏤 𓊹 **Shepset-Áset-urt**, with a similar scene. XXXth dynasty. [No. 8458.]

No. 118. Wooden stele of the lady **Qeresá** 𓈖 𓏭 𓊹, daughter of **Tcha-en-reṭ** 𓈖 𓏲 𓊹, and **Thes-Mut-per** 𓈖 𓊹, with a similar scene. XXXth dynasty. [No. 22,918.]

No. 119. Wooden stele of **Ári-seb-aru** 𓈖 𓏤 𓏭. with a similar scene. XXXth dynasty. [No. 35,625.]

No. 120. Wooden stele of the priest **Nes-pua** 𓈖 𓏭 𓊹, son of **Nes-Ptaḥ** 𓈖 𓊹. Ptolemaïc period. [No. 8473.]

No 121. Wooden stele of **Ānkh-f-Khensu** 𓂋 𓏭 𓊹, son of **Bes-Mut** 𓂋 𓊹, with figures of the deceased adoring Rā-Harmachis and Atmu. The text below consists of two hymns addressed to these deities. XXVIth dynasty. [No. 22,914]

No. 122. Wooden stele of **Nes-Ḥeru** 𓈖 𓊹, son of 𓈖 𓊹 **Peseshet** and **Qebkhu** 𓂋 𓏭 𓐋, with a similar scene. XXVIth dynasty. [No. 21,636.]

G

No. 123. Wooden stele of **Pa-hāp-ḥa-Menthu** [hieroglyphs], son of **Amen-ári** [hieroglyphs], and **Tcheṭ-Ást-ári-ást** [hieroglyphs], with a figure of the deceased adoring Osiris and some of the gods of his company. XXXth dynasty   [No. 8476.]

No. 124. Wooden stele of a priest of Amen-Rā, with a figure of the deceased adoring Rā-Harmachis. XIXth dynasty.   [No. 8451.]

No. 125. Wooden stele of **Nes-qa-shuti** [hieroglyphs], son of **Qāha** [hieroglyphs] and **Mut-á** [hieroglyphs], with a figure of the deceased worshipping Osiris, Isis, Neheb-kau, Nephthys, and the four children of Horus, who stand on a lotus flower. XXVIth dynasty.   [No. 8479.]

No. 126. Wooden stele with figures of **Neb-Ámen** [hieroglyphs], a judge of appeal, and his brother **Áui** [hieroglyphs], adoring "Ámen-Rā, the beautiful prince," who is represented in the form of a ram XIXth dynasty.
                                                        [No. 8485.]

No. 127. Wooden stele of **Tcheṭ-ḥrá** [hieroglyphs] with a figure of the deceased adoring Osiris and certain of his gods XXXth dynasty.   [No. 8475.]

No. 128. Wooden stele of **Petá-Amen-Rā-neb-Uast** [hieroglyphs] with figures of Osiris and the four children of Horus. Ptolemaic period.   [No. 8471.]

No. 129. Wooden stele with a figure of **Ta-qes** [hieroglyphs], a singing woman of Amen-Rā, adoring the triune form of the sun-god. XXth dynasty.
                                                    [No. 27,332.]

No. 130. Wooden stele of **Ṭunf-pa-nefer** , son of Petā-Asàr, with a figure of the deceased adoring Rā-Harmachis and Isis. XXVIth dynasty. [No. 21,639.]

No. 131. Wooden stele of **Ḥeru-utcha** , with a figure of the deceased adoring Rā , the text is a prayer for sepulchral offerings. XXVIth dynasty. [No. 8448.]

No 132. Wooden stele of a daughter of **Nekht-f-Mut** . XXIInd dynasty. [No. 35,895.]

No. 133. Wooden stele of **Maatiu-àriu** , with figures of the deceased and his wife adoring Rā and the four children of Horus. XXXth dynasty. [No. 8474.]

No. 134. Wooden stele of **Petā-Khensu** , an official of the temples of Amen-Rā and Khensu at Karnak , the deceased is repiesented with a large dish of offerings upon his head and a cake in the form of a ciescent moon, symbolic of Khensu. XXVth dynasty. [No. 35,896]

No. 135 Wooden stele of **Nes-ther-en-Maāt** , the daughter of the chief clerk of the works in the temple of Amen, **Ānkh-pa-khraṭ** and **Theshepet** . XXIInd dynasty. [No. 8450]

No. 136. Wooden stele of **Taiàu-khraṭ** , a singing woman in the temple of Amen. XXth dynasty. [No. 8447.]

No. 137. Wooden stele of **Thebnesta** ,

mounted on a pair of steps.   Within an ornamental border
are painted the following scenes :—1.   The sun's disk, with
pendent uræi, shedding rays of light on each side of a
jackal. 2. The soul adoring the dead sun-god Af, who is
seated in his boat ; behind the soul is its " shadow," ⌐,

3. A man, called **Tchabari** [hieroglyphs], probably

the husband of Theb-
nesta, adoring Osiris
and six of the gods
of his company   4.
Row of figures of the
Ṭet [hieroglyph], and the "buckle
of Isis " [hieroglyph].   XXIInd
dynasty
                [No 8463.]
No. 138. Wooden
stele   of   **Nesui**
[hieroglyphs], a priest,
son of   **Takureheb**
[hieroglyphs],
who makes adorations
to the gods in the
boat of Rā, and to
the gods in the Under-
world.   The stele is
beautifully painted in
bright colours on a
No 8468   white   ground, and
stands upon two sup-
ports in the form of the mythological steps [hieroglyph]; it is surmounted by a human-headed hawk, emblematic of the soul
of the deceased, with a gilded face.

This is one of the finest examples of the painted wooden
funeral stelæ in the collection.   XXIInd dynasty.
                [No. 8468.]

No. 139 Wooden stele of **Uah-ȧb-Rā** 𓋹𓏤, a priest of Amen-Rā, son of the "scribe of the wonders of Amen-Rā," **Neb-nest-tauı** ⟨hieroglyphs⟩. This stele is elaborately painted, and contains an unusually large number of mythological scenes, which may be thus described — (1) Gilded disk with wings and uræı ; (2) beetle, from which proceed a number of emblems of life 𓋹𓋹𓋹𓋹, that fall upon the mummy of the deceased ; on each side of the mummy are several genii of the underworld ; (3) representations of the souls of the deceased and his father and mother adoring the dead sun-god and the gods of his company, who are seated ın a boat ; (4) the deceased and

his mother worshıpping the symbol of Osırıs, ⟨hieroglyph⟩, and

various deities , (5) the deceased adoring two rows of gods. On the edge of the stele is a double ınscrıptıon, and on the back is a representatıon of the dısk of the sun shedding rays of light. On the stele the god Amen is descrıbed as, "lord of the thrones of the two lands ın the glory of the monuments," ı e, the great temples of Karnak and Luxor, which were still magnıficent, although the cıty of Thebes itself had been sacked and partly destroyed by the Assyrıans not long before the perıod when the stele was made, XXVIth dynasty. [No. 8461.]

No 140. Wooden stele of **Peṭā-Ȧmen-neb-nest-tauı** ⟨hieroglyphs⟩, ‹on of **Ḥeru** ⟨hieroglyphs⟩ and **Karuthet** ⟨hieroglyphs⟩. The deceased held the offices of (1) " dıvıne father of Amen ın Karnak," (2) "hıgh prıest of Annu-resu (ı e , Dendera)," (3) "he who ıs over the secrets," (4) " lıbatıoner of the god in the most holy places," (5) "great prophet of Khensu in Thebes, surnamed Nefeı-hetep" ⟨hieroglyphs⟩ ⟨hieroglyphs⟩ IIıs father held the

same offices (☖ ⫯⫯⫯). In the registers the deceased's soul
is represented in the act of adoring, in company with two
groups of sacred apes, the dead sun-god Af, who is seated
in his boat, and the deceased, in full priestly attire, is seen
adoring Rā-Harmachis, Atmu, Khepera, Osiris, Isis, Nephthys, and Anubis. On the back of the stele, which is
mounted on two supports in the form of steps, the sun's
disk is depicted shedding rays between the symbols of
East and West.   XXVIth dynasty.   [No. 8462.]

Funeral Boats.— The fine collection of painted wooden
boats with their crews here exhibited is of two classes,
viz., those which are made in the form of the ordinary
funeral or divine bark (*baris*) as represented on the monuments, and those which are models of the ordinary river
boats which were in common use at the time they were
made. In the former the deceased is seen lying upon his
bier under a canopy, sometimes accompanied by Isis and
Nephthys ; sometimes such boats contain figures of rowers,
and sometimes they do not. Boats of this class are found
in all periods, and are of various sizes, but those of the
second class usually belong to the period of the XIth and
XIIth dynasties, about B.C. 2500 2200, and are, relatively,
of large size ; they are always provided with a large crew,
the members of which are often dressed in garments made
of real linen cloth, which is contemporaneous with the
figures themselves Each boat was furnished with masts,
sails (which have now perished), and elaborately decorated
oars, and steering posts, the ends of which are often in the
form of the heads of hawks. The use of the funeral boat
dates from the earliest period, those of the first class represent the actual funeral boat in which the body of the
deceased was ferried across the Nile from the east to the
west bank, where the majority of the cemeteries were
situated, and those of the second class are to be regarded
merely as articles of funeral furniture, and must be placed
in the same category as the models of houses, granaries,
and labourers and tradesmen which are found with them
in tombs of the same period With both classes of boats,
however, was connected another religious idea, namely, the
conception of the boat of the sun-god, called the **" Boat of**

"**Millions of Years**," in which the souls of the beatified were believed to travel nightly in the train of the sun-god as he passed through the Underworld from West to East. The sun-god made his journey by day across the sky in two boats, which were called respectively **Ātet** (or, Mātet) and **Sektet** (or, Semktet). In the former of these he travelled until noon, and in the latter from noon until the evening. During the night, when the sun-god travelled through the Underworld, he was regarded as dead, like the other denizens of the **Tuat** (see page 126), and in this form he appears as a ram-headed being, called **Af, or Auf** (literally, "his, *i e*, the sun-god's, body"), who, as we have seen on the funeral stelæ already described, sits within a shrine which is formed by the folds of the serpent **Mehen.** Finally, the boats of the second class seem to have been placed in the tombs with the view of providing the dead man with the means of sailing about on the streams of the Underworld. By a process of thought common to primitive religions, the Egyptians believed that by the use of words of magical power the "double" (ghost) could transform the models of objects placed in the tombs, including boats, houses, etc, into ghostly representations of their originals upon earth. Thus, provided that such models were placed in the tombs to serve as bases for the ghostly materialization, the deceased could provide himself with anything that he required in the next life. The boat was considered to be such a necessary adjunct to the comfort of the deceased in the next world, that special chapters of the Book of the Dead were compiled for the purpose of supplying him with the words of power necessary to enable him to obtain it. Thus Chapter XCIX. helped him "to bring along a boat," Chapter C enabled him to sail in the boat of Rā, and several other chapters related to the boat of Rā. In Chapter XCIX we have a full list of the magical names of different parts of the ghostly boat in the Underworld, which the deceased was obliged to utter correctly before the boat would allow him to enter. Thus, "Tell us our name," say the oar-rests ; and the deceased answers, "Pillars of the "Underworld is your name." "Tell me my name," saith the Hold ; "Aker" is thy name. "Tell me my name," saith the Sail ; "Nut" (*i e*, heaven) is thy name," etc.

No. 141   **Model of a boat,** painted red, with a crew of nine men ; on the deck is a cabin, which much resembles that in use at the present day. XIth or XIIth dynasty.

[No. 36,422]

No. 142.   **Stone-boat,** with a canopy, beneath which is a figure of a man rolling bread, in the style of the Early Empire ; on the side are reliefs of animal scenes, in the style of the XVIIIth dynasty ; whilst the attendant priests are intended to represent men of a much later period. These anachronisms suggest that the object is a modern forgery. Presented by Captain Taylor, 1841.   [No 9507.]

No 143.   Model of a **ferry-boat,** with a crew of eight rowers, a steersman, and a man who held a punting pole ; the passengers are four in number, two persons of rank, who are seated and wear white cloaks, a servant carrying a pack of luggage on his back, and another servant. XIth or XIIth dynasty.   [No. 35,291]

No. 144   Model of a **ferry-boat,** or **war-boat,** with a crew of fourteen rowers sitting in pairs, the coxswain is provided with a very long and heavy steering oar, and the oars are fastened to the side of the boat by string. XIth or XIIth dynasty.   [No. 25,361]

No. 145.   Model of a boat, of somewhat clumsy build, with a very short keel and overhanging bows and stern XIIth dynasty   [No. 35,292.]

No. 146.   Model of a long **war-boat,** the crew of which consists of six rowers and a steersman. In the centre of the boat, with his back to a mast, is seated a person of quality ; in front of him is a shelter, formed by two of the great cow-hide shields in use in this period, leaning against a post ; under the shields is an object which is probably intended to represent a brazier with fire in it   In the bows of the boat stand five men, each holding a short stick. XIIth dynasty   [No. 35,293]

No. 147   Model of a boat with rowers, each seated upon a separate bench ; a few of these still have upon them their original linen loin-clothes. A person of distinction, wearing a long white cloak, is seated in the bows. XIIth dynasty.   [No 34,273.]

Nos. 148, 149. Two models of **funeral boats**, provided with canopied biers, whereon lie models of the mummies of the deceased persons. At each end of each bier stands a female mourner, who symbolizes one of the two goddesses Isis and Nephthys. Close by stand models of water jars on a frame, and articles of food ; each boat is provided with a steersman, who works two large oars, the handles of which terminate in the heads of hawks. The tops of the steering posts also terminate in the heads of hawks   XIIth dynasty   [Nos. 9524, 9525]

No 9525

WALL-CASES 99-109. Second Shelf. Here is exhibited a representative series of small **portrait statues** and figures, made of hard stone of various kinds, limestone, sandstone, etc., which date from the period of the IIIrd dynasty, about B.C. 3800, to the Roman period, about A.D. 200. Archæologically and artistically this collection is of the highest importance, for from it may be traced the development of Egyptian sculpture in the round, and the modifications which the art of portraiture underwent during the successive great periods of Egyptian history, which taken together cover a space of about four thousand years. From first to last the sculptors made use of the characteristic white limestone of the country, which was generally painted, to a greater or less extent. (See the groups in

Wall-Case 105.] During the period of the Early Empire, hard stones, of fine, close texture, usually black in colour, were employed in making small figures (see Wall-Cases 99, 100); light yellow alabaster was also much used   Under the XIIth dynasty red and white quartzite and green felspar became common (see Wall-Cases 101, 102), under the New Empire black and red granite were in fashion, and under the XXVIth dynasty black basalt was extensively used for statues, chiefly because it was most suitable for cutting the delicately shaped hieroglyphics upon. The best portrait work seems to have been executed under the IVth, XIIth, and XVIIIth dynasties; the archaistic revival of the XXVIth dynasty also gave rise to an attempt to equal the portraiture of the early dynasties. The carefully executed, but somewhat unpleasing portrait statues of the Roman period, are due to the influence of Graeco-Roman art.

The Official Nefer-hi   No. 24,714.

No. 150. Limestone seated figure of the official Nefer-hi 𓏏𓉐𓐎, painted red. IIIrd or IVth dynasty. From Sakkara.
[No. 24,714]

No. 151. Portion of the head of a statue of an official. Found in the workmen's quarters, behind the Second Pyramid of Gizeh   IVth dynasty.   [No 14,288]

No 152. Black granite statue of a nobleman, or official ; over his wig he wears a kind of band, which encircles the head, after the manner of the camel-hair rope worn by Arabs. This is the only example of the head-dress in the collection.   IIIrd or IVth dynasty.   [No. 26,790.]

No. 153. Painted limestone head of an officer. IVth dynasty. From Ṣakkâra [No. 13,346]

No. 154 Painted limestone seated figure of Ānnuá, 〰 ⟨hieroglyphs⟩, a priest and nobleman. Vth dynasty. From Saḳḳâra [No. 32,184]

No. 155 A group of fourteen small black stone portrait figures, of similar workmanship and characteristics VIth–XIIIth dynasties. The chief names are those of Heru-sa-f ⟨hieroglyphs⟩, Ȧnepu, priest of Hathor, and Apep ⟨hieroglyphs⟩; No. 13,320 is a double statue (Antef and his wife Mersebs), and No. 2305 is a triple statue, made in honour of Menthu-hetep, his mother Ȧpu, and wife Met-ta-nebu (?). Most of these statues come from Abydos and the neighbourhood.

No 156. Alabaster seated figure of a priest, whose throne rests upon a step-pedestal of painted limestone. From Abydos. [No. 2313.]

No 157. Similar alabaster figure standing. From Abydos [No 2312.]

Nos. 158, 159. Two painted limestone figures of men, one seated and the other standing. [Nos. 13,318, 36,437]

Nos 156–159 belong to the period which lies between the VIth and the XIth dynasties.

No. 160. Painted limestone figure of Ȧn-kheft-k ⟨hieroglyphs⟩, a "royal relative" ⟨hieroglyphs⟩ and scribe. IVth or Vth dynasty. From Dashâsha. [No. 29,562.]
Presented by the Egypt Exploration Fund, 1897

No. 161. Painted limestone figure inscribed in hieratic with the name Usr ⟨hieroglyphs⟩, and a prayer to Anubis. XIth dynasty. [No. 30,457.]

No. 162. Statue of **Mera** ⌐⊏ ⎔, a royal steward, wearing a skull-cap. VIth–XIth dynasty. From Kûrna. [No. 37,895.]

No. 163. Statue of **Mera**, a royal steward, wearing a wig. VIth–XIth dynasty. From Kûrna. [No. 37,896.] Nos. 162 and 163 are statues of the same person in different costumes; they are of great interest and importance, for they are among the earliest specimens of Theban art, as they date from the period when the Herakleopolite kings ruled over Egypt, and before the founding of the great Theban Empire.

No. 164. Diorite statue of **Sebek-nekht,** the son of **Ānkhet.** Very fine work. XIIth or XIIIth dynasty. [No. 29,671.]

No. 165. Seated statue of **Set-rumi,** an officer of the Temple of Ptaḥ. XIIth or XIIIth dynasty. [No. 29,946.]

No. 166. Upper portion of a portrait figure of an officer. XIIth dynasty. [No. 13,345.]

No. 167. Green felspar statue of **Ānkh-pa-khrat,** a priest of Hathor. This is one of the finest examples of small portrait figures in hard stone in the Museum. XIIth dynasty. [No. 32,183.]

Statue of
Ptaḥ-em-sa-f-senb-tefi.
No. 24,385.

No. 168. Black granite statue of an official; the name is illegible. XIIth dynasty. [No. 35,362.]

No. 169. Rough limestone figure of a man ; poor work. XIth dynasty. [No. 2296.]

No. 170. Red quartzite statue of **Ptaḥ-em-sa-f-senb-**

Statue of Mera. No. 37,895.   Statue of Mera. No. 37,896.

tefi ⬚𓈖𓏏𓁐 〰〰 ⬚ \\, son of Kemt, a royal chancellor and scribe of Lower Egypt. The deceased is dressed in a long garment, which extends from his arm-pits to his feet, this costume is characteristic of the period, and the statue is a fine example of the work of the XIIth dynasty.   [No. 24,385.]

Nos. 171A and B.   Upper portions of two basalt figures of **Amen-em-ḥāt III.**, the greatest king of the XIIth dynasty, about B.C. 2300.   This king is the **Mœris**, or Maros, of the Greeks, and is famous because of his works in connexion with the Fayyûm, and the building of the **Labyrinth** at Hawâra, which is described by Greek and Roman writers.

[Nos. 26,935, 36,298.]

No. 172.   Cast of the head of a figure of **Amen-ḥetep III.**, in the possession of Lord Grenfell.

[No. 18,192.]

No. 173   Seated figure of **Senb-f,** an overseer of artisans.   XIIth or XIIIth dynasty.   [No. 2307.]

No. 174.   Grey granite figure of an official. Since the figure bears no name, it is evident that it formed part of the stock of a funeral furnisher, who kept it in readiness for a possible purchaser, whose name would be inscribed upon it when bought.   XIIth dynasty   [No 2308.]

No. 175.   Limestone standing figure, painted white, and inscribed on the pedestal in hieratic with the name of Usertsen (?), a devotee of the god Menthu.   XIIth dynasty.   [No. 2295.]

No. 176.   Limestone figure ; rude work, and unfinished appearance.   XIIIth–XVIIth dynasty.   [No 32,056.]

No. 177.   Lower portion of a seated figure of a king, made of crystalline white quartzite.   The work and material indicate that this object dates from the XIIth dynasty, and the figure may have been intended to represent Amen-em-ḥāt III.   XIIth dynasty.

[No. 35,361.]

No. 178. Fine green basalt statue of a king. The beard, which was made of gold or electrum, was fastened under the chin by pegs, the sockets of which are still visible. On the base is an unfinished inscription, which reads, "Beautiful Horus, giver of life, the servant of Thoth "(?). XIIIth dynasty. [No. 18,193.]

No. 179. Portion of a limestone figure of the " royal relative" Athembu* ⟨𓊹𓏺⟩ 𓀀 𓏏𓊪. XIIIth dynasty

No. 37,883. [See page 96.]

or later. The form of the name suggests that Athembu was not an Egyptian. [No. 21,878.]

No. 180. Diorite seated figure of Uru (?), son of Ḥetepet. XIIth or XIIIth dynasty. [No. 36,441.]

* Variant ⟨𓊹𓏺⟩ 𓏏𓊪 @ Âthebu.

No. 181. Portion of a grey granite seated figure of

Tchai 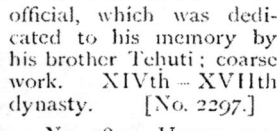, a priest of Ptah and Sekhet at Memphis. XIVth XVIIIth dynasty.   [No. 20,731.]

No. 182. Two black stone seated figures of officials. XIIIth dynasty.   .   [Nos. 32,185, 32,186.]

No. 183. Lower portion of limestone statue of an official, which was dedicated to his memory by his brother Tehuti ; coarse work.   XIVth — XVIIth dynasty.   [No. 2297.]

Statue of Teta-kharṭ.   No. 22,558.

No. 184. Upper portion of a statue of an official wearing a heavy wig. XIIIth XVIIth dynasty.   [No. 36,851.]

No. 185.   Limestone standing statue of **Sebek-nekht,** the son of **Àá,** 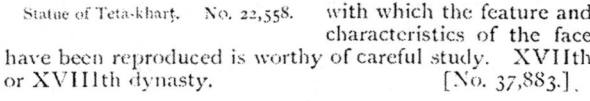. XIIIth-XVIIth dynasty.   [No. 36,850.]

No. 186. Head of a portrait statue of an official in crystalline limestone. This is one of the finest examples of Egyptian portrait sculpture known. The subject was evidently an old man, and the skill with which the feature and characteristics of the face have been reproduced is worthy of careful study.   XVIIth or XVIIIth dynasty.   [No. 37,883.]

No. 187. Portrait figure in fine limestone, painted white, of Queen **Tetà-kharṭ** (*or*, **Tetà-Sheret**) an immediate ancestress of Aāhmes, the founder of the XVIIIth dynasty. It is probable that she was the wife of **Seqenen-Rā Tau-āa I.**, a king of the XVIIth dynasty, B.C. 1700. From Thebes. [No. 22,558.]

No. 188. Limestone kneeling figure of an official holding a stele inscribed with the text of a **hymn to Åmen-Rā.** XVIIIth dynasty. [No. 29,279.]

No. 189. Similar figure in black granite, inscribed with a hymn to Rā; made for Åmen-em-āpt. XVIIIth dynasty. [No. 26,270.]

No. 190. Similar figure in hard, black stone; inscription obliterated. XVIIIth dynasty. From Crocodilopolis. [No. 37,884.]

No. 191. Similar figure in limestone, inscribed with the text of a hymn to Rā. XVIIIth dynasty. [No. 24,430.]

No. 192. Similar figure in black granite, inscribed with the text of a hymn to Rā; it was made for Åmen-em-heb, who was surnamed Māhu. XVIIIth dynasty. [No. 22,557.]

No. 193. Standing figure, with tablet, in sandstone, plastered and painted; it was made for **Usr-Ḥāt**, an official in the temple of Åmen. The text is that of a hymn to Rā. XVIIIth dynasty [No. 2294.]

Kneeling figure of a Priest.
No. 24,430.

No. 194. Kneeling limestone figure of **Seānkh-Åmenqen**, holding an inscribed stele. XVIIIth dynasty. [No. 21,980.]

No. 195. Kneeling limestone figure of a man wearing a side lock, as prince(?), and holding an altar. XVIIIth dynasty. [No. 21,979.]

H

No. 196.   Similar figure holding an altar ; painted black and red.   XVIIIth dynasty.   Fine work.   Nos 194–196 were presented by the Earl of Carlisle in 1889.

[No. 21,978]

No 197 Grey granite kneeling figure of **Ka-em-Uast,** a superintendent of the cattle in the temple of Amen, and a scribe in the palace of Thothmes IV   On the stele which he holds is cut a figure of the ram, sacred to Amen, with floral offerings   XVIIIth dynasty·   [No 37,885.]

No. 198   Similar figure in painted limestone of **Amen- em-heb,** surnamed **Māhu,** the chief goldsmith of the god Amen   XVIIIth dynasty.   [No. 29,944.]

No. 199.   Lower portion of a seated figure of **Ren- senb,** a "clerk of all the works of the king" , the deceased was a man of high rank, and held the dignity of hereditary prince   This statue was dedicated to his memory by the precentor **Hrå-Åmen.** XVIIIth dynasty.   [No 13,368]

Nos. 200, 201.   Heads of portrait figures of persons whose names are unknown ; fine work   XVIIIth dynasty.

[Nos 2339, 2340]

No 202   Steatite figure (sculptor's model ?) of king Thothmes III. ; B C. 1550.   [No. 13,354.]

No 203   Fine steatite figure of king **Amen-hetep III.,** B C. 1450.   From Thebes   [No. 2275]

No. 204.   Fine steatite figure of a king in the form of the god Amen-Rā.   XVIIIth dynasty.   [No 13,353]

No 205   Portion of a standing **figure** of a king which was **usurped** by **Heru-em-heb,** the last king of the XVIIIth dynasty.   [No. 37,639.]
Presented by W McOran Campbell, Esq , 1903

No 206   Portrait figures of **Pa-sheṭu,** and his wife **Ruau,** seated side by side, each with an arm encircling the other ; painted limestone.   XVIIIth dynasty·

[No. 2304]

No. 207. Portrait figures of **Åmen-em-pert**, surnamed Min-Amen (or, **Åmsu-Åmen**), an official of the court of **King Thothmes I.**, and his wife, seated side by side, each with an arm encircling the other ; painted limestone. The upper portions of the figures have been restored. XVIIIth dynasty. [No. 2303.]

No. 208. Similar figures of **Ḥamā** . . . . . . i 𓀀 𓅃, and his wife **Urt-nefert** 𓂋 𓏏 𓄤 𓆓 :

the determinative which follows the man's name shows that he was a foreigner. XVIIIth dynasty. [No. 2302.]

No. 209. Similar figures of a man and wife whose names are wanting. XVIIIth dynasty. [No. 2301.]

No. 210. Seated figures of Min-mes (or **Åmsu-mes**), and his wife and a royal nurse, who was probably a relative ; the deceased was the director of the festival of Osiris and Åmen, and president of the palace of the 'divine wife,' *i.e.*, the reigning queen (?) or priestess. The monument was

Figures of Urt-nefert and her husband. No. 2302.

made by the son of the deceased, who was "chief priest of Osiris," and bore the same name as his father. XVIIIth dynasty. [No. 2300.]

No. 211. Painted limestone figure of a scribe holding before him an image of Osiris. XVIIIth dynasty.

[No. 2292.]

H 2

No. 212.   Portion of the head of a limestone statue of
Åmen-ḥetep IV. (Khu-en-Åten) ; this portrait of the king
was originally very exact.   XVIIIth dynasty.

[No. 13,366.]

Khu-en-Åten (Åmen-ḥetep IV.)   No. 24,431.   [See page 101.]

No 213   Torso of a red sandstone statue of **Amen-hetep IV.** (Khu-en-Aten), holding a crook , on his breast are inscribed the titles of the god Aten   XVIIIth dynasty, B.C 1430.   From Tel' el-Amarna.   [No 12,278]
Presented by the Rev. W. J. Loftie, 1883.

No. 214.   Portion of a painted stone tablet with a portrait figure of **Amen-hetep IV.**, in hollow relief, seated upon a throne , above him are the rays of the god Aten, which proceed from the sun-disk, and which terminate in human hands   The style of the work is curious and interesting.   XVIIIth dynasty.
                            [No. 24,431.]

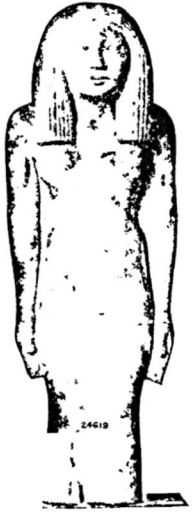

No. 215.   Grey granite head of a statue of **Rameses II.**, B.C   1330   XIXth dynasty.   [No. 37,886.]

No 216.   Upper portion of a painted limestone figure of a princess XIXth dynasty   [No. 29,280]

No. 217.   Upper portion of a black basalt statue of a princess , fine work. XIXth dynasty   From Thebes.
                            [No. 37,887.]

No 218   Fine alabaster standing figure of a princess ; good work. XIXth dynasty.   [No. 24,619.]

No 219.   Upper portion of a granite figure of an officer.   XIXth dynasty.
                            [No 2315]

No 220   Seated granite figure of **Herua,** son of Ptah-mes.   XIXth dynasty   [No. 14,368]

Figure of a Princess.
No. 24,619.

No. 221.   Steatite kneeling figure of **Ptah-meri,** the scribe of the offerings of all the gods, holding the cartouche of **Rameses II.**   XIXth dynasty.   [No. 2291.]

Nos. 222, 223   Heads of two female figures.   XIXth dynasty.   [Nos. 2381, 2382.]

No. 224. Seated statue of **Khert-nefer,** dedicated by his brother Sa-mut, a Judge of Appeal.   XXth dynasty.
[No. 2293.]

No. 225.   Sculptor's model for the head of a royal statue.   XXth dynasty.   [No. 36,849.]

Figure of Harua.   No. 32,555.   [See page 103.]

No. 226.   Portion of a statue of **Khamā - Ḥeru,** a libationer.   XIXth or XXth dynasty.   [No. 14,403.]

No. 227.   Seated, grey granite funeral statue of **Pa-ari.** XXth–XXIInd dynasty.   [No. 37,888.]

No. 228.   Similar statue of **Ámen-ḥetep,** an overseer of the royal granaries and estates. XXth–XXIInd dynasty.
[No. 32,182.]

No. 229. Lower portion of the figure of the royal scribe **Hui,** holding a cynocephalus ape on a shrine. From Tell Basta. XXIInd dynasty.   [No. 13,355.]

No. 230. Part of the statuette of **Thekelethá I.,** a king of the XXIInd dynasty. From Abydos. [No. 37,326.] Presented by the Egypt Exploration Fund, 1902.

No. 231. Kneeling statue of a king holding a memorial tablet ; the base and plinth are uninscribed. XXII-XXVth dynasty.   [No. 26,271.]

No. 232. Grey granite statue of **Queen Amenártás.** XXVth dynasty. About B.C. 700.   [No. 36,440.]

No. 233. Head of a statue of an official of **Queen Amenártás.** XXVth dynasty. B.C. 700.   [No. 14,421.]

No. 234. Seated figure of **Harua,** a high official of **Queen Amenártás,** holding small seated statues of Hathor and Tefnut. XXVth dynasty. [No. 32,555.]

No. 235. Kneeling statue of Khā .... a scribe and overseer of the treasury of Amen, holding a shrine containing a figure of the god Osiris. XIXth dynasty, or later. [No. 37,890.]

No. 37,890.

No. 236. Upper portion of a black basalt statue of an official ; reign of **Psammetichus II.,** about B.C. 596.   [No. 37,891.]

No. 337. Basalt kneeling figure of **Khnemu-em-ḥāt,** a priest, holding a shrine with a figure of Osiris ; it was dedicated to his memory by his son **Sa-pekha.** XXVIth dynasty, B.C. 600.   [No. 29,478.]

No. 238. Upper portion of a black basalt figure of an official XXVIth dynasty, B.C. 600. [No. 37,889.]

No. 239 Upper portion of a black basalt figure of a goddess or woman. XXVIth dynasty. [No. 37,901.]

No 240 Head of a black basalt statue of an official. XXVIth dynasty [No 37,893.]

No. 241. Portion of black basalt statue of an official who flourished in the reign of **Psammetichus II.** XXVIth dynasty. Very fine work. [No. 37,903.]

No 242. Portion of a seated statue of **Heru-utchat.** XXVIth dynasty. [No. 37,902.]

No 243. Limestone kneeling statue of **Psemtek-senb,** a ḤṮ prince, or nomarch. XXVIth dynasty.

[No 16,041.]

No. 244. Black granite kneeling statue of **Pa-ari-àu,** surnamed **Nefer-Nefer-àb-Rà-em-khut,** a priest and judge, who flourished in the reign of Hàà-àb-Rà **(Apries),** about B.C. 590 The deceased has the figure of an ape on his knees. XXVIth dynasty. [No. 37,892.]

No. 245. Black granite kneeling statue of an official, uninscribed. Fine work. XXVIth dynasty. [No. 37,894.]

No. 246. Head of a granite statue of a king. XXVIth dynasty, about B.C. 500. [No. 14,391.]

No 247. Portion of a statue of an official and priest, Psemthek, having on his breast a figure of Osiris. XXVIth dynasty [No. 37,904.]

No. 248. Portion of a limestone figure of a priest of Ptah. XXVIth dynasty. [No. 17,170.]

No. 249. Portion of a green basalt figure of **Khàs-ḥetep,** an official XXVIth dynasty. [No. 15,082.]

No. 250. Portion of a green schist figure of an official, a servant of Amen. XXVIth dynasty. [No. 2348.]

No. 251. Fragment of a kneeling figure of a controller of the temple of Mut, in green schist. XXVIth dynasty.
[No. 14,405.]

No. 252. Black granite statue of an official holding a figure of Osiris, "lord of life." XXVIth dynasty.

[No. 29,947.]

No. 253. Black stone statue of a hereditary prince and officer of the royal wardrobe, holding a figure of Osiris. XXVIth dynasty. [No. 32,629.]

No. 254. Portion of a kneeling figure of **Utchat-Heru-resenet,** son of **Hent-taui.** XXIInd -XXVIth dynasty.

[No 14,366.]

No. 255. Portion of a figure of a priest holding a shrine of Osiris. XXVIth dynasty. [No. 2288.]

No. 256. Portion of a kneeling statue of **Psemthek-sa-Net,** a royal kinsman, holding a shrine containing a figure of the goddess Neith. XXVIth dynasty

[No. 2341.]

No. 257. Portion of a black granite statue of a priest holding a figure of Osiris. On one side of the plinth is a bilingual inscription in Latin and Greek, meaning "Priest bearing Osiris." From Bêrût. Roman period.

[No. 24,784.]

No. 258. Upper portion of a marble figure of a queen holding a votive offering. XXVIth dynasty.

[No 14,397.]

No. 259. Gilded stone figure of a goddess or queen. Ptolemaic period. [No. 2362.]

No. 260 Slab with the figure of a Ptolemaic queen in relief. Sculptor's model ? B.C. 100. [No 14,371.]

Nos. 261–264. Group of kings' heads, torso, etc, in fine limestone, intended to serve as sculptor's models Ptolemaic period, about B.C. 250.

[Nos. 13,352, 14,392, 15,077, 13,316]

No. 265. Black granite head of a queen (?). Ptolemaic period. [No. 2379.]

No 266. Head of a statue of a priest. XXVIth dynasty. [No. 25,253]

No. 267.   Head of a granite portrait statue of a priest.
Ptolemaïc or Roman period.   [No. 37,905.]

No. 268.   Head of a black basalt statue of a priest.
A fine specimen of Egyptian sculpture under the Romans.
[No. 37,906.]

No. 34,270.   No. 22,750.

No. 269.   Black granite portrait statue of a priest in
the temple of Ámen-Rā, called **Ḥeru-utchat-pe-shere-
Bastet,** wearing Roman costume.   About A.D. 150.
[No. 34,270.]

No. 270.   Burnt limestone **figure** of an official in
Roman costume, **with a Demotic inscription** on the base,
From Tanis.   About A.D. 200.   [No. 22,750.]

Presented by the Egypt Exploration Fund, 1885.

No. 271.   Head of a sandstone statue of a man. Late Roman period.   From Aswân.   [No. 21,551.]
Presented by Colonel G. T. Plunkett, R.E.

No. 272.   Portion of a seated statue, in crystalline limestone, of **Tcheṭ-Tehuti-àuf-ānkh,** a high priest and sacred scribe.   XXIInd dynasty.   [No. 37,922.]
Presented by Leigh Sotheby, Esq., 1852.*

No. 273.   Unfinished limestone figure of a king, supported by a deity.   Ptolemaic period.   [No. 2278.]

No. 9708.

No. 274.   A collection of baked clay "**cones,**" stamped with the names and titles of princes, chiefs, and officials who were buried in the necropolis of Thebes, and who flourished between B.C. 1600 and B.C. 1000.   The objects are commonly called **sepulchral cones,** but we know that they were intended to represent the conical or triangular shaped loaves of bread which were placed in the tombs, and were destined to serve as the food for the *ka* or

* On the floor of the case.

"double" Among the many examples of this interesting class of funeral antiquities may be specially mentioned —

1. Cone of **Meri-mes**, prince of Ethiopia, about B.C. 1200.   [No. 9650.]

2. Cone of **Menthu-em-hāt**, a scribe and fourth priest of Amen-Rā. About B.C 1400.   [No 35,681.]

3. Cones of **Sebek-mes**, a chief libationer, B.C. 1400.
    [Nos. 35,684, 35,685]

4 Cones of **Nefer-ḥeb-f**, a priest of Amen-ḥetep II, B.C. 1500.   [Nos 9679, 9690, 9684, 9686]

5. Cone of **Neb-seni**, a priest, B.C. 1600 Presented by Mrs. Hawker, 1900   [No. 33,904]

6. Cone of **Ka[n]ure**, a superintendent of the *Mātchaiu*, a tribe of blacks who policed Thebes. It is interesting to note that this cone has a double impression. XIXth dynasty, B.C. 1300.
    [No. 9729.]

7. Cone of **Rere** ⟨hieroglyphs⟩ a superintendent of the *Mātchaiu*, B C. 1300   [No. 35,650.]

8. Cone of a "steward of the temple of **Khensu**" ⟨hieroglyphs⟩. XXth dynasty   [No. 9641.]

9. Cone of **Nen-tcheser-ka (?)** ⟨hieroglyphs⟩, a libationer, B.C 1500.   [No. 9670.]

On a shelf which runs round the base of **Wall-Cases 97-111** is displayed a large miscellaneous collection of **Canopic Jars**; see Guide to the First and Second Egyptian Rooms, p. 124. On the **floor of these cases** will be found the following :—   [No. 36,906]

No 275 A miscellaneous collection of **flint chips** of the Neolithic period.   No 36,906.]

No. 276. Portion of a **fossilized palm tree** cut and polished to show the grain and fibre. From the fossil remains of the great forest which once existed in the desert to the east of Wâdi Ḥalfa.   [No. 36,873]

No 277 Rungs and ropes from a **ladder.** [No 5042]

No. 278 A miscellaneous collection of **oars, ropes,** and portions of furniture for boats; of various periods, but chiefly of the New Empire, *i e.,* after B.C. 1600.

No. 279. Wooden **spiked club,** probably from Nubia [No 5508]

No. 280. A collection of **foundation deposits,** consisting of a reed mat, a reed vase stand, a terra-cotta vase, model of sledge for transporting stone(?), a bronze axe-head, inscribed with the name of **Queen Ḥātshepset,** a model of a hoe, and a model of a wooden clamp used to fasten together limestone blocks. From the Great Temple at Dêr el-Bahari, Thebes, B.C 1550. Presented by the Egypt Exploration Fund. [No. 26,276.]

No 281. A group of four **wooden hoes.** After B.C. 1600.
[Nos. 22, 863, 5407, 18,154, 5412.]

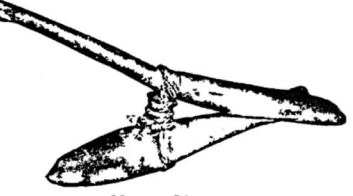

No. 22,863

No. 282 A collection of house **painters' pots and brushes;** in some of the former remains of the paint are still to be seen. After B C. 1600. [Nos. 5992 ff.]

No 283 A collection of **wooden stamps** used by plasterers and brickmakers, several of which are inscribed Among these may be noticed —

1. Stamp with the name of **Âmen-ḥetep III.,** B.C 1450
   [No. 5993]

2. Stamp of the granaries of the Temple of Ptah, of the South Wall, at Memphis. [No. 5595]

3. Long wooden stamp inscribed "Hero, son of Ptolemy," HPⱰNTTTOⱯЄHⱮIOV. B.C 100, or later [No 3220]

No 284   A **drinking horn.**   [No 6037.]

No 285   Massive wooden **wheel of a cart** or trolley for the transport of building materials   From Dér el-Bahari, B C 1550   Presented by the Egypt Exploration Fund, 1898.   [No 29,943]

A collection of baked clay **models of altars, with funeral offerings,** many of which are in the form of houses, with the offerings spread in the courtyards   VIth to XXIInd dynasties.   The following are the most interesting examples :—

> 286 *a–c*   Three plates with the representations of offerings upon them, *i e*, oxen with tied feet, haunches of meat, bread-cakes, etc   [Nos. 24,330, 36,375, 36,376]

> 287.   **Model of a house,** or half of a tomb, with the offerings in front of it ; in the middle are two gutters for carrying off the blood of the slain beasts   VIth dynasty   [No 36,374]

> 288   Stone **model of a mastaba tomb** of the VIth dynasty   The roof is supposed to be removed, and the spectator to be taking a bird's eye view of the interior.   The rectangular cavity represents the tomb chamber, and the round hollow on one side of it is apparently intended to represent the pit which leads to the mummy chamber   The meaning of the smaller perforations is not apparent   On the sides are modelled the false doors of the mastaba and the characteristic crenellations of its brickwork.   VIth dynasty.
> [No. 36,903]

> 289.   Baked clay **model of the front of a tomb,** with a colonnaded entrance, and offerings in front.   In the centre of the court is the rectangular tank for libations, etc., blood from the victims, with a single overflow gutter   VIth–XIIIth dynasty
> [No. 32,613]

> 290.   **Model of a house with two rooms,** each having a separate entrance , above is a flat roof (not represented), with a staircase leading up to it on one side   Against the opposite wall stands a bench

with three *zirat*, or jars for filtering water, and in front are the offerings and a tank with two gutters. VIth dynasty. [No. 32,609.]

291. **Model of a two-storied house.** The main entrance is in the centre of the front, and admits to the lower story only ; the upper story, which consists of a single small room, in front of which stands a water-jar, is approached by a staircase outside the house, and is drained by a gutter which passes through the side wall. The lower story is lighted by a single window, having a single columnar mullion. In the courtyard are the offerings. XIIth dynasty. [No. 32,610.]

Model of a House. No. 32,610.

292. Model of a two-storied house, with two staircases leading to upper story, and continued up to the roof; the house is provided with a balcony. In the courtyard are the offerings. XIIth dynasty, or earlier. [No. 22,783.]

293. Model of a **hut** with a rounded roof; against a wall in the courtyard is a bench with water-pots,

and in the yard itself is a tank with a gutter by which the blood of the victims was removed Near the tank are the offerings. VIth dynasty

[No. 32,612.]

294. Model of a **house and courtyard**, enclosed by a high wall, with a staircase leading up to the roof. In the courtyard are the offerings, including an ox with the feet tied together, and a pillar altar. The gutter passes through the wall by two openings. VIth XIIth dynasty. [No. 32,611.]

295. Model of a **hut**, containing a bench, and supported by a central pillar On the left is a stand for water-jars, and in the space before the hut is the figure of a man seated on the ground, and pouring out wine from a large vessel; round about lie the offerings. The courtyard is provided with a double gutter XIIth dynasty, or earlier. [No. 22,782.]

296 Four models of houses in stone and clay. After the XVIIIth dynasty.

[Nos. 2,462, 18,324, 27,526, 36,904.]

WALL-CASES 111 114. Here is exhibited a collection of painted wooden **sepulchral boxes,** which were used to hold **Canopic* jars** and **ushabtiu* figures**; they belong to the period which lies between the XIth and the XXXth dynasties, i.e., between B.C. 2500 and B.C. 350. Of special interest are the following :—

No 1. *Ushabtiu*-figure box, with two divisions, made for Astit 〔glyphs〕 a singer of Amen. XXIst dynasty. From Dêr el-Baharî. Presented by the Egyptian Government, 1893. [No. 24,895.]

No. 2. Painted sepulchral box of **Kua-ṭep.** XIth dynasty [No. 34,272.]

No 3 *Ushabtiu* box, painted with figures of the gods, and inscribed for **Tche-ḥrá.** An interesting scene is that in which Anpu and Ap-uat are seen drawing back the bolts of the doors of Re-stau, or the tomb From Abydos. XXXth dynasty Presented by the Egypt Exploration Fund, 1902. [No. 37,339.]

* See *Guide to the First and Second Egyptian Rooms,* pp 124, 126.

No 4 **Box for Canopic jars,** made for the lady **Sat-pi** or **Satapa.** XIIth dynasty From Al-Barsha.

[No. 35,286]

No. 5. *Ushabtiu* box, in three divisions, made for **Nesi-neb-taui,** a singer of Amen XXIst dynasty, B C. 1050 From Dêr el-Bahari Presented by the Egyptian Government, 1893 [No 24,894]

No 6 Sepulchral box containing fruit of the *dûm* palm; this is an offering which was made for **Aset-em-kheb,** the sistrum bearer of Amen-Râ, at Thebes About B.C 900. [No. 8532.]

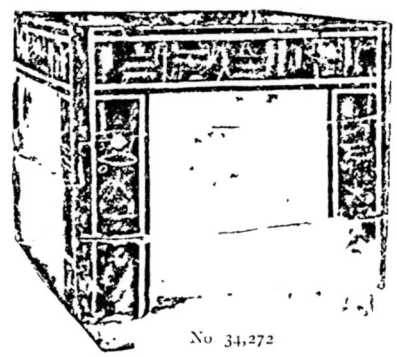

No 34,272

No 7 *Ushabtiu* box, painted white, uninscribed. About B.C 1050 Presented by the Egyptian Government, 1893. [No. 24,893.]

No 8 Painted wooden sepulchral box, made in the shape of a pylon. The sides are ornamented with figures of gods and amulets. From Akhmim, B.C 300

[No 8526]

No 9 Clay sepulchral box, painted white, made for **Nefer-hetep,** the son of Thetui XIIth dynasty

[No. 36,500]

I

No 10. Massive painted wooden **Canopic jar box,** inscribed with the name of **Kua-ṭep,** a high priestly official. Inside are the four alabaster jars, with painted wooden heads, to represent the four children of Horus. XIth dynasty. From Al-Barsha. [No. 30,838]

No. 11 Massive painted wooden Canopic jar box, inscribed with the name of **Sen,** the steward of the palace. The inside of the box is inscribed with religious texts in linear hieroglyphics, and contains four alabaster jars, headless and empty. XIth or XIIth dynasty. From Al-Barsha. [No 30,722.]

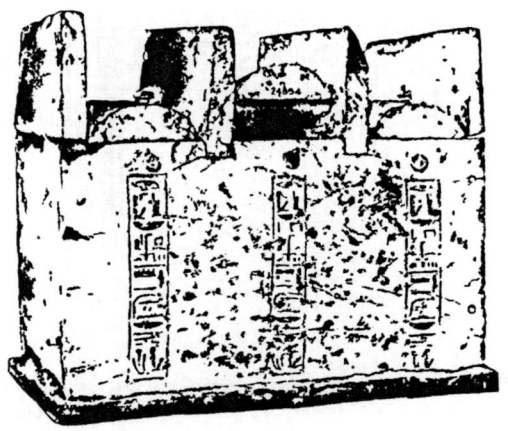

Box for *Ushabtiu* Figures. No 24,894

WALL-CASES 115 118. No. 1. Sepulchral box painted with a scene in which the deceased, Ta-Aut, a singing woman of Amen, is represented in adoration before Rā-Harmachis, Maāt, and Isis. XXIInd dynasty.
[No. 8527.]

No 2 Baked clay *ushabtiu* figure box, with two divisions, and a rough inscription in hieratic. XXth XXIInd dynasty. [No. 29,675]

No. 3. Wooden sepulchral box, which was made for Amen-ḥetep, a priest and doorkeeper in the temple of Amen in Karnak; the inscription is painted in black on a white ground. The box contains a large number of blue glazed faience ushabtiu figures, of which specimens are exhibited on the shelf. XXIInd dynasty or later.

[No. 35,290.]

No. 4. Painted wooden ushabtiu box, made for "the chief cantor of the temple of Amen," whose name was Meri, ⟨hieroglyphs⟩; the deceased was the son of a man who held the same office, and was called "The Dwarf" ⟨hieroglyphs⟩ Pa-nemem. On the cover is the picture of a boat. After the XXIInd dynasty.

[No. 22,820.]

No 5. Wooden sepulchral box, similar in shape and style to No. 3, which was made for Amen-ḥetep, the son of Aha-shere ⟨hieroglyphs⟩, a priest and doorkeeper in the temple of Amen; his father held like offices. The box contains a large number of blue glazed faience ushabtiu figures, specimens of which are exhibited on the shelf. XXIInd dynasty, or later.   [No. 35,289]

No. 6. Small, brightly painted wooden sepulchral box. On one side is a figure of the deceased Apu, who held the office of "incense thrower" (thurifer) ⟨hieroglyphs⟩, burning incense before Osiris, and on the other we see the goddess Nut, who appears from out of a sycamore tree, pouring out celestial water upon the hands of the wife of the deceased and upon a human-headed hawk, the emblem of her soul. XXIst dynasty, B.C 1000.   [No. 35,648.]

No 7. Painted wooden ushabtiu box, with figures of Isis and Nephthys, and symbols of the Sun and Moon, East and West, joy, eternity, gold, etc. XXVIth dynasty.

[No. 35,764.]

No 8   Painted wooden ushabtiu box of **Aset-it**, with a figure of the deceased adoring the four children of Horus On the end is the Utchat, or Eye of Horus (or Ra) XXIInd dynasty   [No. 8543]

No. 9   Large sepulchral chest for holding Canopic jars, made in the form of a pylon, and mounted on runners, so that it might be drawn to the tomb in the funeral procession   On the sides are figures of deities, and texts painted in white on a black ground, on the outside of the cover is a figure of Nut   The chest was made for **Nebi** ⌒ 𓏤𓏤𓈖𓏏. The four Canopic jars are made of alabaster, and have wooden heads   XVIIIth or XIXth dynasty
                                                         [No. 35,808.]

No 10   Similar sepulchral chest, but less well preserved, it was made for a **Kher-heb**, or precentor of Amen, **Amen-em-hāt.**   XVIIIth or XIXth dynasty.
                                                         [No. 35,809.]

Nos. 11, 12.   Two large funeral chests, made in the form of pylons, and painted with figures of gods, amulets, etc   Ptolemaic period.   From Akhmim
                                                  [Nos 18,210, 18,211.]

No. 13   Framework of a canopy of a bier, the cornice of which is ornamented with a row of uræi wearing disks. Roman period.   From Thebes   [No 36,905]

No. 14   Plank from the end of a sepulchral box which seems to have been made for an official who flourished in the time of Cæsar Germanicus (?)   First century A D.
                                                         [No 22,935.]
Presented by F G Hilton Price, Esq., 1898.

WALL-CASES 119 132   Figures of the Gods of Egypt.   In these cases is grouped a collection of figures of Egyptian gods and sacred animals which is probably the largest in the world, and in one form or another there is hardly a god of importance who is not represented in it In the upper group of shelves the figures are of bronze, and nearly all of them served as votive offerings ; many were placed originally in gilded metal shrines in temples, or in private houses, wherein their presence was believed to ensure the protection and favour of the gods whom they represented   The plainer and coarser figures were buried under the doors or corners of houses, and at the boundaries of fields and estates, in order to turn aside from those who made them the attacks of evil influences and spirits, and hostile foreign gods, who were bent on enlarging the space through which they roamed   The Egyptians, in common with many other ancient nations, believed that figures of gods could be inhabited by the gods whom they represented, just as statues of human beings were supposed to form the abodes of the "doubles" of those in whose likeness they were made. Hence it became customary for the man who purchased a figure and dedicated it to the god, to have his own name inscribed upon it, so that when the god visited the figure of himself he might see the name of him that dedicated it, and keep him in remembrance

The greater number of small figures of the gods, chiefly in Egyptian porcelain, which stand on the second group of shelves, were attached to the bodies of the dead, either on necklaces or as pendants, or were laid between the linen swathings of mummified bodies, with the view of securing the protection of the gods thus represented on behalf of the deceased. The 42nd Chapter of the Book of the Dead, which deals with the deification of the members of the body, sets forth what god is to be associated with what member, and there is no doubt that, when the rubric to the chapter was fully carried out, "not a limb of the deceased was without a god." In the Fourth Egyptian Room (Table-Case K) is exhibited a set of figures of the gods and amulets taken from a mummy, the figure of Anubis lay on the breast, and the figures of Isis, Nephthys, Thoth, and another god lay in a row over the diaphragm   These objects date from the XXVIth dynasty, and at that period the figures of gods buried with mummies were fewer than in the period immediately preceding.

On the floor of these cases are a large number of wooden figures of the gods and sacred animals, which were placed either in tombs to protect the coffins and their occupants, or were set up in the temples as votive offerings.

The Greek historian Herodotus affirms (ii. 34) that the Egyptians were "beyond measure scrupulous in all matters appertaining to religion," and the more the hieroglyphic inscriptions are studied, the more true this remark is found to be. No nation of historic antiquity was more religious than the Egyptians, and among none did religious ceremonial and funeral observances form a larger part of the daily life of both priests and people than among the inhabitants of the Valley of the Nile between the foot of the Second Cataract and the sea. Recent discoveries have proved that long before the reign of Mena, or Menes, the first historical king of Egypt, the Nile Valley was occupied by a race of men and women of slender build, who had long narrow heads, long hands, with tapering fingers, feet with high insteps, reddish hair, and probably blue eyes * Those people flourished in the latter part of the Neolithic period, but it is impossible to say whether they were indigenous to the Nile Valley or not ; it is, however, pretty certain that they must be considered to be of north-east African origin, and that they were in no way akin to negro or negroid tribes The graves of large numbers of pre-dynastic Egyptians of this class have been found at Gebelên, Nakâda, and Abydos, and they prove that even at that remote period, which can hardly be later than B.C. 5000, the people believed in a future life of some kind. What kind of life it was cannot be said, but it must have been of a material character, not unlike that which was led by man on this earth at that time, and the place where it was to be lived was thought to be situated at some distance from the present world Well-to-do relatives of the dead placed a supply of food in the graves to sustain them on their journey, and they provided them with flint weapons wherewith to hunt the game which was assumed to exist in the world beyond the grave, and with earthenware vessels filled with the substances which were considered to be essential for the comfort and well-being of the body. We possess no inscriptions or texts of this period, because the Egyptians could not then write, and it is therefore unknown what were the exact views which were held on

* See the ivory figure with inlaid lapis-lazuli eyes in Table-Case L

the subject of the future life ; but it is perfectly certain that the oldest Egyptians known to us both believed in the existence of a heaven and in the possibility of a renewal of life after death on this earth In the latter part of the Neolithic period nothing is known of the predynastic Egyptian conception of God, but there is reason for thinking that the Egyptian peopled heaven with a number of beings who may be termed " gods " , at the same time he certainly paid homage or worship to certain animals, fish, reptiles, etc, *e g*, the bull, cow, crocodile, bear, hippopotamus, tortoise or turtle, cuttle-fish, etc In the dynastic period only the animal of the species which possessed certain distinctive marks was regarded as sacred, *i e*, the incarnation of a god, but whether this idea was evolved in pre-dynastic times cannot be said , it is, however, probable, for the more that is known of the details of the Egyptian religion of the dynastic period, the more clear it becomes that its fundamental conceptions are derived from the predynastic inhabitants of the country. It is, moreover, impossible to believe that the animals chosen for worship were in every respect similar to all the others of the species to which they belonged The cult of quadrupeds, birds, fishes, reptiles, etc., is one of the most persistent characteristics of the Egyptian religion, and it survived the introduction of Christianity into Egypt by two or three centuries

Side by side with the cult of animals there flourished also, probably in the predynastic period, the worship of the

Man-god **Ásár**   or **Osiris,** with whom were associated

his sister-wife **Ast** or **Isis,** and a small group of cognate gods. In the earliest times Osiris appears to have been a water god, or perhaps the god of an arm of the Nile in the Delta, but the tradition of the dynastic period identified him with a king who had once reigned upon earth, and who had been foully murdered by his brother, but who, through the words of power which were uttered by Isis, had been raised from the dead, and appointed the everlasting king and judge of the Underworld. During the rule of the Ist dynasty some important development of the worship of Osiris took place, and the fifth king of the dynasty, who was

called SEMTI,* is mentioned in connexion with the editing
or writing of some portion of the great national funeral
work which was called the " Book of Coming Forth by Day "
(PER-EM-HRU ⬧𓄿𓃭 𓉐 𓆓𓏤), but is now commonly
known as the " Book of the Dead "   In the oldest religious
texts known it is tacitly assumed that the reader is well
acquainted with the details of the life, and death, and resurrection of Osiris, who is treated throughout as the greatest of
all the gods whose names are mentioned in such works,
and as the cause and source of the resurrection and everlasting life   From the allusions found in these texts, we
may conclude that in several parts of Egypt religious
ceremonies partaking of the nature of miracle plays had
been performed annually from time immemorial, with the
object of commemorating the principal events in the original
tragedy of Osiris, and it is clear that such ceremonies were
performed with all the realism which is characteristic of
half-savage, primitive peoples, long after the Egyptians had
become, outwardly at least, highly civilised

   The Book of the Dead is, at base, the book of the cult
of Osiris, and the guide which had the power of teaching
the deceased how to arrive at the kingdom of that god ;
and its principal dogmas and beliefs were clung to
tenaciously in certain parts of Egypt long after the edict
against paganism was promulgated by the orthodox
Emperor Theodosius the Great, in December, A.D. 381
When the great image of Serapis, the god who was
supposed to contain the souls of Osiris and Ptah, was
destroyed in 389 by the Christians, the peoples of the
Delta quietly abandoned their old cult, but those who lived
in Upper Egypt did not do so, and the worship of Osiris
and Isis lasted at Philæ until the reign of Justinian
(527 565). The reason for the popularity of the Osiris cult
is easy to find.   In the first place it absorbed without
difficulty many of the old beliefs connected with the
cult of sacred animals, birds, etc., and its principal gods
appeared in forms half-human and half-animal, or half-
human and half-bird, or wholly animal, and permitted

* His name was formerly read " Hesepti.

the retention of many ancient half-savage rites and customs. Next, it promised to man a resurrection from the dead and an eternal life to be passed in a fertile well-watered region, where the comforts and pleasures of life were abundant, and where there was no labour to be performed

Now, on the eastern frontier of Egypt, and in Syria on the north-east, there lived many tribes and peoples whose principal object of worship was the SUN, and as numbers of these made their way into Egypt and settled down in the region which lay between the Bitter Lakes and Heliopolis, the cult of the sun-god grew and flourished in the Eastern Delta   Another form of sun-worship, which eventually coalesced with this, was introduced into Egypt by conquerors who came from Asiatic territory at a different period, who invaded the country in pre-dynastic times, and, having enslaved the inhabitants, settled down there, and worshipped the god who was best known to them, *i c.*.a form of the sun-god, the closest form of which was at that time Horus, or Horus-Rā

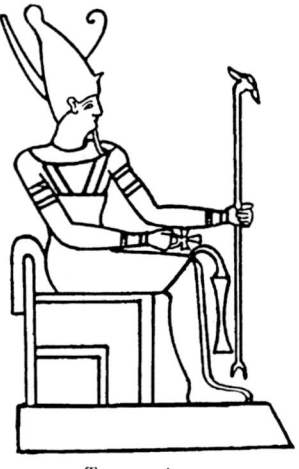

Temu, or Atmu

During the first three dynasties the sun-worshippers, or followers of Rā, do not appear to have possessed any extraordinary political influence, but in the beginning of the Vth dynasty their priests succeeded in acquiring considerable power, and their god Rā became the great god of Egypt, and the king began to call himself " son of Rā," and to adopt a second name as such   The centre of the worship of Rā at this period was Heliopolis, and the priests of this place formulated a system of solar theology, in which the local sun-god **Temu,** who was worshipped under the

form of a man, was made to assume the headship of a
paut ⊖, or "company" of the gods A "company" might
consist of nine or more gods, but nine was the ordinary
number, and the members of the "Company of Annu (i.e.,
Heliopolis) were :—Tem, Shu, Tefnut, Seb, Nut, Osiris,
Isis, Set, Nephthys ; to these were sometimes added Thoth,
Horus, Rā, etc. Now, as the Egyptians divided the world
into three parts, viz , heaven, earth, and underworld, it was
necessary to provide each division with its company of
gods, and thus there were three companies of gods in the
Heliopolitan system, which contained at least twenty-seven
gods, and was expressed in writing thus ⊓⊓⊓⊓⊓⊓⊓⊓⊓
⊓⊓⊓⊓⊓⊓⊓⊓⊓⊓ When the first sun-worshippers
entered Egypt, they merged all the ancient native animal
gods in their own gods, and the Sun-god Rā was
depicted by them in the form of a hawk-headed man,
because the hawk was regarded as a sun-bird by the predynastic Egyptians. The gods who were associated with
him were chosen from a large number of local gods, who
were in turn chosen from the creatures, animate and
inanimate, which were worshipped in predynastic times.
The priests of Heliopolis made the gods of their "company"
to include ancient gods of every kind, and they absorbed
into their theological system legends and beliefs which had
come down to them from their predynastic ancestors , in
fact, they seem to have endeavoured to make their system ·
of religion as much as possible like the old one, with which
the people were so well acquainted. Their chief god **Tem,**
or Temu, included the sun-gods **Rā** and **Kheperà,** with
their feminine counterparts, and was believed to have
produced from himself **Shu** and **Tefnut,** the deities of air,
or sunlight, and water respectively ; these three formed the
great triad of Heliopolis, one of the oldest of the triads of
Egypt. **Seb** and **Nut** represented all the ancient native
gods of sky and earth, and the early legends concerning
them were quietly adapted to the new theological system
of the place. **Osiris** and **Isis,** together with their allied
gods **Set, Nephthys, Horus, Anubis,** etc , as they

represented the ancient native gods of the dead, were introduced in a body into the Heliopolitan company of gods,
but the parts which they played appear to have been
modified somewhat. Speaking generally, the Heliopolitan
system was tolerant, and it admitted within its divine
company almost any ancient local god. It represented a
compromise, of course, and was a mixture of animal and
solar cults, but it satisfied the inhabitants of Lower Egypt
for several centuries, and was even copied in some matters
by the theologians of Herakleopolis, and later even by
those of Thebes.

At the close of the VIth dynasty, about B.C 3100, the
sovereignty passed from Memphis, and the supreme
ecclesiastical power from Heliopolis, and the princes of
Herakleopolis made themselves practically masters of the
country between Memphis and Thebes. As a result the
gods of Herakleopolis assumed prominent positions in
the land, and the religious beliefs and legends of their
priests were grafted on to the theological system of
Heliopolis In process of time the authority of the
Herakleopolitans was broken by the princes of Thebes,
and Amen, whose name means the "Hidden One," the
local god of that city, was proclaimed the "king of the
gods." During the XIIth dynasty (B.C. 2500-2300) the
chief shrine of Ámen was founded, or rebuilt, at Thebes,
on the spot which is marked by the ruins of Karnak, and
his priests began to ascribe to him the powers, and titles,
and attributes of the oldest and greatest gods of Egypt ;
the powers assigned to him included those of all the
animal and solar gods who had been worshipped in the
country. Under the XVIIth dynasty, B.C. 1700, the
Thebans succeeded in gaining the victory in a decisive
battle between themselves and the peoples of northern
Egypt, and the glory and power of Ámen, to whom the
victory was attributed, grew still greater The kings of
the XVIIIth dynasty enlarged his temple, and endowed
the priests with lands and estates, and bestowed upon them
many far-reaching privileges. The brotherhood of the
priests of Amen was one of the richest and most powerful
sacerdotal bodies in ancient Egypt, and they maintained
and increased their influence with such skill, that under

one of the last of the Rameses kings they obtained (about B.C. 1100) authority to levy taxes on the people, and soon afterwards the high priest of Amen became king of Upper Egypt. Speaking generally, Amen was regarded as a great creative god, who united within himself the powers of the solar gods and the gods of generation and of nature; there is no proof that he was considered to be a god of the dead in the earliest times, but after the XIXth dynasty (B.C. 1400 1200) an attempt seems to have been made to make him king of the gods of the dead, and, in fact, to usurp the position and attributes of Osiris.

Under the XVIIIth dynasty the supremacy of **Amen** was challenged seriously by **Amen-ḥetep IV.**, the leader of the **Áten heresy.** Of the origin of the god Aten nothing is known, but there is no doubt that his character was solar, and that he was the god of the disk of the sun, the word Aten means "disk," but the peculiar dogmas which attached to the god himself have not yet been fully made out. It seems, however, that Aten was regarded as the material body of the sun in which Rā dwelt, and also as the visible emblem of the Sun-god, and though followers of Aten were willing to acknowledge the ancient solar gods Heru-khuti (Harmachis), Rā-Heru-khuti, etc, they refused absolutely to admit the claims of Amen, or Amen-Rā, to be the "king of the gods." Amen-hetep IV. asserted the supremacy of Aten in a very definite manner, and his hatred of the god Amen brought him into conflict with the priests of Amen in Thebes. For the first four years of his reign he disputed their contentions vigorously, but finding that they were backed by all the priesthood in the city, and that the people sided with them, he forsook Thebes and settled in a place on the Nile near the modern village of Tell el-ʿAmarna, here he built a beautiful palace and temple, wherein no bloody sacrifice was offered up, but only incense, flowers, and fruits. The new city was called **"Khut-Aten,"** or "Horizon of Aten," the temple was called Ḥet-Benben, or "House of the Obelisk," and the king changed his own name from "Amen-hetep" to **"Khu en Aten,"** i.e., "Glory (or spirit) of Aten." Before he left Thebes he promulgated the edict for obliterating the name of Amen and his figure from every monument in Egypt, and though this was only partially carried out, it practically alienated from him the whole of the people of Upper Egypt. Amen-ḥetep IV, or Khu-en-Aten, lived in his new city for ten or twelve years, and died at a comparatively early age, in less than twenty-five years after his death his city was deserted, the sanctuary of his god was desecrated, his followers were scattered and the triumph of Amen was complete.

The religious texts which were written at Thebes at this period prove that the Egyptians, though accustomed to the worship of many gods, were well acquainted with the idea of monotheism, and numerous passages in the hymns and other works of all periods prove that they believed in the existence of a Being who was immortal, invisible, omnipotent, omnipresent, and eternal, like the Christian God In a manner, the Egyptian religion developed in two directions, i.e. towards polytheism and towards monotheism, but this contradiction is easily explained when we remember that the gods and goddesses of Egypt were only forms, or personifications, of the gods of nature. Heru, Heru-ur, Heru-khuti, Heru-p-khart, Rā, Ptah, Temu, Khepera, etc., are all forms of the Sun-god, and Isis, Uatchet, Neith, and several other goddesses, are only forms or aspects of a predynastic goddess whose attributes and names changed at different periods and in different places In fact, both priests and people united the liveliest sentiment of the spirituality of God to the coarsest representations of different divinities, and a clear and definite belief in the unity of God to an extremely great multitude of divine persons. The popular form of belief was a mixture of crude materialistic ideas and a number of spiritual conceptions of the most exalted character.

Under the XVIIIth and XIXth dynasties it became fashionable among royal personages to have copies of religious works, i.e., the "Books of the Underworld," other than the well-known Book of the Dead, inscribed upon their tombs, and these appear to have been the outcome of a distinct form of religious thought in respect of the future life. The followers of Osiris, as we know from the Book of the Dead, hoped to attain after death to the **Sekhet-**

hetepu, or "Fields of Peace," where they expected to lead to all eternity an existence which had much in common with that lived by prosperous Egyptians in the fertile lands of the Delta. On the other hand, those who were worshippers of the Sun aimed at attaining to a seat in the boat of the Sun, where they hoped to become beings of the same nature as Rā, whose sustenance would be the divine meat and drink of heaven, and whose apparel would be light. They hoped to travel where he travelled, and to rise on the world each day as he did, and to be protected by him to all eternity. To secure such an existence it was necessary for a man to perform all the precepts of the Egyptian religion on earth, and to provide himself with amulets, words of power, magical texts, etc., for without such no soul might hope to pass successfully through the region of the sunset called **Amentet**, *i.e.*, the "hidden" or unseen place, and reach the Tuat, where he would be able to step into the "Boat of Millions of Years."

According to the doctrine of the **Books of the Underworld**, Amentet contained the souls of countless beings, who either through their sins, or because they had been careless of their duties, or because their relatives and friends had failed to provide them with the necessary amulets or words of power, were doomed to remain there, apparently, for ever. Amentet was a place of darkness and terror, and it was the abode of terrible devils and monsters of every description, but the souls therein were cheered once each day by the Sun-god Rā, who passed through it as he journeyed from the place where he set to that where he rose in the morning. The presence of the god brought light and a short period of refreshing daily, but as soon as he reached the end of Amentet, and passed through into the next section of the Underworld, those who were in his boat could hear, as the doors closed after him, the weeping and wailing of the souls who were unable to follow him, and who were forced to remain in darkness until the Sun-god re-visited them next day. Every nome of Egypt was provided with its own underworld, and each underworld possessed its own characteristic inhabitants; the Sun-god Rā was lord of every one of these, except the kingdom of Osiris. Under the New Empire the votaries of Rā formed a numerous and powerful body, and their theologians and priests endeavoured to impress their views on the country in general. This, however, they failed to do, and the old indigenous cult of the deified man Osiris, who had obtained immortality for himself, and made it possible for those who believed in him to obtain it also, continued to keep a firm hold throughout Egypt during the whole of the dynastic period. The Ptolemies supported and amplified the cult of Osiris, and thus, when the Romans took possession of Egypt, B.C 37, the solar cults occupied an inferior place in the affections of the people, and the Egyptians continued to live and die as they had done for about five thousand years, hoping in Osiris, and believing that he was able to give them everlasting life

Ḥeru-ur

WALL-CASES — 119–132. Bronze figures of the gods. Wall-Case 132, Upper Shelf. **Ḥeru-ur,** *i.e.*, "Horus the Aged," the Haroeris of the Greeks, so called to distinguish him from Ḥeru-pakhart, or Harpocrates, *i.e.*, "Horus the Younger." He has the form of a man with the head of a hawk, and under the form of a hawk is one of the oldest of the Egyptian gods In the illustration he wears the crowns of the South and North. The word "Ḥeru" means "he who is above," but later the god came to symbolize the face of heaven, when the sun was the right eye of the god, and the moon the left The most interesting examples of the god here exhibited are :—

1. Bronze seated figure of Ḥeru-ur, hawk-headed, and wearing the double crown ; behind him is an obelisk,

the symbol of the sun The obelisk is called *benben*, and the chief solar temple in Heliopolis, the Sun-city, was called Het-Benben, *i.e.*, "house of the obelisk" [No. 29,608.]

2 Bronze standing figure of Heru-ur, on a double pedestal [No. 930.]

The god Horus possessed fourteen other forms at least, and among these the most important was "Horus of

1. Heru-Behutet   2 Heru-Behutet spearing a hippopotamus

Behutet." *i.e.*, Horus of Edfu ; he represented Horus at mid-day, and so typified the greatest power of the heat of the sun. Horus of Behutet was the god of the people who invaded Egypt from some region in or near southern Arabia, and who conquered the Egyptians in some measure because they were armed with metal weapons. The companions of the god are generally known in the inscriptions as the "Shemsu Heru," or "**Followers of Horus**," and as the "Mesniu" or "**Blacksmiths.**" In illustration No. 1 the god wears the double crown, and in No. 2 we see him holding his characteristic weapon, and spearing a crocodile.

Rā is one of the oldest forms of the Sun-god in Egypt. He was regarded as the maker and creator of the world, and gods, and men, and it is probable that his name has a meaning something like "operative (or creative) power." His worship was associated with that of Ḥeru, the Sky-god, at a very early period, and the hawk was one of his symbols. The visible emblem of Rā was the sun, which was supposed to sail across the sky in two boats ; the morning boat was called "Mātet," and the evening boat "Sektet" ; during the night he passed through the region called the Ṭuat, where he did battle with the hosts of darkness, and whence he emerged victorious each morning. From the XIIth dynasty onwards the attributes of Rā were transferred to those of **Åmen**, the "Hidden god," who was originally nothing but a local god of Thebes, and of little importance. The fortunes of war, which made the princes and kings of Thebes victorious under the XIth and XVIIth dynasties, raised Amen to the position of "King of the gods." Rā is depicted in the form of a hawk-headed man, with the solar disk, surrounded by a serpent twined round it, on his head. The chief characteristic of Amen, or **Åmen-Rā,**

Rā

is the two long plumes which stand above a close-fitting cap or helmet. The examples of Rā of special interest are :—

No. 3. Bronze standing figure of Rā, hawk-headed ; the eyes are inlaid with gold and garnets [No. 343.]

No. 4. Bronze seated figure of Rā, with the solar disk on his head, and a papyrus sceptre on his knees. [No. 346.]

K

No 5. Bronze-seated figure of Rā, with the solar disk on his head, and the feather of Maāt, *i.e.*, right and truth, on his knee. [No. 27,362.]

No 6. Bronze figure of **Rā-Heru-khuti**, or **Rā-Harmachis**, standing upon a pedestal; the eyes are inlaid with gold and garnets. [No. 341.]

Rā-Harmachis united in himself the attributes of Rā and of "Horus of the two horizons" (Heru-khuti).

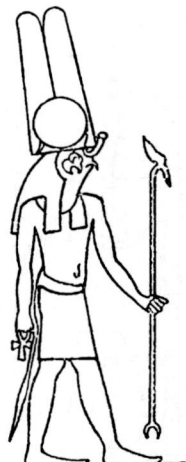

Another well known form of the Sun-god of Egypt was that in which the attributes of Rā and Menthu were united under the form **Menthu-Rā**. The chief seats of his worship were Hermonthis and Thebes. Interesting examples of the god are:—

Nos. 7, 8. Bronze standing figures of **Menthu-Rā**, hawk-headed and wearing the solar disk, with two uræi and plumes, the eyes and necklace are inlaid with gold. [Nos 339, 342.]

9. Pendant bronze figure of the god, with one uræus only. [No. 30,063.]

The next group of gods in Wall-Cases 131, 132 illustrate the great triad of gods of Memphis, namely, **Ptah, Sekhet**, and their two sons, **I-em-hetep** (the Imouthes of the Greeks) and **Nefer-Tem**, or **Nefer-Atmu**.

Menthu-Rā.

Ptah was a form of the morning sun, or was the personification of the rising sun himself, and was the "Opener" of the day; his counterpart was **Temu**, the god of the setting sun, or the "Closer" of the day. In another aspect Ptah was the great cosmic sculptor or artificer, who, with Khnemu, carried out the commands of Thoth, and brought about the creation of heaven and earth. The other principal forms of Ptah are:—**Ptah-Seker**, or **Ptah-Seker-Asàr**, and **Ptah-Tanen.** Ptah-Seker is a form of Osiris, or of the night,

i e, the dead Sun-god   Seker was a god of night, and
represented the inert power of the darkness , he is sometimes depicted in mummy form, and holds the symbols of
the power of Osiris.

Ptah-Seker-Àsar is represented in the form of a pygmy
with a large bald head, and thick limbs , in porcelain
figures he has a beetle on the top of his head   He com-
bined in himself the powers of Amsu, Khepera, and Osiris,

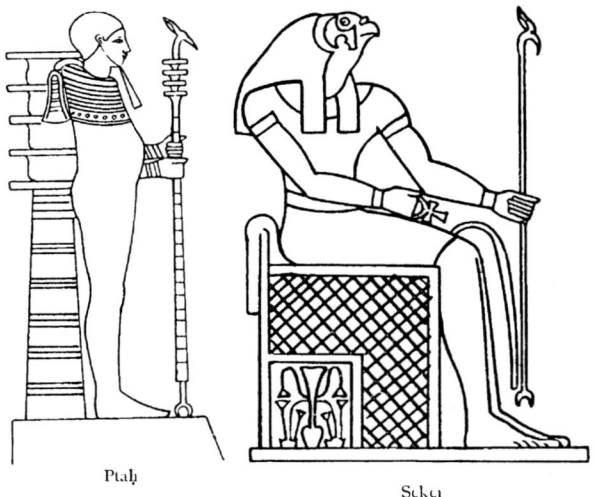

Ptah

Seker

and is such became the type of re-creation, new births,
and the resurrection

Ptah-Tanen represented one of the great creative forces
of the world, and assisted in the creation of the cosmic egg,
out of which sprang the world   Tanen was originally the god
of living but inert matter, but merged into Ptah he became
an active principle of all life, and " the grandfather of the
gods "   He is depicted in human form, with the horns,
plumes, and disk of Tanen and the symbols of Osiris.

Seker as Osiris

Sekhet, the wife of Ptah, is depicted in the form of a woman with the head of a lioness, surmounted by the solar disk, round which is twined the solar uræus. She typified the fierce, scorching, and destroying heat of the sun's rays; she lived on the head of her father Ra and shot out blazing fire upon his enemies. Her son was called **Nefer-Temu,** or **Nefer-Atmu,** and he appears in human form; on his head he wears a lotus flower surmounted by the double plumes of solar gods. Some legends declare him to be the son of Ptah and Bast. Another god who is often mentioned as the third member of the triad of Memphis is **I-em-hetep,** but it is doubtful if he is as ancient as Nefer-Temu, and he appears to have been originally a sage of Memphis, who was deified after death. Examples of these gods worthy of note are —

No. 10. **Ptaḥ,** in mummied form, standing on a rectangular pedestal with steps.   [No. 11,019.]

No. 11. Bronze figure of Ptah, with the attributes of **Amsu** or **Min,** the god of generation.   [No. 11,001.]

No. 12. Bronze figure of Ptah, holding the emblem of "life" $\frac{o}{+}$ [No. 11,038.]

Ptaḥ-Seker-Asar

No. 13. Seated bronze figure of Ptah   [No. 11,016.]

No. 14 **Ptaḥ and Sekhet,** standing on the same pedestal. [No 211.]

No. 15 Seated bronze figure of **Sekhet,** with the head of a lioness, surmounted by a disk and uræus.
[No. 11,068.]

No. 16. Sekhet standing against an obelisk, which, with its pedestal, formed a shrine in which a gold figure of the goddess was probably placed. [No. 27,366.]

No. 17. Bronze ægis of Sekhet ; probably an architectural ornament. [No. 226.]

Ptaḥ-Tanen.

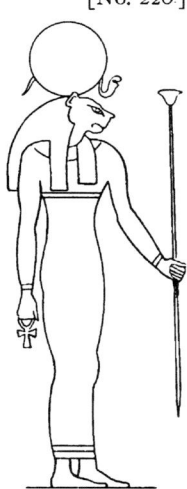

Sekhet

No 18. Fine bronze figure of **Nefer-Àtmu** wearing a lotus flower, symbol of the sun, on his head ; above it are the two solar feathers, and on each side is a *menat* ⌐⌐. symbol of generation (?). In his right hand he holds a scimitar, which has reference to his destroying power as a god of nature. [No. 22,921.]

No. 19   Fine bronze figure of Nefer-Atmu, with the *menats* facing the beholder   In porcelain the figure of this god often stands on a lion.   [No. 11,052.]

No. 20   Bronze figure of **I-em-hetep,** who is seated and holding an unrolled papyrus on his knees, it was dedicated to the god by Ptah-mes

[No. 11,055.]

Nefer-Atmu.   I-em-hetep.

No. 21.   Bronze figure of I-em-hetep, which was dedicated to the god by a devotee of this name.

[No. 11,074.]

No. 22.   Bronze figure of **Seker,** hawk-headed, wearing the double crown.   [No. 11,512.]

No. 23.   Bronze Seker pendant.   [No. 23,867.]

No. 24   Mother-of-emerald seated figure of Seker, hawk-headed, in mummified form.   [No. 397.]

No 25. Bronze figure of **Ptaḥ-Seker-Âsâr.**
[No. 11,046]

No. 26. Blue glazed porcelain figure of Ptah-Seker-Âsar, on his head is a beetle, symbol of new life and resurrection, and on the right of his head is the lock of hair of eternally renewed youth [No. 11,211.]

No 27. Glazed porcelain figure of Ptah-Seker-Âsâr, standing on crocodiles ; on his right hand is Nephthys, on his left Isis, and behind him is Nut. [No. 29,660.]

No 28. Blue glazed porcelain double figure of **Ptaḥ-Seker-Âsâr** and **Bes.** [No. 26,316.]

No. 29. Blue glazed porcelain figure of Ptaḥ-Seker-Âsâr, hawk-headed. [No. 11,260.]

No. 30. Blue paste composite figure of Ptaḥ-Seker-Âsar, Amen (or, Khnemu), Horus, Thoth, Khonsu, etc. [No. 36,453.]

Shu No 1.

According to the doctrine of Heliopolis, the first two gods who proceeded from Temu, and who formed with him a triad, were **Shu** and **Tefnut** ; the former was the personification of sunlight, air, dryness, etc., and the latter of water and of moisture in all forms. Shu and Tefnut are often referred to as the "double lion-god." Shu appears in the form of a man, wearing the feather, the phonetic value of which, SHU, gives the sound of his name, and indicates the word "emptiness," "space" ; in this form he typifies the space between earth and sky. He was, however, regarded as the god who holds up the sun's disk in the sky, and the horizon itself, and in this capacity appears in figure No. 2 Tefnut is depicted as a woman with the head of a lioness, surmounted by the solar uræus. Worthy of note are —

No 31   Ægis with the heads of **Shu and Tefnut,** the latter wearing the solar disk   [No 11,057.]

Nos 32 41   A group of porcelain figures of **Shu** supporting the solar disk.

[Nos 408 410, 415, 416, 418, 419, 439, 440, 442]

The immediate offspring of Shu and Tefnut were **Seb,** the earth-god, and **Nut,** his wife, the sky-goddess   Seb is

Shu, supporting the sun and sky on his hands No. 2   Tefnut.

usually depicted in human form, and is called the " Erpa," *i.e*, the hereditary tribal king of the gods   He usually wears the double crown, with horns, disks, etc. , but often he is seen with the figure of a goose on his head , this bird was sacred to him, because he once transformed himself into a goose in order to make his way through the air   His home was the earth, and his chief throne was at Heliopolis, where, according to a legend, he produced the egg out of which came the sun   His wife was Nut, the sky goddess, who is depicted in the form of a woman and in that of a cow. In the illustration here given she wears the disk, horns, and uræus, which are characteristic of several sky goddesses, and above the disk is the vessel of water, called in Egyptian " Nu," which is at once the symbol and sound of her name. Nut united in herself the attributes of several very ancient sky-goddesses, and especially those of Nut, the female counterpart of the

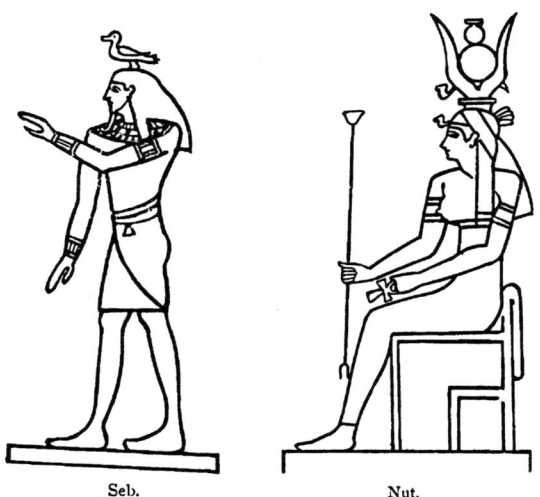

Seb.   Nut.

primeval god Nu, who was the personification of the great watery abyss which existed before all time, and was the source of all life and movement. Nu is depicted in the form of a bearded man, seated on a tank of water, and wearing the solar disk and the double plumes symbolic of air.

Figures of Seb and Nut, in bronze and porcelain, seated or standing, are rare, and the only example of a pendant figure is No. 11,424 (Wall-Case 131, lower shelf); flat figures of the goddess, with outstretched hands and wings, made to be sewn to mummy swathings, will be seen in the Fourth Egyptian Room (Table-Case K).

In the religious texts which treat of the creation of the heavens and the earth, and of the new existence of man in the future life, frequent mention is made of **Thoth** and **Maât.**

Nu.

Thoth was the personification of law, both in its physical and moral aspects, and it was he who formed the plan on which creation was worked out after it had been decreed by Râ, he fixed the positions of the stars and the planets, and the sun and moon, he ordered the seasons, and invented all arts and sciences, and was the patron god of sacred and profane literature, and the "scribe of the gods." He was declared to be the author of the Book of the Dead, and he provided Isis and other deities with the words of power which raised the dead, and which overcame the forces of nature and made them subservient to men. He uttered the word which resulted in the creation, and spoke the decree of everlasting happiness or annihilation of the deceased on the day of judgment in the Hall of Osiris. Thoth is depicted in the form of an ibis-headed man, who wears the *Atef* crown. **Maât,** the female counterpart of Thoth, was the personification of what is right or straight, rectitude, integrity, righteousness and truth. Like Thoth, she was inseparably connected with Râ, the sun-god, who made his course on the lines laid down by her each day. She occupied a place in the boat of the sun when he rose out of the primeval abyss for the first time, and assisted Thoth in determining his course. In connection with Thoth must be mentioned **Sa,** the personification of the divine intelligence and of human reason, who also stood in the boat of the sun; and a sister form of Maât was **Sesheta**, who represented the literary aspect of her character, and was the goddess of painting, writing, etc.

Among the figures of **Thoth** and **Maāt** in Wall-Case No. 131, may be noted :—

No 42   Bronze figure of **Thoth**, ibis-headed, and wearing horns, uræi, plumes, etc   [No 483.]

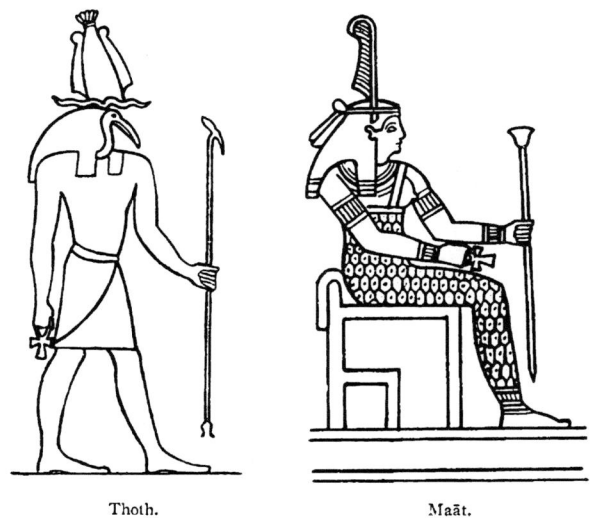

Thoth.   Maāt.

43.   Bronze figure of Thoth, ibis-headed, wearing the crescent moon, with the full moon within it. on his head.
[No. 11,056.]

No 44.   Thoth, ibis-headed, holding in his hands the *utchat* ☜, or Eye of Horus or Rā   He here appears in his capacity of measurer of celestial times and seasons.
[No 481.]

No. 45. Double figure of **Horus and Thoth,** who are engaged in the performance of a mythological ceremony, in which Horus takes the place of Râ.   [No. 484.]

No 46. Bronze figure of **Maât,** wearing on her head the feather which is characteristic, and the phonetic value of which gives the sound of her name.   [No 11,109]

No. 47.   Bronze seated figure of Maât, wearing a feather.   [No. 383.]

Sa.   Sesheta.

In **Wall-Cases 127–130** is exhibited a large and important series of bronze and porcelain figures of the god **Osiris,** and of the members of his divine company. According to the doctrine of Heliopolis, Osiris, Isis, Set, Nephthys, and Horus-Anubis were the offspring of Seb and Nut, the earth-god and sky-goddess respectively In the earliest times, Osiris was a god of water, probably of the Nile, and Isis was the goddess of the land, which was fructified by the Nile   At a later period tradition asserted that Osiris and Isis were the king and queen of a country in the south, that Osiris was murdered by his brother Set, who also hacked the body to pieces, that Isis collected the members of the body and buried them ; that Thoth, by means of his words of power, raised up Osiris to life in the next world, where he became the king and judge of the dead, and the giver of immortality and everlasting life to man The Egyptians, in the burial of their dead, imitated all the ceremonies which tradition asserted had been performed at the burial of Osiris, and they recited the words which had been composed by Thoth for Isis and Horus, believing that the words and ceremonies together would secure for them acquittal in the judgment, and a happy eternal life in the **Sekhet-hetep** or "Field of Peace" The Egyptian hoped that, through the sufferings and death of Osiris, his body might rise again in a transformed, glorified, and incorruptible shape. and the devotee appealed in prayer for eternal life to him who had conquered death and had become the king of the underworld through his victory and prayer   For illustrations of figures of Osiris and Isis, and of the judgment scene, see Standard Cases F. and G

The Tet, or symbol of the tree trunk in which the body of Osiris was hidden by Isis, with the attributes of Osiris.

Isis, the sister and wife of Osiris, is usually represented in the form of a woman, who wears on her head the throne 𓊨, the phonetic value of which, "Ast," gives her name The legends about the goddess state that on certain occasions she took upon herself the form of a bird, as, for example, when she hovered over her husband's dead body, and when she escaped from her enemies , in the Book of the Dead she once appears as a hawk and once as a serpent. She is commonly called the "lady of words of power,"

and the " mother of the god," and her incantations, which
she had learned from Thoth, were declared to be irresistible.
When her son Horus was stung to death by a scorpion,
the appeal for help which she addressed to the sun-god Rā
was so effective, that he stopped in his course, and sent
Thoth to teach her the words which, if properly recited,
would restore Horus to life. When Isis had made use of

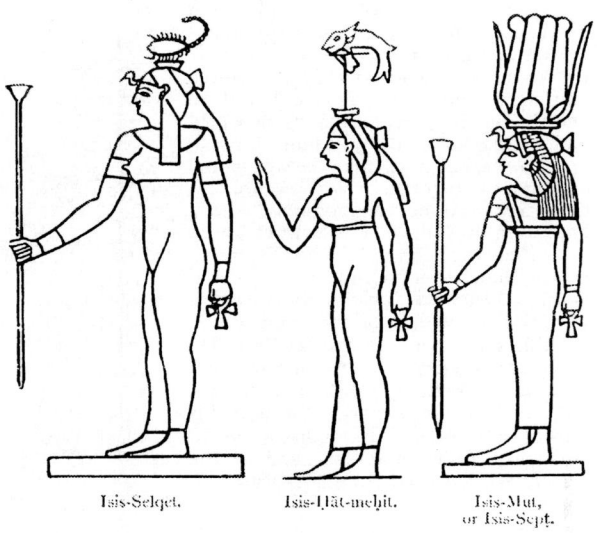

Isis-Selqet.   Isis-Ḥāt-meḥit.   Isis-Mut,
                                              or Isis-Sept.

the words, life returned to her child, and then Thoth re-
entered the boat of the sun and Rā went again on his way.
Isis possessed many attributes, and was identified with
many goddesses, e.g., with **Selqet**, the scorpion-goddess,
with **Sept**, the goddess of the star Ṣothis, with **Ḥāt-meḥit**
a local fish-goddess, who was widely worshipped in the
Delta, and with **Mut, Hathor,** etc. The form, however,
under which she most appealed to the Egyptians was that

of the loving, protecting mother, and she was held to be
the mother of the dead as well as of the living. The
figures of this goddess commonly represent her in the act
of suckling her child Horus, and the British Museum collection comprises about 140 such figures, 40 in bronze, and
100 in porcelain.

Closely connected with Osiris and Isis were **Set** and

Isis-Sept.   Set.   Nephthys.
(Isis-Sothis).

Nephthys, the former of whom murdered Osiris ; Nephthys,
however, was closely associated with her sister Isis in the
funeral ceremonies which were performed for Osiris, and
in funeral scenes she always appears as the friend and
helper of Isis in her efforts to benefit the dead. Set is
depicted with the head of an unknown, probably predynastic,
animal, and Nephthys with the symbols ⎕ upon her head ;
the phonetic values of these, " NEBT-ḤET," form her name.

Set was originally a nature power and was the personification of night, but in later days he was regarded as a power of moral, as well as of physical, evil. He waged war against Horus the Aged, then against Ra, and finally against Osiris, whom he slew. Horus the son of Osiris and Isis met him in combat, and did battle with him for three days and three

Heru-pa-khart (Harpocrates).

nights, and at length Set was overthrown; henceforth this form of Horus was called "Heru - netch - tef - f," i.e, "Horus, the avenger of his father." This god is sometimes confused with Heru-pa-khart, or "Harpocrates," who was declared to be originally the offspring of Heru-ur, a very ancient sky-god

The son of Set and Nephthys was called **Anpu**, or **Anubis**, who is always depicted in the form of a jackal-headed god. Anubis was the god of the tomb, and of embalmment, and of all kinds of funeral ceremonies In the funeral papyri he is seen standing by the bier of the dead, and he receives the mummy at the door of the tomb, in order to take it to his abode in the underworld. Beneath the bier in the accompanying illustration are four vases, each having a cover made in a different form These represent the **four children of Horus**, who were called **Mestha, Ḥāpi, Tuamutef**, and **Qebhsennuf.** Originally these gods represented the four pillars which held up the iron plate that formed the sky, but at a later period they were associated with Horus and Anubis in the performance of the ceremonies which were connected with the funeral of Osiris. Each was supposed to take under his protection one of the four principal internal organs of the body, and the covers of the jars in which the organs were placed after embalmment were made in the forms of the heads of the gods who guarded them.

Examples of figures of the gods of the company of Osiris are :—

No. 48. Bronze **Osiris**, bearded, and wearing the *Atef* crown, *i.e.*, the crown of the South, with plumes, and holding the flail ⚚ and crook, symbols of power and dominion.

[No. 11,054.]

Anubis standing by the bier of the dead.

No. 49. Bronze Osiris, wearing the *Atef* crown with horns, pendent uræi with disks, etc.; the eyes are inlaid with gold.   [No. 34,868.]

No. 50. Bronze seated figure of "Osiris the Moon," wearing the crescent moon and lunar disk on his head.

[No. 738.]

No. 51. Bronze seated figure of "Osiris the Moon," holding in his hands an Utchat, or " Eye of Horus."

[No. 12,589.]

L

No 52.   Bronze seated figure of Osiris

[No 12,592.]

No. 53   Bronze seated figure of **Isis**, suckling her son Horus , on her head she wears a crown of uræi surmounted by a pair of horns and a disk   In the inscription on the pedestal she is called " great one, god-mother "

[No. 24,726.]

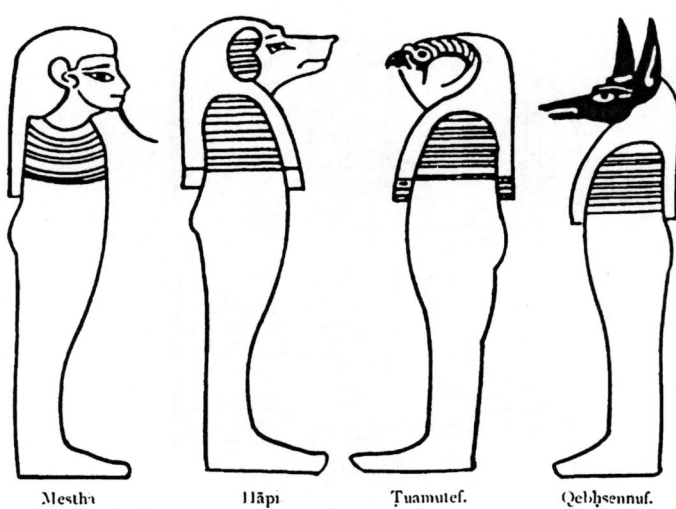

Mestha   Hāpi   Ṭuamutef.   Qebḥsennuf.

No 54.   Bronze standing figure of Isis, wearing the usual crown, and with her winged arms held out before her to protect Osiris or Horus.   Late, but fine work.

[No 12,588.]

No. 55   Bronze seated figure of **Isis-Hathor-Selqet**; very rare.   [No 26,943.]

No. 56   Bronze seated figure of **Isis-Sothis**, the goddess of the Dog-Star.   [No 110]

No 57. Bronze standing figure of **Isis-Sothis,** the goddess of the Dog-Star.   [No. 11,143.]

No. 58 Bronze standing figure of **Isis-Hathor.**
[No. 26,746.]

Nos 59, 60. Seated porcelain figures of the goddess **Ḥāt-meḥit ;** late period   [Nos 909, 27,380.]

No 61. Bronze standing figure of the god **Set,** wearing the crowns of the South and North , the upper part of the body and the head were gilded   At the end of the period of the new Empire the worship of Set became unfashionable in Egypt, and the statues and figures of the god were broken, and he himself was included among the devils who were hated and feared throughout the country
[No 18,191.]

No. 62. Small bronze standing figure of the god Set , poor work, of a late period.   [No. 22,897.]

No. 63. Bronze standing figure of the goddess **Nephthys.**   [No 11,504.]

Nos 64, 65. Glazed porcelain figures of the goddess Nephthys, with the symbols of her name ⫝̸ on her head
[Nos. 871, 13,527.]

No 66 Bronze standing figure of **Ḥeru-pa-khrat,** or Harpocrates, wearing the crowns of the South and North , on the right of his head is the lock of hair symbolic of "youth," and he holds his right hand to his mouth in the attitude common to children.   [No 11,525.]

No. 67. Bronze seated figure of Harpocrates, wearing on his head horns, plumes, and a disk, which are the attributes of several solar gods   [No 26,296.]

No 68 Bronze seated figure of **Ḥeru-sa-Aset,** i e, " Horus, son of Isis."   [No. 998.]

No 69 Gilded seated bronze figure of **Ḥeru-pa-neb-ta,** i.e., " Horus, the lord of the world," wearing the triple crown.
[No. 11,495.]

Nos 70, 71 Glazed porcelain amulets, with figures of Horus, Isis, and Nephthys.   [Nos. 913, 26 317.]

No 72   Porcelain hollow-work figures of six goddesses, viz, Hathor, Nephthys, Isis, Mut, Tefnut, Bast

[No 929]

Between the Saite and Roman periods, i.e., between B.C 600 and B C 20, the Egyptians employed as talismans for the protection of houses and other buildings small rounded stone stelæ, with projections at the feet, whereon stood figures of Horus in the form of the "aged god who reneweth his youth" To this class of objects the name **Cippi of Horus** has been given   The god stands with each foot on the head of a crocodile, and in his hands he grasps serpents, scorpions, gazelle, etc , which typify powers of evil ; on his right and left are symbols of Upper and Lower Egypt   Above his head is the head of Bes, who here symbolizes the aged Sun-god, who becomes young again under the form of Horus   On each side of the sculptured figure of the god is a series of mythological scenes, all of which have reference to the power possessed by Horus over noxious animals and reptiles and evil spirits   On the back and sides of the cippi are inscribed series of magical texts, which usually tell the story of how Horus was restored to life after he had been stung to death by a scorpion.

No 73. Black stone **Cippus of Horus,** of the early Ptolemaic period   [No. 36,250]

No 74   Black steatite cippus of Horus, of the late Ptolemaic period.   [No 30,745.]

No 75   Grey steatite cippus of Horus.   In this example Horus stands above six hippopotami, and on the back are two mythological scenes not usually found on cippi of Horus   [No. 27,373.]

No. 76. Bronze standing figure of Anpu or **Anubis,** jackal-headed, and wearing the crowns of the South and North.   [No. 22,923.]

No. 77.   Bronze standing figure of Anubis

[No. 29,197.]

No 78. Bronze figure of Anubis with the attributes of Horus. Roman period.   [No. 11,513]

No. 79.   Bronze figure of Anubis.   Roman period.
[No. 11,529.]

No. 80.   Bronze figure of Anubis with the attributes of
Ptah-Seker-Asâr, Horus, etc.   [No. 22,930.]

Of the **Four Children of Horus** a large number of porcelain figures will be found on the second group of shelves in Wall-Cases 127 and 128; these were not worn as pendants like the figures of the other gods, but were sewn to the swathings of mummies, and are generally found lying over the breasts of the dead.

In **Wall-Case 125** are exhibited a number of bronze figures

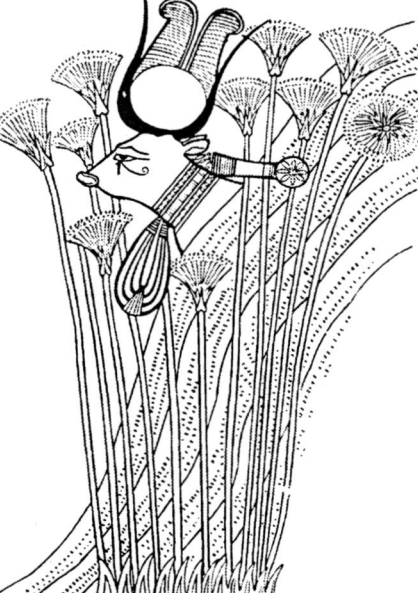

Hathor, or a goddess of the dead, looking forth from the necropolis in the Theban hills.

of some of the great goddesses of Egypt.   First among these comes **Hathor,** who was worshipped in pre-dynastic times under the form of a cow; her name in Egyptian is "Het-Hert," and means the "house of Horus," and as such she is the personification of that portion of the sky where Horus was born, i.e., of the place of sunrise. The worship of the **Cow goddess Hathor** was universal in Egypt, and in course of time her attributes became merged in those of almost every great local goddess throughout the country. One of her principal forms is that shown in the accompanying illustration (No. 1), where she appears in the form of a woman, and holds the sceptre of the goddesses of Upper Egypt. On her head is the head-dress of **Mut**, the wife of Ȧmen-Rā, the king of the gods, and this is surmounted by the horns of the Cow of Hathor, the solar disk,

Hathor. No. 1.

which indicates her relation to Horus, and the feather of the goddess **Maāt**. In illustration No. 2 the goddess appears both in the form of a cow and in that of a woman ; the object here represented is a portion of the *menȧt* amulet, and is inscribed with the prenomen of Ȧmenḥetep III. ⬭, a king of the XVIIIth dynasty, about B.C. 1450 ; it is important as illustrating the dual character of the goddess at a comparatively early period. In the Book of the Dead Hathor plays a very prominent part, for it is she who provides

Hathor. No. 2.

nourishment for the deceased in his new life in the other world. Closely connected with her is **Meḥ-urt,** the personification of the overflowing celestial stream wherein the gods were produced and lived ; she also symbolized the source of matter, and at a very early period was identified with the primeval creative principle. Her typical form is that of a cow-headed woman, who wears the horns, disk, and plumes of Hathor. Meh-urt is, according to some late texts, a form of **Nehemāuait,** a goddess whose head is surmounted by the sistrum of Hathor and the cat of Bast, and who holds in her hands the symbol of Maāt and the papyrus sceptre. The attributes of Nehemāuait

Meḥ-urt.

are not clearly defined, and her worship is not ancient. Among the Hathor goddesses, who are sometimes said to be seven in number, and sometimes twelve, must be mentioned **Meskhenet,** who presided over the birth of gods and men. She appears in the Judgment Scene of the Book of the Dead in connexion with **Renenet,** the celestial nurse who appears there before the gods to speak on behalf of the deceased. Renenet is sometimes depicted in the form of a snake-headed woman suckling a child ; the two plumes on her head indicate that she was recognized both in Upper and Lower Egypt

Nehemāuait

The four great divisions of Egypt, South, North, East and West, were represented by the goddesses Nekhebet, Uatchet, Bast and Neith. **Nekhebet** appears in the form of a winged serpent, wearing the crown of the South, and also in the form of a woman wearing the crown of the South, with plumes attached, and holding in her hand a papyrus sceptre, round which a serpent is entwined.   The worship of the goddess is very ancient, and dates from pre-dynastic times.   **Uatchet** appears in

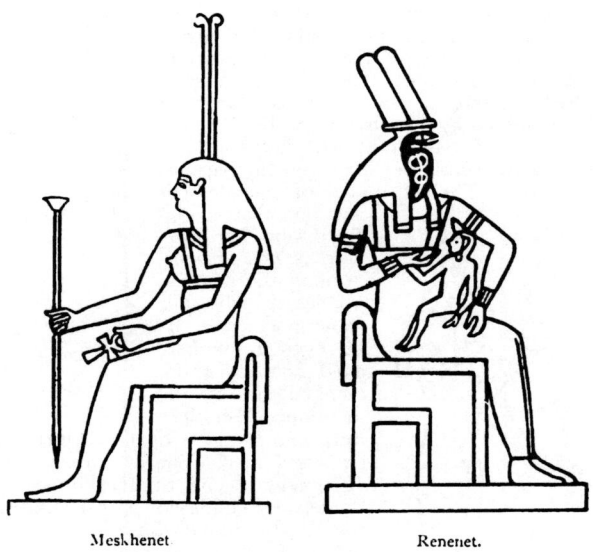

Meskhenet   Renenet.

the form of a winged serpent wearing the crown of the North, and also in the form of a woman, wearing the crown of the North, and holding in her hand the lotus sceptre.   The centre of her cult was at Per-Uatchet in the Delta, and it seems that the serpent which represented the goddess was worshipped there from time immemorial **Bast** is usually depicted in the form of a cat-headed woman, and the cat was sacred to her.   The home of her

THE GODDESSES OF THE FOUR DIVISIONS OF EGYPT.

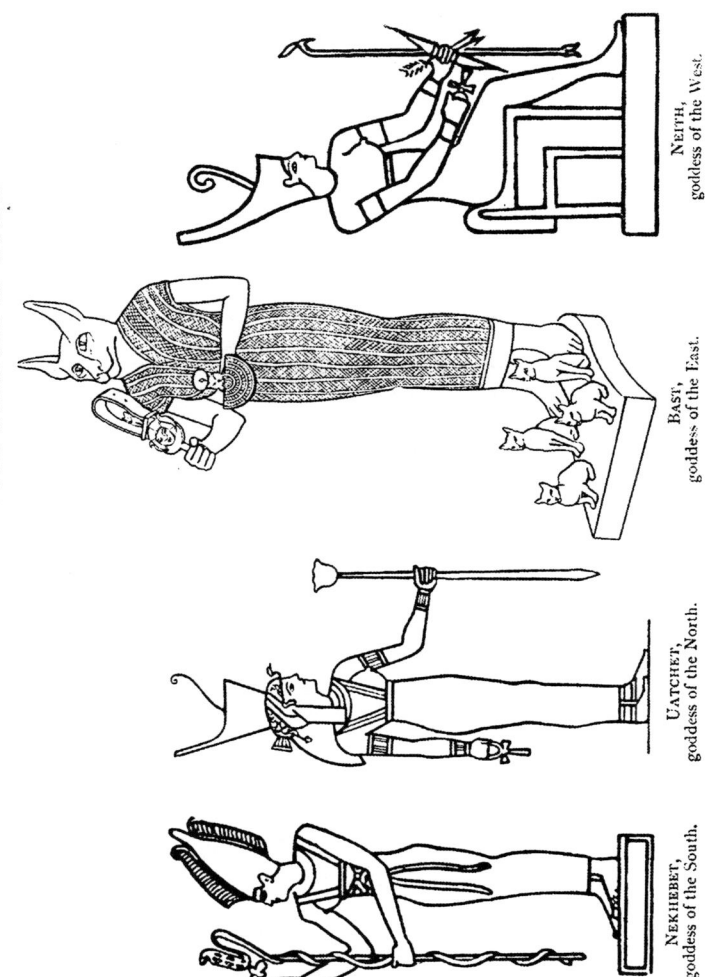

NEKHEBET,
goddess of the South.

UATCHET,
goddess of the North.

BAST,
goddess of the East.

NEITH,
goddess of the West.

cult was Pa-Bast, in the Eastern Delta, a city which is mentioned in the Bible under the form of Pi-beseth (Ezekiel xxx, 17.

Nekhebet.

Originally she seems to have been a foreign goddess, but in very early times she was identified with the female counterparts of Rā and Tem, of which gods she was declared to be the "Eye." One legend makes her to be the "soul of Isis." **Neith** was one of the oldest of the Egyptian goddesses, and her worship seems to have been common in the Western Delta in pre-dynastic times. She is depicted in the form of a woman, wearing the crown of the North, and holding in her hands a bow and two arrows, or a shuttle, and sometimes she is accompanied by two crocodiles. According to one view she was the goddess of war and the chase, and according to another she was a personification of a

Uatchet.

form of the great, inert, primeval watery abyss which was endowed with the power of self-creation and reproduction.

A selection of bronze and porcelain figures which illustrate the above paragraphs is exhibited in **Wall-Case 125.**

No 81. Bronze standing figure of **Hathor,** wearing horns and solar disk, she probably held between her hands a vase.   [No 30,713.]

No. 82. Bronze standing figure of Hathor, bearing on her head a sistrum and uræus.   [No. 29,606.]

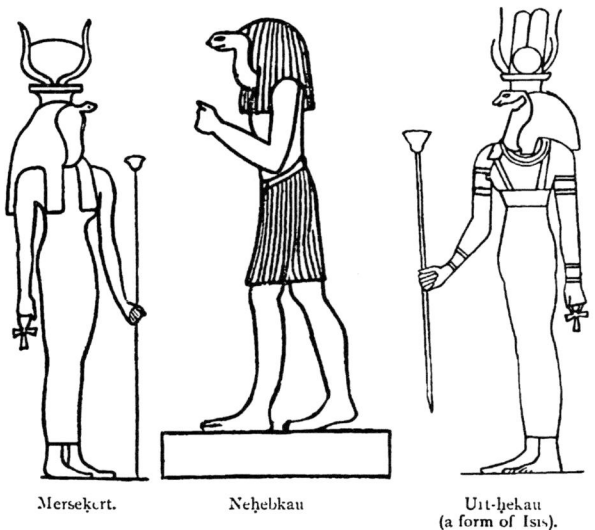

Mersekert.   Neḥebkau   Uıt-ḥekau
                                       (a form of Isıs).

No. 83. Portion of a *menât* amulet illustrating the two principal forms of Hathor, *i e*, those of a woman and a cow.   [No. 300.]

No 84 Bronze figure of the goddess **Meḥ-urt,** cow-headed, and wearing plumes, uræus, and solar disk.   [No. 22,925]

No 85 Bronze figure of the goddess **Neḥemāuit.**   [No. 303]

Nos. 86, 87.   Bronze figures of the goddess **Mersekert,**
under the form of a human-headed snake
[Nos. 2007, 29,415.]

No. 88.   Bronze figure of the snake-headed goddess
Nehebkau.   [No. 11,517]

No 89   Wooden figure of Nehebkau, carrying the
Utchat ☞.   [No. 11,779]

Nos. 90, 91.   Porcelain figures of Nehebkau.
[Nos 1197, 24,748]

No. 92.   Bronze standing figure of **Bast,** cat-headed.
[No. 11,036.]

No. 93.   Bronze standing figure of Bast, holding an
ægis and a sistrum.   [No. 11,033]

No. 94.   Bronze figure of Bast, standing on a pedestal
made in the form of the symbol of her name ∬.
[No. 11,582]

No. 95.   Bronze figure of **Bast with kittens.**
[No. 12,590]

No. 96.   Bronze seated figure of Bast, wearing a disk
and uræus.   [No. 11,047.]

No. 97.   Bronze standing figure of the cat-headed
goddess **Menhi,** wearing horns, disk and plumes.
[No. 11,017.]

Nos. 98 100.   Three lapis-lazuli figures of the goddess
Selqet, wearing on her head a scorpion, her symbol.
[Nos. 375, 11,381, 11,382.]

No. 101.   Bronze figure of the goddess **Neith,** of Saïs,
wearing on her head the crown of the North.
[No. 24,722]

No. 102.   Bronze seated figure of Neith.
[No. 11,008.]

No. 103.   Bronze ægis of Neith.   [No. 72]

No 104.   Blue paste head of the goddess **Uatchet,** on
a papyrus sceptre   [No. 13,405.]

No. 105. Bronze figure of a form of the hippo-potamus-goddess **Ta-urt** or Thoueris, with the head of a lion Very rare The goddess usually has on her head a disk and a pair of horns ; she holds in her right paw a torch (?) and in her left, which rests on the sign of magical protection 𓏃, the symbol of "life" 𓋹.

[No 27,585] ☥

Nos 106, 107. Fi-gures of Thoueris [Nos 1321, 29,667.]

WALL - CASE 124.

No. 108. Bronze standing figure of **Hāpı**, the **Nile-god**, who holds before him an altar from which he pours forth a stream of water On his head are a cluster of papyrus. or lotus plants, and the Utchat 𓂀. [No. 11,069]

The Egyptians thought that the Nile rose from between two mountains near the Island of Philæ, and that it came from the great celestial stream

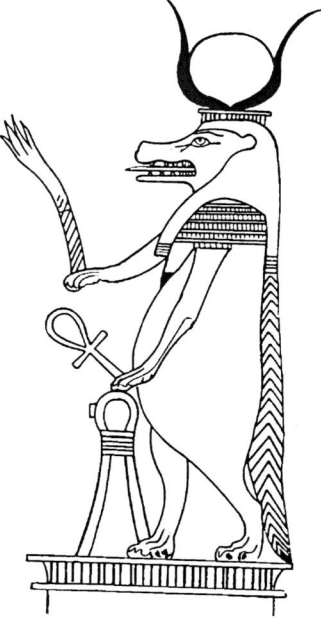

Ta-urt (Thoueris).

Nu Like Egypt, the Nile was divided into two sections, each section being presided over by a god. In the accom-panying illustration the two Nile-gods are tying the stem of a lotus plant and the stem of a papyrus plant in

a knot round the symbol *sma* 𓊽 , which means "to unite,"

and the union of Upper and Lower Egypt is indicated by this ceremony.

No. 109. Bronze standing figure of the Crocodile-god **Sebek**, wearing on his head a pair of horns, a solar disk with a uræus, and a pair of plumes.   [No. 22,924.]

The god of the South Nile.   The god of the North Nile.

Sebek, the **Souchos** of the Greeks, was at a very early period identified with that form of the Sun-god Rā who was held to be the son of Neith, and with Set the murderer of Osiris. In some parts of Egypt crocodiles were hunted and killed as noxious beasts, but at Thebes and near lake Moeris they were accounted sacred, and their devotees put crystal and gold earrings in their ears, and bracelets on their fore-paws.

No. 110. Bronze standing figure of the god **Maahes**, with the head of a lion. The god usually wears the crown of the South, to which are attached the two feathers , he is generally considered to be a form of the god Shu

[No. 11 115]

No. 111.   Portion of a bronze standing figure of Maahes, with crown imperfect.   [No. 12,543.]

Nos. 112, 113.   Porcelain figures of Maahes.   [Nos. 394, 395.]

No 114   Bronze standing figure of Án-her, the Onouris of the Greeks.
[No. 36,311.]

An-her was the god of the under-world of the city of Abydos, and his common title was "Governor of Ámentet" (Khenti Amentet); when, however, Osiris became the great god of the dead of Abydos, this title was transferred to him, and An-her was relegated to the position of a god of secondary importance.   An-

Sebek.

her appears to have been originally a personification of the reproductive power of nature, with especial reference to the sky and atmosphere, and in some of his aspects he resembles Shu.

Nos. 115, 116.   Bronze standing figures of Ámsu, or Min, a very old personification of the generative and reproductive powers of nature.   Like Amen, or Ámen-Rā, he wears on his head a disk and plumes, and he is usually depicted as an ithyphallic god, with his right hand and arm raised in the act of holding up a flail

[Nos. 43, 45]

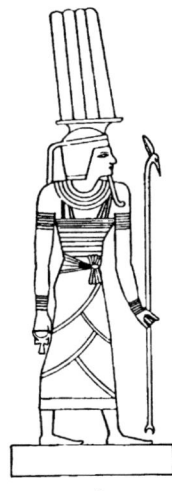

An-her

No 117 Bronze pendant with three bronze figures of the gods of creation, **Rā, Amen**, and **Amsu**, or Min

[No. 18,681.]

Nos 118, 119 Glazed porcelain figures of Amsu.

[Nos. 13,520, 22,168.]

In **Wall-Case 123** will be found grouped figures of Amen-Rā, Mut, and Khonsu, who formed the triad of great gods of Thebes. **Amen-Rā** represents the fusion of Amen and Rā, and the cult of this dual god is one of the most remarkable phases of Egyptian religious belief. Originally Amen was a local god of Thebes, who sprang into prominence immediately after the rise to power of the princes of Thebes, about B.C. 2600, the kings of the XIIth dynasty either founded or added to a temple to the god at Thebes, and their successors continued to pay great honour to him. When Seqenen-Rā, a king of the XVIIth dynasty, defeated the Hyksos, and so made himself master of all Egypt, the power and glory of Amen were further magnified, and under the XVIIIth dynasty he was definitely proclaimed "king of the gods," and he was made to usurp all the titles and attributes of Rā, the Sun-god. The name "Amen" means "hidden," and he appears to be the personification of the invisible, all-pervading, all-creating generative male principle, which made itself visible in the great operative powers of nature His female counterpart was **Mut**, who is depicted in the form of a woman, and may be regarded as the type of the Egyptian "world-mother" in the latter half of the dynastic period. The third member of the triad of Thebes was the Moon-god, who existed in two forms, which are called **Khonsu** and **Khonsu Nefer-ḥetep.** Khonsu possessed many of the attributes of Horus, and is depicted as a hawk-headed man, with the lunar crescent and disk on his head. Khonsu Nefer-hetep has the head of a man, and was believed to possess the power of driving out evil spirits, and of curing those who were sick of diseases caused by the supernatural and unfriendly powers.

No. 120. Bronze standing figure of **Amen-Rā**, king of the gods, with the solar disk and plumes on his head.

[No. 9]

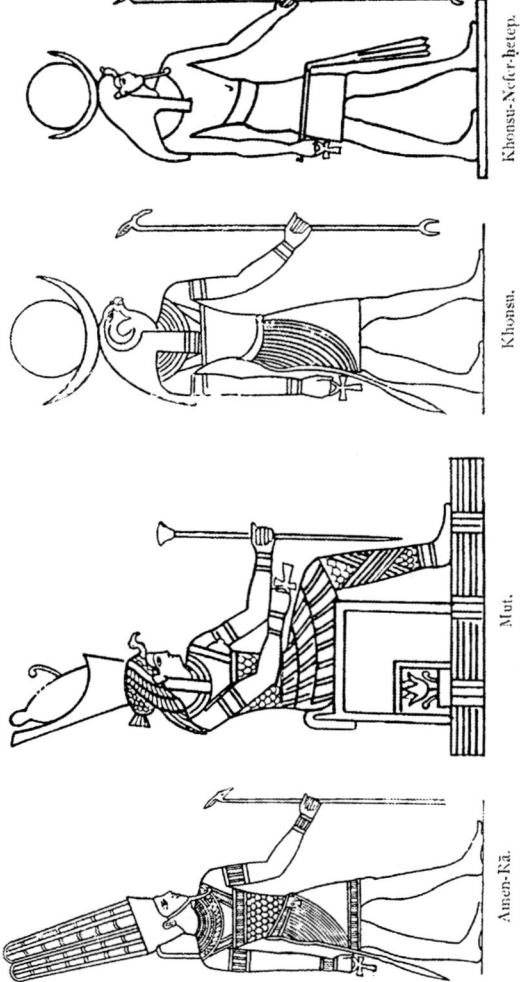

THE TRIAD OF THE GREAT GODS AT THEBES.

Amen-Rā. Mut. Khonsu. Khonsu-Nefer-hetep.

M

No. 121.   Bronze seated figure of Ámen-Rā.
[No. 11,003.]

No. 122.   Bronze seated figure of Amen-Rā, ram-headed.   [No. 11,233.]

No. 123.   Bronze shrine containing a seated figure of Amen-Rā. This object was a votive offering made by Shabataka, a king of Egypt of the XXVth dynasty, about B.C. 650.   [No 11,013.]

No. 124.   Wooden plaque inscribed with figures of " Amen-Rā, king of the gods," and " Ptah, the begetter of the gods "; between them is the cartouche of **Seti II.**

Mer-en-Ptah  , a king of Egypt, B.C 1300
[No 38.]

No. 125.   Bronze seated figure of Ámen-Heru-pa-khart (**Amen-Harpocrates**).
[No 34,937.]

No. 126.   Bronze seated figure of **Mut**   [No. 58.]

No. 127.   Bronze standing figure of Mut.   [No. 11,022.]

Nos. 128, 129.   Two porcelain figures of the goddess Mut in the character of Isis suckling Horus.
[Nos. 11,158, 13,519.]

No. 130.   Bronze figure of **Khonsu**, hawk-headed.
[No. 87.]

No. 131.   Gold figure of Khonsu, with lunar crescent and disk.   [No. 86.]

Khnemu.

Nos. 132, 133.   Bronze figures of Khonsu, wearing the triple crown and attributes of Harpocrates.
[Nos. 11,045, 35,417.]

No. 134.   Bronze figure of Khonsu, holding the *Utchat* of the moon.   [No. 12,587.]

No. 135.   Bronze figure of Khonsu, wearing the crown, horns, etc., of Osiris.   [No. 583.]

In **Wall-Case 122** are exhibited figures of the gods of the triad of Elephantine, which consisted of Khnemu, Satet, and Ānqet. **Khnemu** was probably a god of the pre-dynastic Egyptians; he is usually depicted in the form of a man, with the head of a flat-horned ram, an animal which appears to have been introduced into Egypt from the East, and which is not represented on the monuments after the period of the XIIth dynasty. Above his horns is often seen the jug ⴺ, the phonetic value of which, "Khnemu," forms the god's name. The name Khnemu means the "moulder," and he is described as the "builder of "men, the maker of the gods, the "Father who was in the beginning, the "creator of the things which are, and "of the things which shall be, the "source of all that existeth, Father of "fathers, Mother of mothers, the lord "who maketh things to come into "being from himself, creator of heaven, "earth, underworld, water and moun- "tains, who raised up heaven on its "four pillars, and who holdeth up the "same in the firmament." The female counterpart of Khnemu was **Sati** or **Satet**, who appears to have been the goddess of the Inundation of the Nile. She was identified with Isis-Sothis, Isis-Hathor, Ament, Menāt, Renpit and other goddesses. Her sister goddess was **Ānqet**, a personification of the waters of the Nile.

No. 136.   Bronze standing figure of **Khnemu**, ram-headed, wearing the *Atef* crown with disk, uræi, etc.

Satet, or Sati.

[No. 92.]

M 2

No 137.   Bronze figure of Khnemu, weaiing a disk.
                                                [No 11,040.]
No 138.   Lead seated figure of Khnemu.
                                                [No. 11,067.]
No 139   Bronze ægis of Khnemu   [No. 37,470]

No. 140.   Wooden figure of **Sati** or Satet.
                                                [No 11,487.]

Among the foreign gods of unusual type preserved in the collection may be mentioned Bes and Reshpu. The

origin of **Bes** is still an open question, but judging by the feathers on his head, his home was the northern portion of Central Africa. He is depicted in the form of a large-headed bearded dwarf, with bowed legs, and he wears the skin of the *Bes* 𓃹, an animal of the panther class, from which he appears to derive his name. Bes was the god of war, music, laughter, and of merry-making of all kinds, and he was the protector of children and the patron of beauty. In the later dynastic period he was identified with Horus and other solar gods, and became the type of the "old god who reneweth his youth."

No. 141.   Bronze figure of **Bes**, whose plumes are surmounted by an ægis of Khnemu. [No. 11,503.]

No. 142.   Bronze figure of Bes, with two uræi on his head.
                                                [No. 11,530]

No. 143.   Bronze figure of Bes on a standard   [No. 15,291.]

Bes.

No. 144.   Bronze figure of Bes standing on a seat supported by sphinxes.   [No 1208]

No 145.   Bronze figure of Bes standing on two lions.
                                                [No. 35,978.]

No. 146. Wooden figure of Bes, holding a tambourine, and dancing on a lotus flower. [**Wall-Case 129.**]

[No. 20,865.]

Among the other foreign gods worshipped in Egypt may be mentioned **Ānthât,** a goddess of war, who is probably to be identified with **Ānthretha, Āstharthet,** or **Ashtôreth, Qetesh, Kent, Āāsith,** Bār or **Baal, Baıltha** or **Beltis,** and **Reshpu.** Ānthât holds a spear and shield in her right hand, and brandishes a club in

Reshpu.

her left, Reshpu is depicted in the form of a man who is armed with shield, spear, and club; projecting from his turban is the head of a gazelle, which animal appears to be a very ancient symbol of the god. Figures of Ānthât and Reshpu may be seen on Stele No. 191 in the Northern Egyptian Gallery.

In **Wall-Case 122** are exhibited several examples of "polytheistic figures," *i.e.,* figures of a composite god who, in the Ptolemaïc period, was endowed with all the chief attributes of all the ancient gods of Egypt. See Nos. 17,169, 1205, 35,720, etc.

In **Wall-Cases 119–123** will be found specimens of figures of nearly all the sacred animals, reptiles, birds, etc., of Egypt. Among these may be specially mentioned :—

Bronze figures of the **hawk,** sacred to the Horus gods [Nos. 11,593, 11,594, 1844, 36,313], and figures of a hawk with the attributes of Menthu and Khonsu [Nos. 1859, 1861]. Figures of the **man-headed lion,** or Egyptian **Sphinx,** symbol of Rā-Ḥeru-Khuti or Rā-Harmachis [Nos. 11,891, 24,700, 35,725, 11,552]. Figures of the **lion,** sacred to Horus, Aker, and other gods [Nos. 11,553, 11,936] Figures of Ḥāp or **Apis,** the sacred bull of Memphis, and of Mei-ur, or **Mnevis,** the sacred bull of Heliopolis The cult of these gods is very ancient, and continued until the latest times [Nos. 1608, 35,721, 11,617, 11,616; examples in porcelain are 1624, 11,949] Figures of the **ibis,** sacred to Thoth [Nos. 1925, 11,619, 36,218; ibis with figure of Maāt [No. 36,451]. Figures of

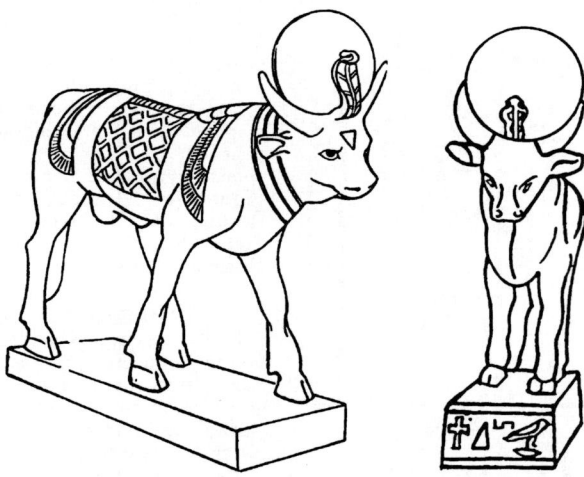

The Bull Apis   The Bull Mnevis

the **shrewmouse,** sacred to Horus [Nos. 1604, 26,335]. Figures of the **dog-headed ape,** having on his head the lunar disk and horns. He was the companion of Thoth, whom he assisted in calculating times and seasons, and in weighing the souls of the dead in the Judgment [Nos. 1443, 35,401, 12,561, 32,197, 11,898]. Figure of the animal, symbol of **Set** [No. 30,460]. Figures of the **jackal** sacred to Ȧnpu (Anubis) and Ȧp-uat [Nos. 11,532,

11,895, 22,928]. Figures of the **cow,** sacred to Hathor [Nos. 1631, 36,447, 11,579, 11,585]. Figures of **fish,** sacred to Hathor, Nehemāuit, and Hāt-mehit [Nos. 11,624, 11,626, 12,041, 37,376, 37,449] Figures of the **cat,** sacred to Bast [Nos. 1546, 1552, 11,556; a figure in crystal No. 11,918]. Figures of the **crocodile,** sacred to Sebek [Nos. 1941, 22,154, 23,049]. Figures of the **ram,** sacred

The Ram of Mendes.

to Khnemu, and later to Amen [Nos. 11,720, 22,887]. Figures of the **vulture,** sacred to Mut [Nos. 12,022, 12,030]. Figures of the **ichneumon,** sacred to Uatchet, [Nos. 11,590, 29,602, 35,091] Figures of the **uræus,** sacred to Rā and other gods [Nos. 1994, 24,727]. Figures of the **sow,** sacred to Isis [Nos. 1700, 1795]. Figures of the **hare,** sacred to Osiris [Nos. 1731, 11,983]. Figures of the **scorpion,** sacred to Selqet [Nos. 2017, 12,033].

Figures of the **frog**, emblem of the resurrection and fertility [Nos. 2019, 11,620]. Figures of the horned **beetle**, sacred to Rā [Nos. 2042, 11,630, 12,040]. Figure of the **hippopotamus**, sacred to Hathor [No. 34,275]

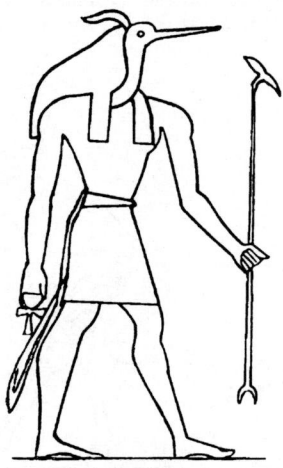

The god Bennu, *i e* , the Phœnix god.

On the floor of **Wall-Cases 118- 132** will be found an interesting collection of figures of the gods who have already been referred to, in wood, bronze, stone, terracotta, clay, etc.

FOURTH EGYPTIAN ROOM.

In this room are exhibited large collections of Jewellery, Amulets, Scarabs, Portrait figures in bronze and wood, Vases and other Vessels in various kinds of limestone, diorite, porphyry, earthenware, porcelain, glass, etc.; some fine specimens of Furniture, sun-dried Bricks, glazed Tiles, terra-cotta figures of the Ptolemaic and Roman periods, and a large number of miscellaneous antiquities of great general interest. The period covered by these objects ranges from about B.C. 4000 to A D. 400. In Standard-Case A are musical instruments, ivory amulets, figures, plaques for inlaying in toilet boxes, etc, spoons in various ornamental forms. Table-Case B contains a large and varied collection of glazed porcelain beads, necklaces, ornamental pendants, etc. In Standard-Case C are groups of toys, including dolls in wood, earthenware, bronze, etc., figures of animals, some having moveable limbs, draughtboards and draughtsmen, etc. In the same case are fine painted wooden models of houses, granaries, boats, etc., and a number of inscribed bronze libation buckets, libation vases, censers, and other vessels, many of which were used in the public and private worship of the gods. In Table-Cases D, E, G, I, is exhibited a collection of scarabs which is the largest and most representative in the world ; many of them are inscribed with royal names, and are very fine, and some of them record the names of kings of whom no larger monuments exist. The custom of wearing scarabs with the view of obtaining the protection of Kheperà, the creator of gods and men, began early in the dynastic period, and continued until long after Egypt had become a Roman province ; the large green stone scarabs, of which so many fine examples are exhibited in Table-Cases G and I, were laid in or on the bodies of the dead at a still earlier period, and the idea most prevalent in connexion with them had reference to the resurrection of the dead. All the principal varieties of inscription, device, ornament, and style are well represented here. Table-Case F contains an important group of hard stone **amulets,** which were used chiefly in connexion with the Book of the Dead, and many of the varieties are inscribed with extracts from chapters in that work Here too are a number of fine **necklaces,** formed of beads in gold and hard stone, of the period of the XIXth and following dynasties; the older specimens of this class of object will be found in **Table-Case J. Table-Case H** contains an ancient **Chair of State** inlaid with silver, a set of fine draughtsmen, etc. In **Table-Case J** is exhibited an important series of groups of **jewellery,** among them being a long **necklace of scarabs** set in gold frames, of the period of the XIIth dynasty, a number of massive inscribed **gold rings,** a pair of **bracelets** inlaid with plaques of coloured stones and paste, of a unique character, and several interesting objects of the Græco-Roman period. **Table-Case K** contains a large miscellaneous collection of objects in **porcelain,** and pendants, plaques, etc., of **glass.** In **Standard-Case L** are several fine inlaid **chairs** of the XVIIIth and XIXth dynasties, a **table,** the frame of a bed, a **toilet box** of the XVIIIth dynasty, etc. Græco-Roman antiquities and **Coptic ostraka** will be found in **Table-Case M,** and **Table-Case N** contains **Gnostic Gems.** The **Gnostics** were a Christian sect which flourished in the third century, and their doctrines were a mixture of Christian and pagan beliefs, which they expressed symbolically. Many of the gems here exhibited are of great interest and importance.

The **WALL-CASES 137–142, 194 204** contain an extremely comprehensive collection of **vases, jars, bowls,** cups, saucers, jugs, etc., which were placed in the tomb to hold wine, oil, honey, unguents, cosmetics, etc. They have been arranged in chronological order, and cover practically the whole range of Egyptian dynastic history. During the Archaic period **vessels** of this kind were usually made of dark coloured and variegated stones, but from about the Vth dynasty onwards alabaster and arragonite, or zoned-alabaster, were commonly used.

In **WALL-CASES 143–164** are fine series of **earthenware and porcelain vessels,** which illustrate the potter's art from the time when painted earthenware vessels and models in wood were made to take the place of variegated stone vases to the Roman period. The forms of many of the porcelain objects are very graceful, and the colours very beautiful, and they well illustrate the high pitch of perfection to which the ceramic art of Egypt was brought under the XVIIIth and XIXth dynasties. In **Wall-Case 175** are sun-dried **bricks,** made of mud and sand which were bound together by broken pottery and straw. Among the names of kings inscribed on them are **Thothmes I.,** B C **1633; Thothmes III.,** B.C. **1600; Thothmes IV.,** B.C. **1533; Amen-hetep III.,** B.C. **1500;** and **Rameses II.,** B C **1333,** for whom the children of Israel built the store cities of Pithom and Raamses.

In **WALL-CASES 182–187** are **Articles for the Toilet,** including combs, hair pins, hair tweezers, bronze mirrors and mirror cases, handles of fans, tubes and boxes in various shapes and forms for holding *kohl, i.e.,* antimony or bismuth, for the eye-lids, unguents, perfumes, etc. ; on the floor of the cases are specimens of petrified wood.

In **WALL-CASES 188–193** are groups of models of men engaged in cooking, slaughtering animals, etc., and a fine series of wooden **Portrait Figures,** the oldest of which date from the XIth or XIIth dynasty.

On the south wall of the room is a large **painted cast** on which is represented the **conquest of the Nubians by Rameses II.,** and the receipt of tribute by the king. Rameses sits under a canopy, and his officers lead before him Nubians, who bring as gifts apes, leopards, a giraffe, Sûdân cattle, a hunting dog, a lion, an ostrich, gazelle, and pieces of ebony. On the north wall is another large **painted cast,** on which is a series of scenes representing the conquest by the same king of Libyans and Syrians. The casts were made from the walls of the little rock-hewn tomb which Rameses II. built to commemorate his victories over the Nubians in the city of Thelemset, the Talmis of classical writers, and the modern Kalâbshah, about 40 miles south of Aswân These casts were made by Mr. Bonomi for Mr. Hay, and were carefully coloured after the originals, and they are the only evidences extant of the beauty of the wall decorations of the temple, for every trace of colour has now vanished.

Rameses II. [No. 30,448.]

On entering the room to the right is exhibited a beautifully sculptured head from a quartzite-porphyry statue of **Rameses II.**, king of Egypt about B.C. 1333, as a young man ; notwithstanding the extreme hardness of the stone, the features are cut with a delicacy and finish which makes this object one of the finest examples of portraiture in stone of the period.   From Thebes.

TABLE-CASE A. Musical instruments, inscribed
shells, ivory and wooden **spoons,** etc. The following are
of special interest :—

No. 1. **Harp,** the body of which is made in the form
of a woman, wearing the crowns of the South and North,
and a pectoral, the two ends of which terminate in hawks'
heads and disks. This very interesting instrument is made
of wood, covered with painted plaster, and the upper part
of it is inlaid with plaques of blue, green, and red glazed
porcelain. When fully strung the instrument possessed

Harp. No. 24,564.

five strings. From the tomb of Ani at Thebes. XVIIIth
dynasty. [No. 24,564.]

No. 2. Four-stringed harp, the body of which is
formed by pieces of skin stretched over a wooden frame.
[No. 38,170.]

No. 3. Four-stringed harp, with the sound board made
in the form of a shell. No. 4. Tortoise shell, which once
formed the sound board of a small harp.
[Nos. 6381, 38,171.]

No 5   **Reed flute**, with four holes [No 6385]   No 6.
Bronze flute with four holes, and ornamented with incised
rings [No 12,742]   No 7   Portion of a reed **whistle**, with the
remains of an inscription in Greek uncials   [No 16,232.]

No. 8   **Bells**   Bronze bell, ornamented with the head of
Bes [No 6374]   No. 9   Bronze bell, ornamented with the
heads of cats in relief [No 38,160].   No 10 Bronze bell, ornamented with the head of an animal [No 17,094]   No 11
Bronze bell with figures of lizards, the head of a bull, the head
of a hen, the head of Bes, the god Ptah, and *utchats*, or symbolic eyes in relief [No. 30,062].   Many, if not all, of the bells
here exhibited were attached to the garments of priests and
ministrants when engaged in the performance of services in
the temples, and the sounds which the clappers made were
thought to be effectual in driving away evil spirits. Nos. 12
and 13 were probably used for signalling
purposes   [Nos 32,212, 32,213.]

No 13.   **Cymbals**.   Pair of bronze
cymbals, fixed in their original frame or
holder, which is ornamented with an incised
diamond pattern, they were probably
carried by a priestess, who suspended the
holder from her girdle [No. 26,260]   No
14. Pair of fine bronze cymbals, with the
original linen cord [No 6373].   No. 15.
Two pairs of cymbals, unmounted.
[Nos 15,774, 17,084]
No. 16.   **Sistra**.   Massive bronze sistrum, the upper part of the handle of
which is in the form of the head of Hathor,
who wears a tiara composed of uræi
wearing disks.   The small bronze disks
which produced the sound moved on three
wires, which are made in the form of uræi;
the heads of these project from one side,
and the tails from the other.   Sistra were

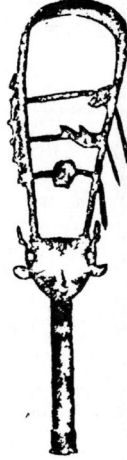

Bronze Sistrum
[No 36,310]

usually carried by priestesses in processions in the temples, and the noise made
by the bronze disks when shaken was
believed to drive away evil spirits [No. 36,310]   No 17.

Bronze sistrum, the upper part of which is ornamented with designs representing the goddesses of the South and North carrying sistra, the goddess Bast, etc [No 38,172]. No 18. Bronze sistrum ornamented with figures of cats and a bird [No. 30,735]. No 19 Green glazed porcelain sistrum, the upper part of which is in the form of a shrine of Hathor ; it was made for a king or prince called **Psammetichus**, , whose name it bears [No 6359]. No 20 Model of a sistrum made of wood, and a reed painted [No. 6358] No 21. Cast of a sistrum, with a handle formed by a figure of Bes and a head of Hathor. The ends of the wires are in the form of heads of ducks [No. 6365]. Nos. 22, 23. Green glazed porcelain models of sistra.

[Nos. 6361, 6362.]

No. 24.   A group of **Shells**, inscribed with the prenomen and nomen of **Usertsen I.** , , the prenomen of **Amenemhāt II.** , and the prenomen of **Rameses II**, the Great .

[Nos. 15,423, 20,754, 27,723, 29,434, 30,056, 30,057, 30,731, 36,499]

On the sloping sides of the case are exhibited —

No. 1.   Semicircular ivory object, amulet (?) with rounded ends, inscribed with figures of the two-headed lion god Aker, heads of crocodiles, lions, serpents, a serpent-headed god holding a serpent in each hand, a beetle, a frog, the hippopotamus goddess Thoueris, etc.   On the reverse, among other figures, is that of a hawk-headed leopard, with wings and a human head growing out of his back.   A short inscription indicates that the object was made to give " magical protection to the lady of the house," whose name was SENEB   From Thebes XVIIIth dynasty or earlier.   [No. 18,175.]

No. 2. Stamp, with figures of the two **Nile-gods** uniting the South and the North, and the goddesses Nekhebet and Uatchet, in the forms of a vulture and a serpent, seated on clusters of papyrus and lotus plants [No. 35,421]. No. 3. Ivory plaque from a box made in the form of a pylon of a temple [No. 29,371]. No. 4. Rounded plaque from a box, with a figure of Rā or Rā-Harmachis in relief. Fine work [No. 38,183]. No. 5. Ivory figure of a woman wearing a close-fitting cap and a pig-tail. Fine work [No. 38,185]. No. 6. Ivory seated figure of a boy [No. 30.467]. No. 7. Ivory hippopotamus

Ivory amulet made for the lady Seneb. [No. 18,175]

[No. 35,426]. No. 8. Ivory figure of a god wearing the triple crown [No. 35,423]. No. 9. Ivory box in the form of a water-fowl, which is giving a fish to its young [No. 5946]. Nos. 10, 11. Portions of ivory spoons [Nos. 5975, 5955]. Nos. 12-16. Pieces of ivory coloured for inlaying [No. 32,697, etc.]. Nos. 17-19. Three ivory legs from a box made in the form of lions' legs [Nos. 30,465, 30,466, 29,433]. No. 20. Ivory spoon, the bowl of which is in the shape of the shell *Indina Nilotica* [No. 5957].

Nos 31-68. A fine series of **spoons** made of wood, carved in various ornamental shapes, many being painted and inlaid. The most interesting are —No 36. Spoon,

the bowl of which is in the form of a duck, and the
handle in that of a woman lying full length [No. 38,186].
No. 47. Bowl of a spoon carved with lotus flowers
[No. 5971]. No. 48. Spoon, with flat, hollow-work handle,

No. 37,924.

SPOONS.

No. 5966.

in which is a figure of a woman walking among lotus
plants [No. 38,188]. No. 49. Spoon, with flat, hollow-
work handle, in which is a figure of the god Bes
[No. 5954]. No. 50. Spoon, with handle in the form of
a human hand and arm [No. 5962]. No. 51. Spoon, with

N

bowl in the form of a vase, and the handle in that of a woman with an elaborate head-dress, who is carrying the bowl on her shoulder [No. 37,924]   No 52 Spoon, painted with lotus flowers and inlaid [No. 5965].   No 53. Spoon in the form of a lotus flower, with two buds on stalks [No 5966]   No 56. Double spoon, with bowls in the form of cartouches, and ornamented with designs of water-fowl and papyrus plants   In the flat handle are two figures of the god Bes   The substance in the spoon is wax [No 5953]   No 63 Spoon, with handle in the form of a flat fish [No 5952]   No 65 Spoon, with a handle in the form of a jackal [No 38,187]   No 66 Spoon, with the bowl in the form of a fish, and the handle in that of a jackal, which is seizing the fish by its tail [No. 5945]

Nos. 69 96   Models of **hands and arms**, in ivory and wood   These objects are usually found lying on the breasts of mummies, and they appear to have been placed there with the view of procuring the " magical protection " of the gods for the dead.   The finest examples are — No. 74. Ivory object, with one end terminating in the head of a ram or oryx [No 18,186].   Nos 75, 76, 94, 95 Ivory hands and arms with annular ornaments [Nos. 20,859, etc.]   Nos 78, 79. Pair of horns, ornamented with incised lines [Nos. 30,728, 30,729].   Nos. 83, 84. Ivory hands and arms, ornamented at the wrists with heads of Hathor [Nos. 20,779, 20,780].   No 87 Ivory scarab, inscribed [No 30,730]

Nos 98-148 A large miscellaneous collection of bone and ivory objects, of various periods, from B.C. 1500 to the late Coptic period   Among these may be specially noted :—Nos. 113–116. **Theatre tickets** [Nos 14,493, etc.]. Nos 128 131 **Ivory boxes**, some of which are ornamented with annules [Nos 18,187, etc.].   No 133 Ivory box in the form of a pylon [No 16,021]   No. 134. Round ivory box with a lid [No. 38,246]   No 136ff A collection of bone and ivory bracelets [No 26,741]   No 147. Round ivory box, in the shape of a two-eared vase, ornamented with incised lines [No. 29,662]   Nos 149 194 A fine series of carved bone and ivory **plaques for inlaying** in boxes, with corner ornaments, etc.   These belong chiefly to the Roman period. No. 199. Figure of a dog holding a bird in his mouth, his collar is of gold [No. 13,596]. No. 200 Bust of an Egyptian royal personage [No. 35,422]. No. 201. Head of Venus Anadyomene [No 20,995]. No 221. Ivory altar. Coptic period. [No. 37,451]. Nos. 246, 247. Handles of knives, with ends in the form of lions' heads [Nos. 13,966, 14,467]. No. 251. Head of a lion. Very fine work [No. 38,197]. No. 260. Ivory figures of Isis and Horus. Roman period [No. 26,225]. No. 262. A deity in a shrine, holding a bull's head [No. 20,875]   Nos. 267, 268. Ivory pomegranates, coloured red [Nos. 17,064, 18,189].

TABLE-CASE B. Herein is exhibited a large collection of Egyptian **porcelain beads,** glazed in blue, green, red, yellow, and other colours. The greater number of them were found in tombs in Upper Egypt, and were collected from coffins, into which they had fallen from the necks of mummies; many necklaces have been re-strung, but in some cases the ancient linen thread has been preserved   They belong chiefly to the period of the XXVIth dynasty, about B.C. 600. The following are of special interest :—No. 1. Necklace of blue porcelain bugle beads, with pendent scarab [No 32,482]. No. 55. Necklace formed of a series of rectangular plaques of porcelain, inscribed with the name of Psammetichus □ ⌐⌐⌐ [No. 24,312]. No. 56. Similar necklace, the plaques being inscribed with the name of Osiris ⌐⌐ [No. 24,313]. No 70. Necklace composed of porcelain scaraboids and porcelain disks [No 20,586]. No. 71. Necklace of thick, short, tube-shaped blue porcelain beads [No. 30,337]   No. 87. Necklace of circular greenish-blue porcelain beads [No. 18,168]. No. 88. Necklace of round, blue glazed porcelain beads, with yellow disks, a figure of Bes, and two plaques, one with the figure of a hippopotamus, and the other with a lion's head, in relief [No. 3334]. No 112. String of flat, circular beads, glazed in blue, green, red, yellow, and white colours [No. 14,451]. Nos 138, 139 Massive blue glazed porcelain beads [Nos. 7789, 7790]. No. 149. Necklace of blue porcelain beads, made in the form of Egyptian

N 2

gods and amulets [No 38,003] No 188. Necklace made of oval, serrated plaques of glazed porcelain, stamped with a cross of double lines [No. 20,593]. No 215 Necklace of blue porcelain beads, made in the form of uræi, cartouches, etc., some of the cartouches are stamped with the prenomen and nomen of one of the Rameses kings [No 14,790] No. 216. Necklace of blue porcelain beads, with pendants of the same material in the form of Harpocrates, a snake, a bird, etc. [No. 29,468] Nos 235 242 A group of fragments of ancient bead-work, which formed part of the coverings of mummies in their coffins No. 243 has been carefully restored, but many modern beads have been added

[Nos 7160, 18,167, 14,627, 14,665, 7159, etc.]

STANDARD-CASE C. Bronze bowls, vessels, implements, etc., **toys, models of houses, a granary,** etc From B C 2500 to the Roman period.

Shelf 1. No. 1 Bronze **libation vase,** inscribed with the name of **Nesi-ta-neb-asher** [hieroglyphs] [No. 25,567] No. 2 Libation vase inscribed with the names of **Ast-em-khebit** and **Rā-men-kheper,** two prominent members of the family of the priest kings of Egypt of the XXIInd dynasty [No 25,566] Nos 3 11 Bronze bowls, with feet, handles, spouts, etc [Nos. 29,174, etc.] No. 12. Iron object of unknown use [No. 38,236]

Shelf 2 Children's Toys, Dolls, etc Nos. 13 15 Wooden dolls, ornamented with coloured patterns Nos 16 17. Wooden dolls, with figures of a mythical monster painted on them Nos 20 23 Wooden dolls, with strings of mud beads to represent hair Nos 24 26. Wooden dolls, made in the form of Nubian women No. 31 Painted earthenware doll in the form of a captive with his hands tied behind him, and a duck's head [No 32,201]. No. 32. Bronze doll, woman bearing a pot, or tiara, on her head [No. 36,076] No. 33 Earthenware doll, woman carrying her child [No 30,725]. No 34. Earthenware doll, woman nursing her child [No. 23,424] No 35 Earthenware doll, good work [No 2363] No 36. Limestone doll, with head-dress painted black [No 37,925]. No 37 Painted

PLATE V.

EGYPTIAN TOYS.

1. Negro pursued by an animal.
2. Painted, flat, headless wooden doll.
3. Bronze doll, with moveable arms.
4. Wooden doll, with mud beads for hair.
5. Wooden lion.
6. Cat, with moveable jaw.
7. Wooden calf.
8. Wooden fish.
9. Porcelain elephant and rider.
10. Draughtsman, with the head of Bes.
11. Draughtsman, with head of Anubis.

[To face page 180.]

earthenware doll, with head-dress painted !black and surmounted by a cone [No 21,953]. No 38. Blue glazed
porcelain doll [No 29,408] No 39 Bronze doll, with
moveable arms [No. 37,162] No 40. Portion of a glazed
porcelain doll, woman tiring her hair [No. 22,510] No. 41.
Model of a Nubian woman carrying two children in a
basket, or bag, on her back [No 32,594] No. 42. Stone
figure of a man playing two pipes [No 14,399] No 43
Two wrestlers [No 24,701] No 44 Ape driving a chariot
[No. 21,984] Nos. 45 47. Groups of apes [Nos. 1460,
11,549, 11,888] No 48. Toy, man and moveable figure
of a dog [No 26,254] No 49 Blue glazed porcelain
dwarf, with the head of a cat, XIIth dynasty [No 22,883]
No 50 Porcelain **elephant**, which originally had moveable
legs [No 17,059] No 51. Wooden **cat**, with inlaid eyes
of crystal and moveable jaw [No 15,671]. Nos. 52, 53
Wooden **cows** [Nos. 21,891, 21,892] No 54 Blue glazed
porcelain **lion** killing its prey [No 22,876]. No 55 Blue
glazed porcelain **lion** couchant [No 22,797] No. 56
Porcelain **dog** [No 22,877] No 57 Porcelain **hippopotamus** [No. 22,880] Nos. 58-63. Children's **balls**, made of
blue glazed porcelain, papyrus, leather stuffed with chopped
straw, leather stuffed with hair, thread, etc [No 6467, etc.]
Draught boxes and draughts No 64 Wooden draught
box, with drawer, and eleven pieces [No. 24,424] No 65.
Portion of a **stone draught board**, with nine pieces made
of earthenware [No 14,315] Late period. No. 66 Set of
draughtsmen, ten with heads of Bes, and seven with heads
of a jackal [Nos 24,668, etc.]. No 67 A miscellaneous
group of draughtsmen, in porcelain and wood [Nos 30,789,
etc.] No. 68. Limestone draughtsmen inscribed with the
titles and prenomen of **Necho II.** ⸮⸮⸮⸮⸮⸮⸮,
king of Egypt, about B.C. 630 [No 38,254]. **Dice** No 69.
Crystal die [No 37,467]. Nos 70 73. Bone dice [Nos. 6457,
etc.]. No 74. Stone die [No 37,466]. No 75 Stone
object, with twenty facets, on each of which is cut a letter
of the Greek alphabet, probably used in working magic
or for purposes of divination [No. 29,418] No 76.
Wooden **knot**, inscribed in gold with the prenomen of
Thothmes III, or of a king of the XXIInd dynasty

[No. 18,195]. No. 77. Wooden model of a **horse on wheels**. Late period [No. 38,142].

On the floor of the case are :—No. 78. Wooden **model of a granary**, from a tomb of the VIth dynasty at Aswân in Upper Egypt. The model contains seven bins, into which the grain is supposed to be poured through holes in the roof, and each is provided with a sliding door, over which

Wooden Model of a Granary, B.C. 3500.   [No. 21,804.]

the name of the grain inside is written in hieratic. By the side of the wooden stairs which lead to the roof stands the keeper of the granary, and near him is the grain measure which he uses. This model represents a building about 60 feet long by 15 feet high, and is one of the oldest known. Presented by Lord Grenfell, 1888 [No. 21,804]. Nos. 79–81. Limestone and wood **models of houses** [Nos. 36,872, etc.]. No. 82. **Model of a door** plated with

electrum, or gold. ⟩ In relief is a kneeling figure of
Nectanebus II., king of Egypt about B.C. 350, making an
offering of an utchat 👁, and above are his titles and
prenomen ⦰, and a row of uræi with
disks [No. 38,255]. No. 83. Model of a man rolling dough
[No. 18,177]. No. 84. Bronze **table of offerings,** the upper
part of which is in the form of an altar ⌐⊥⌐, with a com-

INTERIOR OF THE MODEL OF A GRANARY.   [No. 21,804.]

(The side has been removed in order to show the names of the grain, written
in the hieratic character, which are above the shutters of the bins. The
keeper of the granary, with his measure, stands close to the steps.)

plete series of models of libation vases, saucers and other
vessels. This very interesting group was made for the
"chief reader" Áṭená ⦰, whose alabaster
pillow and vases are exhibited in Wall-Case No. 138.
VIth dynasty [No. 5315]. No. 85. Basalt socket for a door
to work in [No. 2446]. No. 86. Toy house, with moveable
door.   [No. 23,075.]

Shelf 3. On the small glass shelves is a series of **bronze vases, jugs,** etc, of various periods, chiefly of the XXIInd and XXVIth dynasties. Suspended from the frame are the following —No. 87. **Ladle,** with handle terminating in a duck's head No. 88 Ladle with jointed handle No. 89 **Lamp,** with three feet, and long handle terminating in a duck's head [No 38,244, etc.] No. 90. Pair of bronze tongs for use at the altar [No. 20,817] On the large shelf are:—Nos. 91, 92. Heads of bronze **ceremonial standards,** with figures of crocodiles, arrows, etc. [Nos 5498, 5499] No. 93. Head of a standard with a figure of Horus [No 5500] No. 94 Head of a lotus standard, with figures of a cat and two kittens [No 38,245]; it was dedicated to Bast No. 95. Head of a lotus standard with a seated figure of Harpocrates [No 29,603] Nos. 96 - 100. Bronze ends of standards, one of which (No 96) is ornamented with a figure of Bes [Nos. 23,457, etc.]. Nos 101 103. Bronze **votive buckets,** ornamented with figures of gods and goddesses, animals, birds, etc, in relief. No 101 was dedicated by Petā-Amen [symbols] (?) [No. 36,319]. No 104. Bronze pan from a pair of scales, ornamented with linear designs, figures, etc. [No. 38,241]

Shelf 4. No. 105 Bronze **measure (?)** inscribed with the name of Amenartās, son of Aāḥmes [symbols] [No 37,640]. No 106. Bronze bowl, with ornamental border on the edge, and a rosette at the base [No. 37,915]. No. 107. Bronze cup of fine metal [No.38,202]. No. 108 Bronze **wine-strainer,** perforated with holes in ornamental patterns and the inscription DIONYSIOSEPO [No. 36,322]. No 109 Bronze **incense burner,** with receptacle for incense braced on the handle [No. 38,209] No 110 Bronze **libation vase** [symbol] [No. 36,318] No. 111. Bronze **shovel** or spoon for use at the altar [No 38,210]. No. 112. King kneeling before a libation vase in the form of a cartouche [No. 5296] Nos. 113, 114. Handles of bronze censers in the form of the heads of hawks [Nos. 5297, 38,247]. No. 115. Bronze vase, in the form of a flat fish [No. 37,469] No. 116. End of a bronze *menât,*

ornamented with a design in which Horus is seen standing
among lotus flowers [No. 38,225] Nos. 117–119. Models
of **bronze altars** [Nos. 2287, etc.] No. 120 Bronze ægis
of Horus, dedicated by Pef-ā-Heru, son of Puher and of
Tāt-Ast □
[No. 38,208]. Nos. 121, 122. Bronze vases, of the late
Coptic period [Nos. 20,781, 30,738]. No 123. **Lead vase,**
with cover having handle [No 5339]

On the **floor of the case** are :—No. 124. Massive **lead
jar,** with cover, which has been securely fastened ; contents
unknown [No. 22,111]. Nos 125–134. A group of fine
bronze vases, bowls and jars [Nos. 5326, etc]. No. 135.
Large wooden model of a house and granary enclosed
within walls. The grain is supposed to be stored in three
bins, each of which is provided with a sliding door. Under
the stairs which lead to the roof is the apartment in which
the guardian and his wife live, and on the roof is a small
chamber, open towards the north, in which the guardian of
the granary kept watch. Before him, on a small stand,
are the remains of his food, which consisted of grapes,
dates, some fruit of the cherry class, and grain. In the
courtyard below is a model of his wife or daughter, who is
rolling dough on a kneading trough, at one end of which is
a hollow for flour [No. 2463]. Suspended from the roof
of the case are the three following very fine specimens of
libation buckets, ornamented with inscriptions and figures of
gods, etc. :—No. 136. Libation bucket made for **Peṭā-Amen-
neb-nest-taui** [No. 38,212]. As the deceased was a priestly
official of king **Nekht-Heru-heb** ,
this object must have been made about B.C 378. No. 137.
Libation bucket made for **Rā-mes** , the son of
a priest and a sistrum bearer of Heru-Behutet [No. 38,213].
No. 138. Libation bucket of a "scribe of the wonders of
Āmen," called "**Peṭā-Amen-neb-nest-taui**" □
, the son of Pekhar-Khensu □ and the
lady Ast-em-khebit [No. 38,214 .

WOODEN MODEL OF A HOUSE. [No. 2463.]

(The side has been removed in order to show the arrangement of the grain bin
in the courtyard, and the figure of the woman making dough.)

TABLE-CASES D, E, G and I. Here is exhibited a large and exceedingly fine collection of **scarabs**, that is say, models of a certain beetle which have been found inside the swathings of mummies, and in rings on their fingers, and in chambers of tombs, and in ruins of temples and other buildings in Egypt and other countries, the inhabitants of which had trading and other relations with the Egyptians. These models are made chiefly of steatite, glazed with blue, green, and other colours ; hard stones, *e.g*, amethyst, carnelian, onyx, mother-of-emerald, basalt, green schist, and of porcelain, wood, and, though rarely, of gold and bronze *
The beetle which was copied in this manner belongs to the family called by naturalists *Scarabæidæ* (Coprophagi, *i.e*, dung-eaters), of which the *scarabæus sacer* is the type. The species are generally of a black hue, but among them are to be found some adorned with the richest metallic colours. A remarkable peculiarity exists in the structure and situation of the hind legs, which are placed so near the extremity of the body, and so far from each other, as to give the insect a most extraordinary appearance when walking This peculiar formation is, nevertheless, particularly serviceable to its possessors in rolling the balls of excrementitious matter in which they enclose their eggs. The balls are at first irregular and soft, but by degrees, and during the process of rolling along, become rounded and harder ; they are propelled by means of the hind legs. The balls are from one to two inches in diameter, and in rolling them along the beetles stand almost upon their heads, with their heads turned from the balls, which are rolled into holes previously prepared by the insect.   At a very early period the Egyptians evolved some remarkable ideas concerning this particular kind of beetle. Because it flew during the hottest part of the day, it was believed to be connected with Rā, the Sun-god, and a deceased king is said to have entered the boat of the Sun in the form of the scarab. The ball of dung containing its eggs was compared with the sun itself, and because it was rolled along the ground as the sun's globe was rolled across the sky, and because both it and the sun were sources of life, the beetle was called the " roller," in Egyptian " Kheprerā "

* Nos. 30,701, 30,713   (Table-Case D, No 1257, and Table-Case G, No. 805.)

and was connected by the Egyptians with the great god **Kheperá**, who was a form of the Sun-god, and was one of the chief gods of creation known to them. Now the eggs of the beetle were hatched by the heat of the sun, and the young larvæ fed upon the matter of

The god Kheperá

which was made the ball in which they had been laid, and this fact suggested to the early Egyptians the comparison between the egg-ball of the beetle and the dead human body, for each was formed of corruptible matter, and each contained a living germ, or potential life. the egg-ball covering the germs which would develop into beetles, and the dead material body the germ of the incorruptible spiritual body which would, under proper conditions, be developed from it. Now, the god Khepera also represented inert but living matter which was about to begin a course of existence, and at a very early period he was regarded as a god of the **Resurrection**; and since the scarab was identified with him, that insect became at once the symbol of the god and the type of the resurrection. And as the beetle had given potential life to its eggs in the ball, so, it was thought, would a model of the scarab, itself the symbol of Khepera, also give potential life to the dead body upon which it was placed, always provided that the proper "words of power" were first said over it or written upon it. When once the custom of burying scarabs with the dead became recognized, the habit of wearing them as ornaments by the living came into fashion, and as a result scarabs of almost every sort and kind may be found by the thousand. Besides being enclosed between the swathings of mummies, large numbers of scarabs have been found lying loose in coffins, and even in shallow holes dug in the tomb under the place where the coffin rested. It is recorded that in 1854, in a tomb at Thebes, the late Sir J. G. Wilkinson found, buried beneath the sepulchral stele that stood near the head of the coffin, a hoard of scarabs, some thousands in number, which had been placed there to insure the resurrection of the occupant of the tomb.

In **TABLE-CASE D** are arranged chronologically stone and porcelain **scarabs, cylinder-seals**, etc., inscribed with the names and titles of kings and queens of Egypt, and other royal personages, and scarabs inscribed with imitations of royal names ; all the important dynasties from about B.C. 4400 to about B.C. 500 are represented. Scarabs were not in common use during the Ptolemaïc and Roman periods, and there is no evidence that they were ever used as money. Nearly every scarab in this case has been selected for exhibition for some peculiarity of form, or colour, or inscription, and the collection as a whole is the most typical and representative known. Noteworthy scarabs and cylinders are :—

No. 1. Cylinder-seal of a king of the Ist dynasty, B.C. 4400 No. 2. Cylinder-seal of **Ath**, (?) a king of the Ist dynasty. No. 7. Scarab of **Khufu**, or **Cheops**, the builder of the Great Pyramid at Gîzeh, B C. 3700. No. 12. Scarab of **Khâfrā**, or **Khephren**, the builder of the Second Pyramid at Gîzeh No. 19. Scarab of **Menkaurā**, or **Mycerinus**, the builder of the Third Pyramid at Gîzeh. No. 23. Cylinder-seal of **Sahurā**, B.C. 3533. No. 25. Cylinder-seal of **Userkaf**, B.C. 3500. No. 32. Scarab of **Unās**, the builder of a pyramid at Sakkâra, B C. 3333. No. 38. Cylinder-seal of **Pepi I**. Meri-Rā, B.C 3233. No. 39. Bronze cylinder-seal of **Pepi I**. Meri-Rā. No 40. Massive cylinder-seal inscribed with the name of **Pepi I.**, Meri-Rā. No. 48. Scarab of **Pepi II.**, B.C. 3166. No. 63. Scarab of **Amenemḥāt I.**, B.C 2466. Nos. 67, 70 and 76. A bead, a cylinder-seal, and a scarab of **Usertsen I.**, B C. 2433 No. 91. Cylinder-seal of **Amenemḥāt II.**, B C. 2400 No. 94. Cylinder-seal of **Usertsen II.**, B.C 2366. No 103 Cylinder-seal, fluted, of **Usertsen III.**, B.C. 2333. Nos. 111–130. Cylinder-seal and scarabs of **Amen-**

emhāt III., B.C. 2300. No 134. Cylinder-seal of **Sebek-neferu**, B.C. 2250; beautiful work. No 141. Scarab of **Sebek-hetep II.**, B.C. 2200. Nos. 146 155. Scarabs of **Sebek-hetep III.**, B.C. 2150 No. 159. Scarab of **Queen Sat-Sebek**, B.C. 2200 No. 161. Scarab of **Queen Anna**, B.C. 1900. No. 167. Scarab of **Uatchkarā**, B C 1900. Nos 196, 197 Scarabs of **Khian**, B.C. 1800. No 215. Cylinder-seal of **Antef V.**, B C. 1850. No. 228. Blue glass scarab of **Aāhmes I.**, B.C. 1700. Nos. 230, 231. Carnelian beads of **Queen Nefert-ari**, B.C. 1700. Nos. 246 297 Scarabs, plaques, and cylinder of **Amen-hetep I.**, B C. 1666. Nos. 302 320. Scarabs, etc, of **Thothmes I.**, B.C. 1633. Nos. 321 323. Scarabs of **Thothmes II.**, B.C. 1600. Nos. 324 358. Scarabs, etc, of **Queen Hātshepset**, B.C. 1600 Nos. 359 758. Scarabs of **Thothmes III.**, B.C 1600. Nos. 759–767. Scarabs with the prenomens of Thothmes III. and other kings Nos 768 811. Scarabs of **Amen-hetep II**, B.C. 1500. Nos 812 833. Scarabs, rings, etc., of **Thothmes IV.**, B.C. 1500. Nos. 834 976. Scarabs, rings, etc, of **Amen-hetep III.**, and of **Queen Thi**, B C 1466.

Among the scarabs of Amen-hetep III. here exhibited is a group of large **historical scarabs** which were made to commemorate such events in his reign as he considered of great importance. Nos. 922–924 record the names and titles of Amen-hetep III and the Mesopotamian princess **Thi** ⟨𓂋𓈖𓇋⟩, the daughter of Iuaa and Thuau ; they also state that the boundary of his kingdom in the south was at Karei 𓈎𓂋𓇋𓈖, and in the North at Neharina (Northern Mesopotamia) 𓈖𓉔𓂋𓈖𓅆. No. 923 was presented by C. Innes Pocock, Esq., 1884 Nos. 925–929 are inscribed with the names and titles of Amen-hetep III and Thi, and the statement that during the first ten years of his reign the king shot 102 fierce lions with his own hand 𓀀

𓂋𓏏𓂻𓅆𓏏𓏤𓇋𓈖𓂋𓈖𓎡𓇳𓈖

On each side of No. 927 is the cartouche of Amen-hetep III.

Neb-Maāt-Rā ⟨○🪲◡⟩.   No. 926 was presented by
G. Bullock, Esq., 1856; and No. 929 by Mrs. Eustace
Smith.   On scarabs of Amen-hetep III. the prenomen of
Thothmes III. is sometimes found ; see Nos. 977–979.

    Nos. 980–1002. Scarabs, rings, a mould, etc., of **Amen-
hetep IV.** or Khu-en-Àten, B.C. 1430. Nos. 1036–1042.

No. 922.   Scarab of Amen-hetep III.,
recording the names of the parents
of Queen Thi. [No. 29,437.]

No. 929.   Scarab of Amen-hetep III.,
recording the slaughter of 102 lions
by the king, in the first ten years
of his reign. [No. 12,520.]

Scarabs and ring of **Ai,** B.C. 1460.   Nos. 1043–1055.
Scarabs, etc., of **Heru-em-heb,** B.C. 1466.   Nos. 1056–1062.
Scarabs of **Rameses I.,** B.C. 1400.   Nos. 1063–1103.
Scarabs of **Seti I.,** B.C. 1366.   Nos. 1104–1185. Scarabs
of **Rameses II.,** B.C. 1333.   No. 1203. Scarab of **Amen-
meses,** B.C. 1250.   No. 1205. Scarab of **Seti II.,** B.C. 1230.

Nos. 1217–1235. Scarabs of **Rameses III.,** B.C. 1200.
Nos. 1236 1252. Scarabs of **Rameses IV.,** B.C. 1166.
Nos. 1253, etc Scarabs of **Rameses VIII.,** B.C. 1150. No.
1268 ff Scarabs of **Shashanq I.** (Shishak), B.C 975. No
1296 ff. Scarabs of **Pamai,** B.C. 825.   No. 1309. Lapis-
lazuli scarab of **Queen Åmenårtås,** B.C. 725. No 1328 ff.

Scarabs of **Shabaka,
Shep-en-Åpt, Taharq**
(Tirhakah), **Psammeti-
chus I.,** and **Psammetichus II.,** of the XXVIth
dynasty, B.C 666 600.

At the end of this
case is a large group
(Nos. 1373 1587) of
scarabs, etc, which are
inscribed with names
imitated from royal
prenomens and nomens ,
they belong to various
periods, and a few of
them are probably copies
of genuine scarabs, of
local manufacture, which
were made during the
Roman period, or in
modern times. It must
be noted that the dates
given in the above para-
graphs are those of the
reigns of the kings

No. 921 Scarab recording the names
and titles of King Amen-hetep and
Queen Thi [No. 29,438.]

whose names are found
on the scarabs, and they do not therefore always represent
the age of the objects mentioned. The names of favourite
kings were inscribed on scarabs for hundreds of years after
those who bore them were dead, e.g., RĀ-MEN-KHEPER

⊙ 𓏴 𓎯, the prenomen of Thothmes III., was used as a

talisman or amulet from the date of his reign to the Ptolemaïc period, indeed it seems to have been copied on scarabs
long after its meaning had been forgotten.

TABLE-CASE E.   Scarabs—continued.   Here are exhibited some eighteen hundred scarabs made of steatite, glazed blue or green, amethyst, carnelian, lapis-lazuli, blue paste, etc., inscribed with the names of gods, priestly and other officials, and private persons, and a number of cylinder-seals, rings, plaques : some of them forming the bezels of rings, beads, and amulets in the form of frogs, etc   The dates of these objects cover the best periods of Egyptian dynastic history.   The oldest object in the case is the cylinder-seal of **Ru-nefer,** an official of the Ist dynasty, about B.C. 4400; it was presented by Mr. Somers Clarke in 1899 [No 1.] The most important group in the case is that containing the cylinders and scarabs inscribed with the names and titles of officials who flourished under the first six dynasties (Nos. 1–186), and many of the rings (Nos. 1109 ff) are remarkable for the beauty of their colour.   Some of the objects in carnelian are worthy of note, especially the bead, No. 1634, inscribed with the name of "**Amen-hetep,** the overseer of the treasury," who flourished about B.C. 1500.

TABLE-CASE F.—See page 209.

TABLE-CASE G.   Scarabs—continued.   A miscellaneous collection of stone and porcelain scarabs, plaques, rings, seals, etc., inscribed with the names of private persons, emblems, floral and other designs, from about B.C. 1500 to the end of the dynastic period, about B.C 350. The materials employed consist of steatite, hard stone, *e.g.*, basalt, carnelian, lapis-lazuli, blue paste, glass, etc , and the fine group of rings (Nos 3057 ff) in glazed porcelain illustrates the skill of the workman and the pitch of perfection to which the art of working this difficult material was brought in the XVIIIth and XIXth dynasties.   Not the least interesting object in this case, from an archæological point of view, is the bronze scarab No. 30,713, which is probably unique.

TABLE-CASE H.—See page 214.

TABLE-CASE I.   Funeral scarabs.   The greater number of these measure from half an inch to two inches in length, and they are usually made of porcelain,

steatite, green schist, slate, basalt, granite, carnelian, lapis-
lazuli, etc. See Nos. 1 250 Belonging to the same class
are the green basalt scarabs which were laid upon the
breasts of mummies, and were sometimes placed inside
the bodies of the dead, and were intended to take the
place of the heart Of this section there are many
varieties, but the form most approved by the Egyptians
seems to have consisted of a scarab of fine, hard basalt,
let into a gold frame, to which was attached a fine gold
wire for hanging round the neck The bases of large
funeral scarabs are usually inscribed with the text of
the XXXth Chapter of the Book of the Dead, but sometimes we find on them only figures of the gods, cut in
outline ; occasionally the inscriptions are merely written,
and not cut into the stone. Funeral scarabs formed part
of the stock-in-trade of the Egyptian undertaker, and a
blank space was often left at one end of the base wherein
the name of the deceased person for whom it was intended
could be inserted The text which is inscribed on the
base of funeral scarabs is commonly known as the
" Chapter of a heart of green jasper," or the " Chapter
of not allowing the heart of a man to be repulsed in the
Underworld," and it is undoubtedly very ancient, for
tradition asserted that the composition was known in the
reign of **Semti**, the fifth king of the 1st dynasty, about
B.C 4400. According to the rubric of the XXXth or
LXIVth Chapter of the Book of the Dead, it was to
" be recited over a scarab of green jasper, which was to
" be mounted in a frame of *smu* metal, and to be provided
" with a silver ring, and then laid upon the neck of the
" deceased." A rendering of the inscription on funeral
scarabs is as follows :—" O my heart, my mother ; O my
" heart, my mother ! O my heart of my existence upon
" earth. May naught stand up to oppose me in judgment
" in the presence of the lords of the trial; let it not be
" said of me and of that which I have done, ' He hath
" done deeds against that which is right and true '; may
" naught be against me in the presence of the great god,
" the lord of Amentet. Homage to thee, O my heart !
" Homage to thee, O my heart ! Homage to you, O my
" reins ! Homage to you, O ye gods who dwell in the

"divine clouds, and who are exalted (or holy) by reason
"of your sceptres! Speak ye [for me] fair things to Rā.
"and make ye me to prosper before Nehebka And
"behold me, even though I be joined to the earth in the
"mighty innermost parts thereof, let me remain upon the
"earth and let me not die in Amentet, but become a spirit
"(*Khu*) therein." The most noteworthy scarabs in this
case are:—

No. 290. Scarab with a figure of the *Bennu* bird, and
inscribed, "heart of Rā, the divine one." [No. 7878.]

No. 291. Scarab made for a scribe and steward of the
palace of a queen called Tetthi, [No 7877.]

No. 300. Scarab inscribed on the base with figures of
Osiris, Isis, and Nephthys. [No. 7930.]

No. 301. Hard green crystalline stone scarab, on a
plinth in the form of a vase, made for the lady Aui
. On the back of the scarab is a prayer that the
deceased may have a boat in which to sail, that her eyes
and her ears may be given to her, and that she may see
the "land of the gods." [No. 7925.]

No. 310. Scarab inscribed on the back with figures of
the gods Rā and Temu, the two *utchats*, and the
lunar crescent with disk. [No. 7886.]

No. 364. Stone heart, in the form of a vase, inscribed
with a figure of a beetle on one side, and a copy of
Chapter XXXB of the Book of the Dead in paint on the
other. [No. 8003.]

No. 371. Green stone heart, inscribed for the royal
scribe Nekht-Amen. [No. 15,619.]

No. 373. Wooden funeral scarab, inscribed with a
prayer for sepulchral offerings on behalf of Reru, a singing
woman in the temple of Amen. [No. 24,752.]

No. 377. Green basalt scarab, sculptured with a human
face [No. 15,516.]

No. 389.   Green schist heart scarab, set in a frame of gilded metal, to which portions of the substances used in mummifying the body wherein it was found still cling.

[No. 29,439.]

No. 402   Black stone scarab, on a plinth in the form of a pylon; it was made for Piaai ⌂ 𓆼 𓅿 𓇳 𓀀   In the design on the plinth the oval of the scarab is seen above the symbol of the horizon.   [No. 7858]

No. 408.   Green schist heart-scarab, on the vase of which the name and titles of the deceased have been painted and varnished   From Kûrna.   XIIth dynasty.

[No. 29,224.]

No. 409.   Green stone heart-scarab, with human head in relief.   [No. 7999]

No. 416

"Heart" scarab, inscribed with a version of Chapter XXXB of the Book of the Dead.   [No. 7899]

No. 416.   Black stone heart-scarab, inscribed with a copy of Chapter XXXB of the Book of the Dead on behalf of Ani 𓆼 𓇳 𓀀   [No 7899]

No. 417   Cobalt coloured porcelain scarab, painted with a figure of the *Bennu* bird

[No 15,439]

No. 418.   Similar scarab, with human face inlaid in red porcelain.   [No. 29,440.]

No. 419.   Stone human-headed heart, inlaid with the figure of a *Bennu* bird; at the back of the head are the remains of a bronze pin.

[No. 8006]

No. 420   Portion of a dark stone human-headed heart, inlaid with a figure of the soul in red and blue porcelain.   [No 8005]

In the last section of the case is a fine collection of blue and green glazed porcelain **pectorals,** or breast ornaments, for mummies, and funeral scarabs of the same material. The most interesting are :—

No. 499. Massive blue glazed porcelain funeral scarab.
[No. 30,050.]

No. 506. Cobalt and yellow glazed pectoral in the form of a pylon, ornamented with a figure of Anubis and the winged *utchat.*   [No. 7853.]

Pectoral, with human-headed Heart-Scarab.
[No. 29,369.]

No. 507. Pectoral, similarly shaped, in blue porcelain.
[No. 14,654.]

No. 515. Yellow porcelain pectoral inlaid with figures of Isis and Nephthys, and symbols of amulets, and a heart - scarab, inscribed with the name of the lady Pen - seneb ⌂ 〰〰. [No. 7865.]

No. 520. Similar object inlaid with a boat and figures of Isis and Nephthys, and a human-headed heart-scarab, which takes the place of the solar disk in the boat. On the back are painted symbols of stability and the blood of Isis.   [No. 29,369.]

LIST OF THE PRINCIPAL EGYPTIAN KINGS
WHOSE NAMES ARE FOUND ON SCARABS.

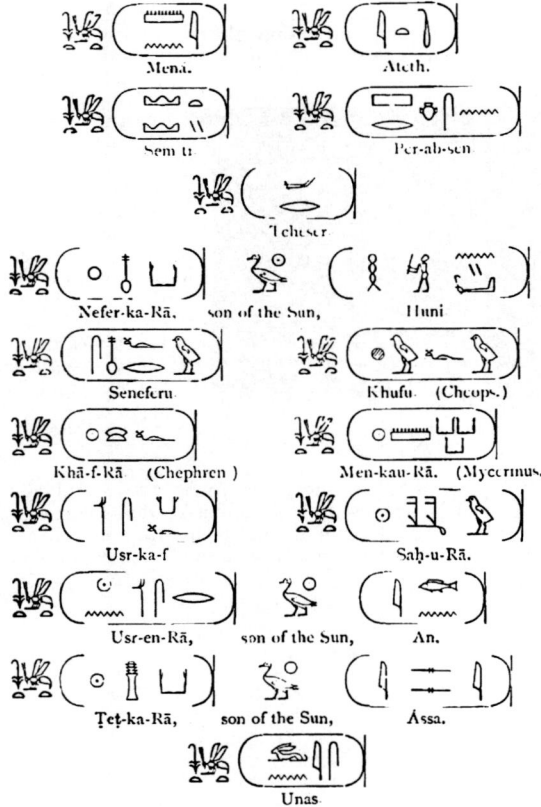

Mena.

Atcth.

Sem ti

Per-ab-sen

Tcheser

Nefer-ka-Rā.   son of the Sun,   Huni

Seneferu

Khufu   (Cheops.)

Khā-f-Rā   (Chephren)

Men-kau-Rā.   (Mycerinus.)

Usr-ka-f

Saḥ-u-Rā.

Usr-en-Rā,   son of the Sun,   An.

Ṭeṭ-ka-Rā,   son of the Sun,   Assa.

Unas

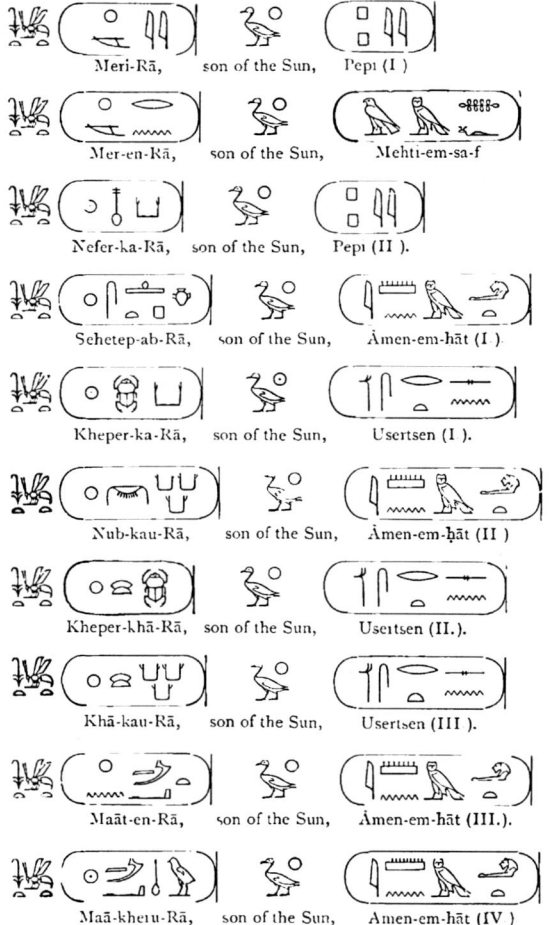

Meri-Rā,	son of the Sun,	Pepi (I)
Mer-en-Rā,	son of the Sun,	Mehti-em-sa-f
Nefer-ka-Rā,	son of the Sun,	Pepi (II).
Sehetep-ab-Rā,	son of the Sun,	Åmen-em-hāt (I)
Kheper-ka-Rā,	son of the Sun,	Usertsen (I).
Nub-kau-Rā,	son of the Sun,	Åmen-em-ḥāt (II)
Kheper-khā-Rā,	son of the Sun,	Useitsen (II.).
Khā-kau-Rā,	son of the Sun,	Usertsen (III).
Maāt-en-Rā,	son of the Sun,	Åmen-em-hāt (III.).
Maā-kheru-Rā,	son of the Sun,	Amen-em-hāt (IV)

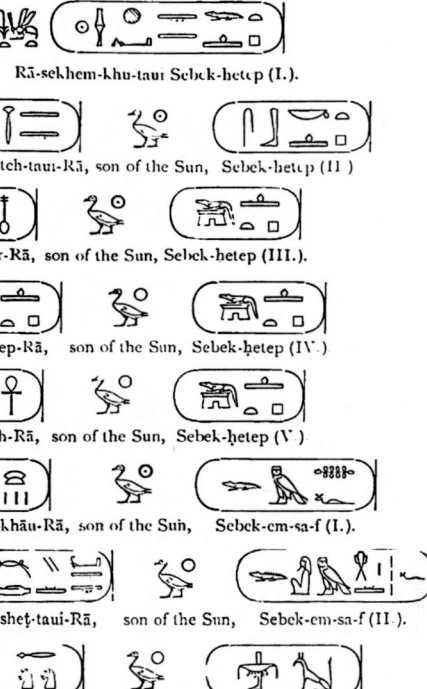

Sebek-neferu-Rā.

Rā-sekhem-khu-taui Sebek-hetep (I.).

Sekhem-senatch-taui-Rā, son of the Sun,   Sebek-hetep (II.)

Khā-nefer-Rā, son of the Sun, Sebek-hetep (III.).

Khā-hetep-Rā,   son of the Sun,   Sebek-ḥetep (IV.)

Khā-ānkh-Rā,   son of the Sun,   Sebek-ḥetep (V.)

Sekhem-uatch-khāu-Rā, son of the Sun,   Sebek-em-sa-f (I.).

Sekhem-sheṭ-taui-Rā,   son of the Sun,   Sebek-em-sa-f (II.).

Āa-peḥ-peḥ-Set,   son of the Sun,   Nub-Set (?).

Neter nefer   Āa-ab-taui-Rā,   son of the Sun,   Āpepa.
Beautiful god,

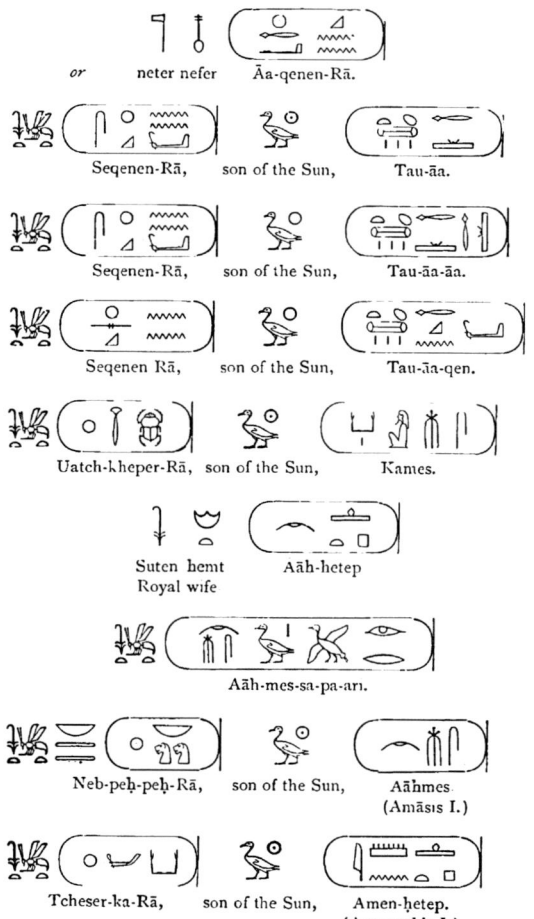

or   neter nefer   Āa-qenen-Rā.

Seqenen-Rā,   son of the Sun,   Tau-āa.

Seqenen-Rā,   son of the Sun,   Tau-āa-āa.

Seqenen Rā,   son of the Sun,   Tau-āa-qen.

Uatch-kheper-Rā, son of the Sun,   Kames.

Suten hemt   Aāh-hetep
Royal wife

Aāh-mes-sa-pa-ari.

Neb-peḥ-peḥ-Rā,   son of the Sun,   Aāhmes
                                       (Amāsıs I.)

Tcheser-ka-Rā,   son of the Sun,   Amen-ḥetep.
                                       (Amenophis I.)

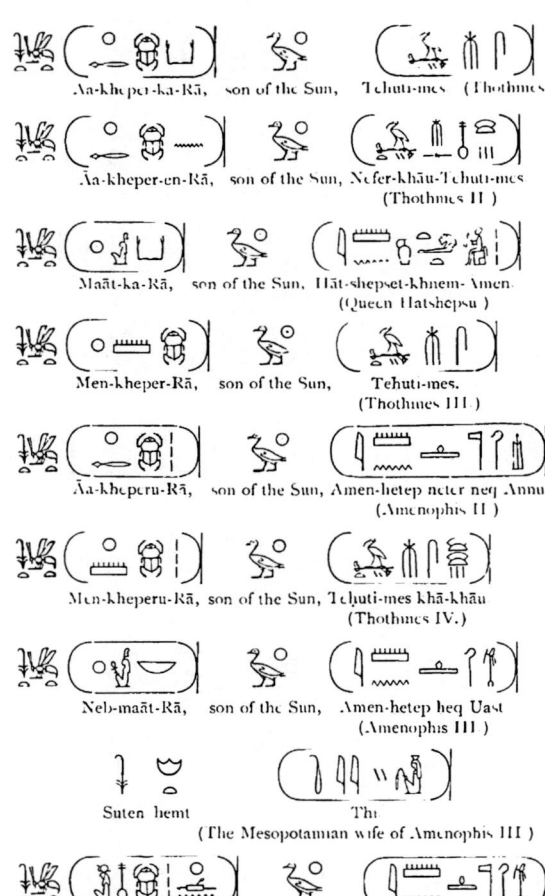

Aa-kheper-ka-Rā,   son of the Sun,   Tehuti-mes   (Thothmes I)

Aa-kheper-en-Rā,   son of the Sun,   Nefer-khāu-Tehuti-mes
(Thothmes II)

Maāt-ka-Rā,   son of the Sun,   Hāt-shepset-khnem-Amen-
(Queen Hatshepsu)

Men-kheper-Rā,   son of the Sun,   Tehuti-mes.
(Thothmes III)

Aa-kheperu-Rā,   son of the Sun,   Amen-hetep neter neq Annu
(Amenophis II)

Men-kheperu-Rā,   son of the Sun,   Tehuti-mes khā-khāu
(Thothmes IV.)

Neb-maāt-Rā,   son of the Sun,   Amen-hetep heq Uast
(Amenophis III)

Suten hemt   Thi
(The Mesopotamian wife of Amenophis III)

Nefer-kheperu-Rā-uā-   son of the Sun,   Amen-hetep neter heq
en-Rā,   Uast (Amenophis IV)

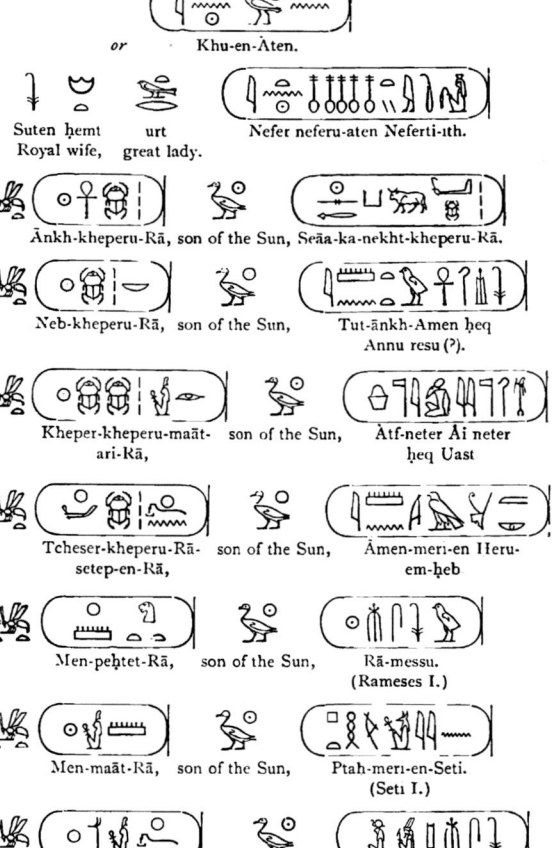

or   Khu-en-Âten.

Suten ḥemt   urt
Royal wife,   great lady.

Nefer neferu-aten Neferti-ıth.

Ānkh-kheperu-Rā, son of the Sun, Seāa-ka-nekht-kheperu-Rā.

Neb-kheperu-Rā, son of the Sun,   Tut-ānkh-Amen ḥeq
Annu resu (?).

Kheper-kheperu-maāt- son of the Sun,   Àtf-neter Âi neter
ari-Rā,   ḥeq Uast

Tcheser-kheperu-Rā- son of the Sun,   Âmen-merı-en Heru-
setep-en-Rā,   em-ḥeb

Men-peḥtet-Rā,   son of the Sun,   Rā-messu.
(Rameses I.)

Men-maāt-Rā,   son of the Sun,   Ptah-merı-en-Seti.
(Setı I.)

Usr-maāt-Rā setep-en-Rā, son of the Sun,   Rā-messu-merı-Âmen.
(Rameses II.)

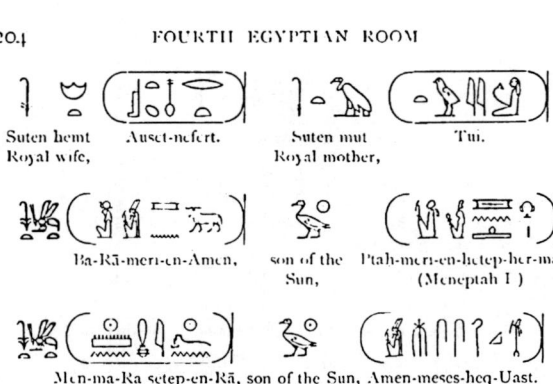

Suten hemt   Auset-nefert.   Suten mut   Tui.
Royal wife,   Royal mother,

Ba-Rā-meri-en-Amen,   son of the   Ptah-meri-en-hetep-her-maāt
Sun,   (Meneptah I)

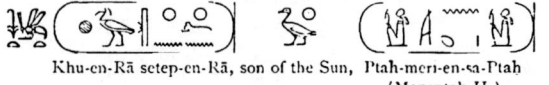

Men-ma-Ra setep-en-Rā, son of the Sun,   Amen-meses-heq-Uast.
(Amen-meses)

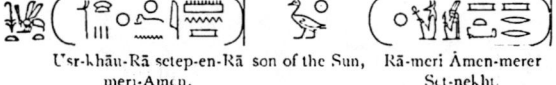

Usr-kheperu-Rā-meri-Amen, son of the Sun,   Seti-meri-en-Ptah
(Seti II)

Khu-en-Rā setep-en-Rā, son of the Sun,   Ptah-meri-en-sa-Ptah
(Meneptah II)

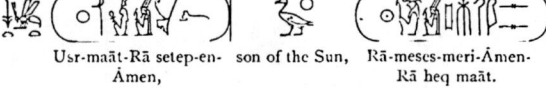

Usr-khāu-Rā setep-en-Rā son of the Sun,   Rā-meri Åmen-merer
meri-Amen,   Set-nekht
(Set-Nekht.)

Usr-maāt-Rā-meri-Åmen, son of the Sun,   Rā-meses-heq-Annu.
(Rameses III)

Usr-maāt-Rā setep-en-   son of the Sun,   Rā-meses-meri-Åmen-
Åmen,   Rā heq maāt.
(Rameses IV.)

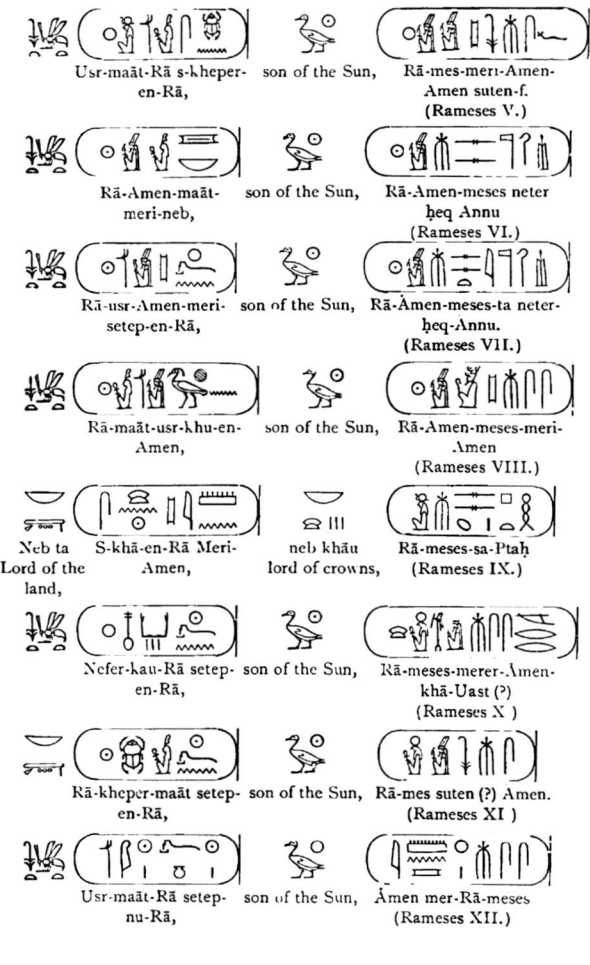

Usr-maāt-Rā s-kheper-en-Rā, — son of the Sun, — Rā-mes-meri-Amen-Amen suten-f. (Rameses V.)

Rā-Amen-maāt-meri-neb, — son of the Sun, — Rā-Amen-meses neter ḥeq Annu (Rameses VI.)

Rā-usr-Amen-meri-setep-en-Rā, — son of the Sun, — Rā-Amen-meses-ta neter-ḥeq-Annu. (Rameses VII.)

Rā-maāt-usr-khu-en-Amen, — son of the Sun, — Rā-Amen-meses-meri-Amen (Rameses VIII.)

Neb ta Lord of the land, — S-khā-en-Rā Meri-Amen, — neb khāu lord of crowns, — Rā-meses-sa-Ptaḥ (Rameses IX.)

Nefer-kau-Rā setep-en-Rā, — son of the Sun, — Rā-meses-merer-Amen-khā-Uast (?) (Rameses X)

Rā-kheper-maāt setep-en-Rā, — son of the Sun, — Rā-mes suten (?) Amen. (Rameses XI)

Usr-maāt-Rā setep-nu-Rā, — son of the Sun, — Āmen mer-Rā-meses (Rameses XII.)

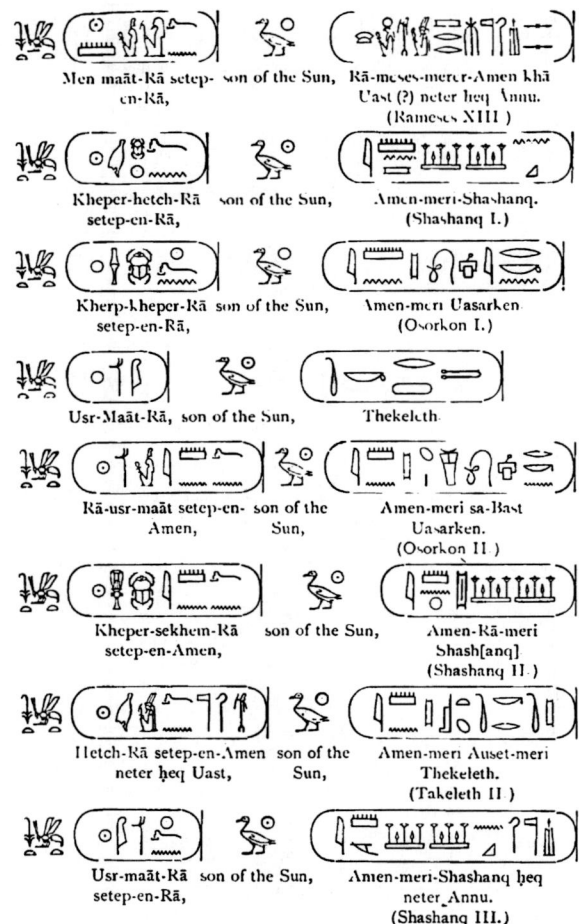

Men maāt-Rā setep-en-Rā, son of the Sun, Rā-meses-merer-Amen khā Uast (?) neter ḥeq Annu.
(Rameses XIII.)

Kheper-hetch-Rā setep-en-Rā, son of the Sun, Amen-meri-Shashanq.
(Shashanq I.)

Kherp-kheper-Rā setep-en-Rā, son of the Sun, Amen-meri Uasarken
(Osorkon I.)

Usr-Maāt-Rā, son of the Sun, Thekeleth

Rā-usr-maāt setep-en-Amen, son of the Sun, Amen-meri sa-Bast Uasarken.
(Osorkon II.)

Kheper-sekhem-Rā setep-en-Amen, son of the Sun, Amen-Rā-meri Shash[anq]
(Shashanq II.)

Hetch-Rā setep-en-Amen neter ḥeq Uast, son of the Sun, Amen-meri Auset-meri Thekeleth.
(Takeleth II.)

Usr-maāt-Rā setep-en-Rā, son of the Sun, Amen-meri-Shashanq ḥeq neter Annu.
(Shashanq III.)

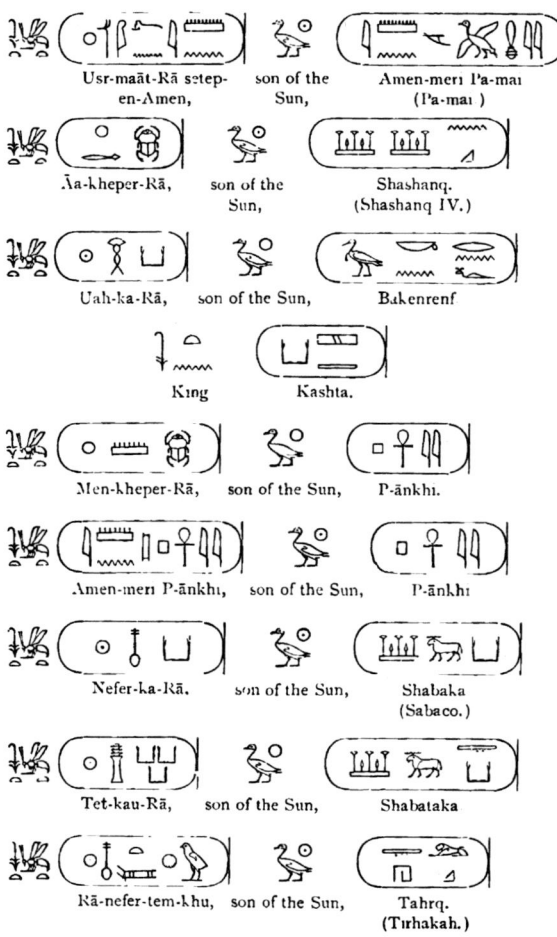

Usr-maāt-Rā setep-
en-Amen,

son of the
Sun,

Amen-meri Pa-mai
(Pa-mai)

Āa-kheper-Rā,

son of the
Sun,

Shashanq.
(Shashanq IV.)

Uah-ka-Rā,

son of the Sun,

Bakenrenf

King

Kashta.

Men-kheper-Rā,

son of the Sun,

P-ānkhi.

Amen-meri P-ānkhi,

son of the Sun,

P-ānkhi

Nefer-ka-Rā,

son of the Sun,

Shabaka
(Sabaco.)

Tet-kau-Rā,

son of the Sun,

Shabataka

Rā-nefer-tem-khu,

son of the Sun,

Tahrq.
(Tirhakah.)

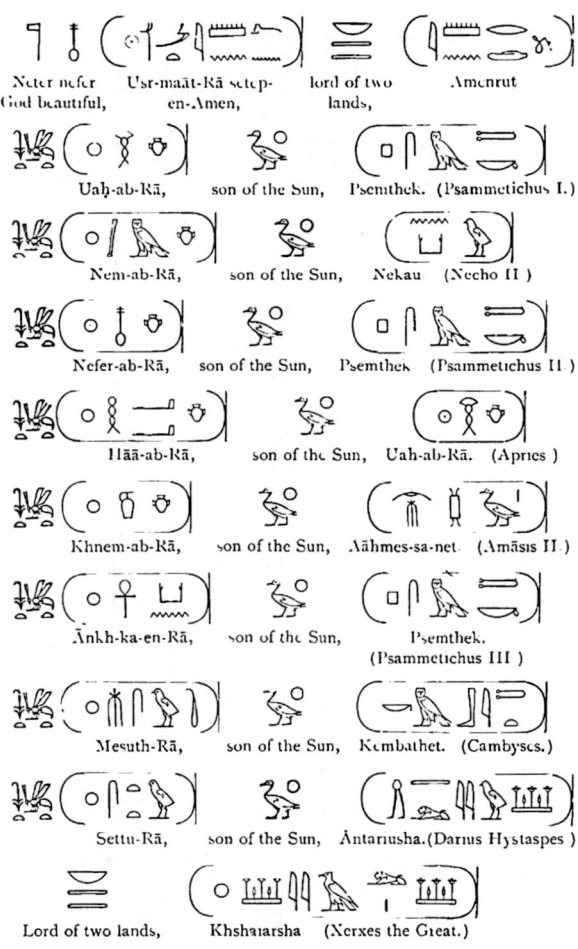

Neter nefer   Usr-maāt-Rā setep-   lord of two   Amenrut
God beautiful,   en-Amen,   lands,

Uah-ab-Rā,   son of the Sun,   Psemthek. (Psammetichus I.)

Nem-ab-Rā,   son of the Sun,   Nekau   (Necho II.)

Nefer-ab-Rā,   son of the Sun,   Psemthek   (Psammetichus II.)

Haā-ab-Rā,   son of the Sun,   Uah-ab-Rā.   (Apries.)

Khnem-ab-Rā,   son of the Sun,   Āāhmes-sa-net.   (Amāsis II.)

Ānkh-ka-en-Rā,   son of the Sun,   Psemthek.
                                     (Psammetichus III.)

Mesuth-Rā,   son of the Sun,   Kembathet.   (Cambyses.)

Settu-Rā,   son of the Sun,   Āntariusha.(Darius Hystaspes.)

Lord of two lands,   Khshaiarsha   (Xerxes the Great.)

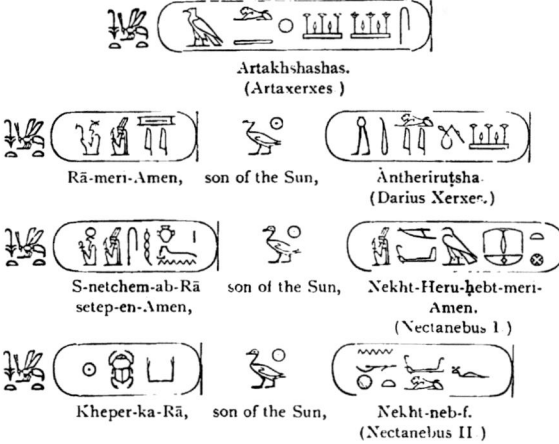

Artakhshashas.
(Artaxerxes)

Rā-meri-Amen,   son of the Sun,   Antherirutsha-
(Darius Xerxes.)

S-netchem-ab-Rā   son of the Sun,   Nekht-Heru-hebt-meri-
setep-en-Amen,   Amen.
(Nectanebus I)

Kheper-ka-Rā,   son of the Sun,   Nekht-neb-f.
(Nectanebus II)

TABLE-CASE F.   Amulets, Necklaces, Pendants, etc.

On the west side of this case is exhibited a large and
important series of Egyptian **amulets**, *i e.*, objects and
ornaments which were worn to protect the human body,
either living or dead, from baleful influences and from the
attacks of visible and invisible foes.   The word amulet is
derived from the Arabic, and means " that which is worn,"
but it has been somewhat loosely applied to any talisman
or ornament to which supernatural powers are ascribed.
The Egyptians employed amulets in large numbers for the
protection of the dead, and they placed them either on the
mummy itself, or between the mummy swathings , the use
of amulets probably dates from the end of predynastic
times, and it seems as if it was believed even in the earliest
period that in the stones which were selected magical
powers were inherent.   When inscribed with the names of

P

gods, or with magical formulæ of a certain character, the power of amulets was thought to be irresistible. The common name for words of power of all kinds is "hekau" ⟨hieroglyphs⟩, and whether they were inscribed upon amulets, or merely recited over them, the effect was the same. The earliest use of "hekau" is mentioned in a text which was copied upon a wall in the tomb of King Unas (line 584), king of Egypt, about B.C. 3300.

Nos. 1–45. Carnelian, red jasper, and red glass amulets of the **Buckle of the girdle of Isis** ⟨hieroglyph⟩; they symbolize the "blood of Isis, and the strength of Isis, and the power of Isis," and were believed to protect the wearer from every kind of evil. The texts inscribed on Nos. 21, 22, 28, 30, etc., are portions of the CLVIth Chapter of the Book of the Dead.

Nos. 46–68. Amulets of the **Snake's head** ⟨hieroglyph⟩. These were placed in tombs, to prevent the deceased from being bitten by snakes in the underworld, and some are inscribed with portions of the XXXIVth Chapter of the Book of the Dead. This amulet appears to have been associated with Isis.

Nos. 69–136. Amulets of the **Heart** ⟨hieroglyph⟩, in carnelian, lapis-lazuli, mother-of-emerald, breccia, steatite, etc. These amulets were connected with Chapters XXVII–XXXB of the Book of the Dead, and they were supposed to bring to the wearer the protection of these all-powerful compositions.

Nos. 138–140. The Amulet of the **Menát** ⟨hieroglyph⟩ was symbolic of nutrition, strength, and the powers of generation and reproduction.

Nos. 142, 143. The Amulet of the **Human-headed Fly** conferred on the wearer the power to ascend to heaven, like a certain species of fly which was associated with Rā.

Nos. 145–187. The Amulet of the **Tet** ⟨hieroglyph⟩. This object symbolizes the tree trunk in which Isis concealed the body of Osiris, and the four bars indicate the four branches of the great World-tree, and typify the four cardinal points. The " setting up of the Tet " was a ceremony which was performed annually with great reverence at Busiris in the Delta, and at Abydos in Upper Egypt, and it was always associated with the building up of the backbone, and reconstitution of the body of Osiris. The Tet represents neither a mason's table nor a Nilometer. It was worn as a symbol of " stability," and the amulet was sometimes inscribed with the CLVth Chapter of the Book of the Dead.

Nos 188–237. The Amulet of the **Papyrus Sceptre** ⌠ was intended to give youth, vigour, virile power, etc., to the wearer. In late times it typified the power of Isis, who derived it from the god of harvest, and it was worn as a symbol of sound health ; it is sometimes associated with Chapters CLIX and CLX of the Book of the Dead.

Nos 239 268 The Amulet of the **Pillow** ⏑ is usually made of hæmatite, and is inscribed with the text of the CLXVIth Chapter of the Book of the Dead; it symbolized the " raising up of the head " of the deceased, and it was placed with the dead to prevent the head from being carried away.

Nos. 270–277. The Amulet of the **Cartouche** ⌷, *i.e.*, of the oval made of rope tied into a knot at one end, which is depicted on the monuments, and which encloses the names of royal personages, is the symbol of the " name " of a man or woman, and it was worn with the view of preventing the name from being blotted out in the next world.

Nos. 278–302. The Amulet of the **Two Plumes** ⍦, with and without the cartouche, symbolized the power or height of heaven, and of the great gods of light and air, *e.g*, Shu, Amen, etc , when the feathers refer to the two Maāt goddesses, they signify right or truth.

Nos. 306–336. The Amulet of the **Nefer** ⌠ signifies " good luck," " happiness," and cognate ideas.

Nos. 337 470.   The Amulet of the **Utchat** 𓂀
is symbolic of the Eye of Horus, and was intended to
bring the wearer strength, vigour, protection, safety, good
health, etc   When two Utchats are together 𓂀𓂀 they
typify the Sun and the Moon   The word *utchat* means
primarily "strength," and it was applied to the Sun at the
summer solstice, *i e*, when it was in its greatest strength
and was most powerful on earth.

Nos. 472–501   The Amulet of the **Two Fingers**
appears to have reference to the two fingers, index and
medius, which Horus stretched out to help his father up
the **ladder** which led from earth to heaven   Concerning
Pepi I, king of Egypt about B C 3300, it is said in a text,
" Pepi hath gathered together his bones, he hath collected
his flesh, and he hath gone quickly into heaven by means of
the Two Fingers of the god of the Ladder" (*i e*, Horus).
This amulet is found in the interior of mummies, and is
usually made of obsidian or hæmatite

No. 505   The Amulet **Pesh-ken**, surmounted by the
head of a goddess   The exact signification of this amulet
is unknown, but it appears to have been connected with
the idea of birth.

Nos. 510–520.   The Amulet **Sma** 𓄓 symbolizes
physical happiness

Nos. 555 564.   The Amulet of the **Angle** symbolizes
rectitude.

Nos. 565–577.   The Amulet of the **Plummet** symbolizes
moral integrity.

Nos. 578–590   Mother-of-emerald   plaques,   which
were   intended   to   be   inscribed   with   extracts   from
Chapter XXXB of the Book of the Dead

Nos 595–621   The Amulet of the **Sun's Disk** on the
horizon symbolized new birth, resurrection, etc.

Nos. 622–718.   A miscellaneous group of amulets in
carnelian, red stone, lapis-lazuli, etc   One of the most
interesting of these is No 626, which is in the form of an
elephant; No. 644 represents a bull being attacked by

some wild creature, probably a serpent. The exact use of
the split rings and their signification are unknown.

In the east side of the case is exhibited a fine
collection of **necklaces**, belonging to various periods
between B.C. 1700 and A.D. 100. The most interesting
are —

No 741 Necklace of variegated glass beads and
carnelian *nefer* pendants. No. 742 Necklace of small
gold and stone beads, with scarabs, and gold pendants
in the form of fish No 751 Necklace of small gold
and stone beads, with *nefer* pendants in gold, carnelian,
porcelain, glass, etc No 753 Necklace of garnet and
amethyst beads No. 757 Necklace of carnelian and
garnet beads, with pendants in the shape of hands ⤳,
fish ⤠, utchats ⤡, wasps ⤢, etc No. 758 Necklace of carnelian and amethyst beads, with gold pendant
inscribed with figures of Mut and Khonsu No. 760.
Necklace of gold, lapis-lazuli and other beads, with
metal shells, and pendants in the forms of locks of hair,
fish, and the lotus, to which is attached the emblem of
millions of years ⤣. No. 762. Necklace of carnelian
beads, with bud and lizard pendants in gold. No. 763
Necklace of blue glazed faience beads, with a gold knot-
fastening No 766. Necklace of gold and carnelian beads,
with inlaid pendants in the form of the fruit of the persea
tree. No 767. Necklace, with scorpion and " millions of
years " pendants ⤤ in gold No. 768 Twenty-two
lapis-lazuli and agate (?) beads, each banded with gold.
No 784 Necklace of carnelian beads capped with gold,
with gold pendants inlaid with topaz and garnet, and a
double fish with three pendent uræi , Greek or Roman
period No 791. Necklace of a triple row of annular
gold beads, with gold chain fastenings terminating in
lapis-lazuli knobs. No 792 Necklaces of gilded glass
beads, some of which are fluted. No 797. Necklace of
gold beads, with a pendant in the form of a vase or heart.
Many of the other necklaces here exhibited are worthy
of examination, for they well illustrate the pitch of

perfection to which the art of making glass and porcelain beads was carried in the Ptolemaic and Roman periods. Under the Greeks and Romans variegated glass beads were greatly in fashion, and the use of the stones which were associated with the dead by the ancient Egyptians was not so widespread as in the dynastic period.

TABLE-CASE H contains a group of interesting antiquities from Thebes, which were presented by Jesse Haworth, Esq., 1887. These are:—

No. 1.   Legs and part of the frame of a large **Chair of State.** The legs are in the form of bulls' legs, and the hoofs were originally covered with plates of silver, each leg is ornamented with a pair of gilded uræi, which represent the sovereignty over the South and North.   The frame was covered with plates of silver, which were held in position by bronze nails with gilded heads. The angle supports of the back are ornamented each with a uræus, inlaid with silver annules. This important object was found in the famous pit of Dêr al-Bahari with the portion of the wooden oval (No. 2) that bears the names of Queen Hātshepset, about B.C. 1600, and it has been thought that it was the great queen's throne; but the evidence which connects the chair with the wooden oval is very slight, for it is well known that the pit contained many objects which must have been hidden there some hundreds of years after the original deposit was made. [No. 21,574.]

No. 2.   Portion of a wooden oval which, when complete, bore the name of **Queen Hātshepset** ⟨hieroglyphs⟩,
and that of a king.   [No. 21,575.]

No. 3.   **Wood and Ivory draughtboard,** with sliding drawer and two draughtsmen.   The square which marked the winning point of the game is inscribed with the sign ⟨sign⟩.
                                                      [Nos. 21,576, etc.]

No. 4   Portion of an inlaid **ivory and blue glazed porcelain draughtboard,** with one porcelain draughtsman.
                                                 [Nos. 21,577, 21,602.]

Nos 5–8. **Ivory draughtsman,** in the shape of a lion's head, two ivory reels, and one astragalus.

[Nos. 21,580, 21,603 21605]

Nos 9–27   Wooden draughtsmen, in the shape of lions' heads   [Nos 21,592, etc.]

Nos 28, 29   Two wooden figures of men , fine work.

[Nos. 21,578, etc]

No. 30.   Alabaster **shell,** which was used at the toilet for holding unguents   [No 21,612]

No 31   Slate **shell,** with the handle in the form of the symbol of life.   [No 21,611.]

Nos 32, 33   Portions of two blue glazed porcelain **bangles.**   [Nos. 21,609, 21,610]

Nos. 34, 35   Portions of two blue glazed porcelain cylindrical objects   [Nos. 21,607, 21,608]

TABLE-CASE J.   Jewellery, bracelets, rings, neck-laces, etc.   The following objects are worthy of note —

No 19   Gold spray, set with pearls [No 16,979]   No 47. Gold breastplate, with ends terminating in hawks' heads. No. 50 Gold heart, bequeathed by Dr. J. Anthony, 1895 No 66 Gold ægis of Bast, or Sekhet   No 69 Two gold figures ; late period   No 72. Gold plate, stamped with the cartouches Ka-en-Rā and Senefer-ka

No 92   Bust of a deity wearing a disk.   No. 94 Green stone " Heart-scarab," set in a massive gold frame. No 96 Necklace of gold beads, with pendants indicating " millions of years."   No 101   Jackal-headed gold pendant. No. 105. Gold uræus, wearing the Teshert crown, symbolic of sovereignty over Lower Egypt.   No 107   Pair of massive gold bracelets ; Ptolemaic or Roman period. No 114. Gold Harpocrates   No 116   Plaque, with head of Hathor in relief   No 132. " Heart-Scarab," with massive gold setting and collar by which to fasten it to the neck of the dead   No 133   Hawk of gold, with outstretched wings, inlaid with pieces of carnelian and lapis-lazuli , the claw grasps ☯ *shen*, the symbol of eternity

Nos 134, 135 Pair of gold bracelets, inlaid with lapis-lazuli and blue paste. The centre scene represents Harpocrates sitting on a lotus flower between two uræi wearing disks Inside is inscribed in hieroglyphics a short text which says that these bracelets were " made for the princess, 'the daughter of the chief of all the bowmen, **Nemareth,** " whose mother was the daughter of the prince of the land " of Reshnes." Nemareth was the descendant in the fifth generation of Buiu-uaua, a Libyan prince, and the father of Shashanq I, Shishak of 1 Kings xiv, 25, King of Egypt about B.C. 966

No 136 " Heart-Scarab," with massive gold setting and gold wire collar by which it was suspended from the neck No 137. Gold necklace ornament, or pendant, with hinged lid, it was probably used as an amulet case The zig-zag ornamentation is a fine example of this class of work, and it should be noted that each small gold bead has been soldered on separately No 138 Gold pendant in the form of king seated on a throne The face was probably inlaid with lapis-lazuli, and the rich featherwork tunic, the collar and necklace, etc, with red, blue, and green paste The ornament of the plinth of the throne, formed by sceptres and symbols of " life" $\bigcap \varphi \bigcap \bigcap \varphi \bigcap$, was filled with coloured paste. The reverse of the pendant is carefully chased with delicate feather work, the symbol of the union of the two countries, etc. XIXth dynasty, or a little later No. 140 Flat gold bangle, with figures of various amulets and animals in gold and silver alternately, a very rare and interesting specimen of Egyptian jewellery Nos 142 and 143 Hollow gold scarabs, the bases of which are stamped with the prenomen of Thothmes III, or that of one of the priest kings Presented by T. Gibson, Esq, 1897. No 154. Portion of a fine gold fibula No 156 Human-headed hawk, symbol of the soul, with outspread wings, inlaid with lapis-lazuli and mother-of-emerald No 157. Portion of a gold pendant, two birds, standing, one on each side of a cluster of lotus plants. No 175 Gold lion; fine work On the base is inscribed $\bigcap | \bigcap | \text{(hieroglyphs)}$ Nos 176, 177 Pair of gold lions, man-headed.

No 182. Pendent head of Hathor, with necklace inlaid with white and blue enamel (?)

No 195. Fine green stone scarab, with human face, set in a plinth of gold On the base of the plinth are stamped extracts from Chapters XXXB and LXIV of the Book of the Dead, and on the edge is cut, " King Sebek-em-sa-f," 𓏏 . Sebek-em-sa-f was a king of the XIVth dynasty, B.C. 2300, and it is probable that this most important object was made for him It was found at Kûrna (Thebes) by Mr Salt [No. 7876.]

Nos 197-266. **Gold rings,** set with scarabs, plaques, etc., from the XVIIIth dynasty to the Roman period The most interesting are :—

No 198 Gold ring, with lapis-lazuli bezel inscribed with the prenomen of **Thothmes III.** .

[No 14,349]

No 199 Gold ring, with bezel inscribed with a scorpion , and surmounted by a frog [No 2923]

No 201. Gold ring, with lapis-lazuli scarab, inscribed, " Maāt-ka-Rā, flesh and blood of Amen-Rā " Maāt-ka-Rā is the prenomen of **Queen Hātshepset.**

[No. 2933]

No 202 Gold ring, with rectangular lapis-lazuli plaque. On the one side is inscribed , and on the other a man-headed lion crushes a prostrate foe with his paw Above are the prenomen and titles of Thothmes III, " Beautiful god, conqueror of all lands, Men-kheper-Rā [No 2934.]

No 203 Modern ring, set with a plaque of mille-fiori glass, with a figure of a human-headed hawk, symbolic of the soul. [No 20,871]

No 204 Gold ring, set with a steatite scarab, inscribed with the name of Ptah-mes , an official who was a *Sem* priest and the high priest of Memphis. [No 2939]

No 217.   Gold ring, set with a steatite scarab inscribed with the prenomen and nomen of **Shishak I.**

[No. 14,345]

No. 222.   Gold ring, inscribed with the name **Rā-neferu**

[No. 36,467.]

No. 223.   Gold ring, inscribed **ΕΠΑΓΑΘΩ**

[No. 26,322.]

No 225   Gold ring, set with a green stone scarab inscribed with four uræi and four cartouches containing the symbol of "life."   [No. 36,466.]

No. 227   Gold ring, set with a scarab inscribed with the symbols of "life", and "vigorous, healthy existence"   Bequeathed by Dr J Anthony, 1895.

[No. 23,429.]

No. 228.   Gold ring, set with a scarab inscribed with the figure of a scorpion.   [No. 27,732]

No 233.   Gold ring, with three uræi having the heads of Serapis, Isis, and Harpocrates, late Ptolemaic period

[No. 2965]

No 234   Gold ring, on the bezel of which is inscribed a male figure dancing; on his head is a cluster of lotus flowers (?)   [No. 17,822.]

No 236.   Gold ring, on the bezel of which is inscribed a figure of a god with a serpent on his head, a scorpion in his left hand. and a staff or bow in his right.   [No 26,323]

No. 237.   Gold ring, inscribed with the name of **Ptolemy III.,** son of Rā

This is probably the official ring of a priest who belonged to one of the orders of priests established by Ptolemy III.

[No. 36,468]

No. 238   Gold ring, on the bezel of which is inscribed the figure of a goddess seated in a boat under a canopy, the pillars of which are made in the form of papyrus sceptres

[No 16,977.]

No. 239. Gold ring, on the bezel of which is inscribed a seated figure holding the feather of Maāt, the solar disk with uræi, the symbol of "life" $\frac{Q}{T}$, and a flabellum $\frac{Q}{\parallel}$.

[No 32,723.]

No 240. Gold wire ring, set with a circular plaque, on which in relief, within a rectangular border, is a figure of the god Osiris. On the right of the frame is the headless hide of a bull suspended by the tail over a vase, which catches the blood, and on the left is the hawk of Horus. Ptolemaic period (?). [No 23,299.]

No 246 Gold ring, the bezel of which is inscribed with a figure similar to that of No 234. [No. 2948.]

No. 247. Gold snake ring, Græco-Roman period.

[No. 15,840.]

No. 248 Gold ring, the rectangular bezel of which is inscribed with $\cap\cap$, the emblem of the eight gods of the company of Thoth (?). [No 14,374]

No. 249 Gold ring, with the bezel in the form of a rectangular plinth surmounted by a frog, on the base of the plinth is inscribed the figure of a cat seated on the symbol for gold $\overset{\curvearrowleft}{\underset{\frown}{\triangle}}$. [No. 2928.]

No 251 Gold ring, with a rectangular solid gold bezel , on one side is the figure of a king wearing the crown of the North, and on the other a seated figure of a man holding a flower in his left hand On the edges are two ornamental borders. [No 2924]

No 252 Gold ring, inscribed with the figure of a deity , compare No 236. [No 26,326]

No 266. Gold ring, inscribed with the prenomen of Amen-hetep III , King of Egypt about B.C. 1450 $\left\| \underset{\wwww}{\overset{\text{mmm}}{\Longleftarrow}} \underset{\zeta}{\underset{\circ}{\multimap}} \uparrow \text{\%} \right\|$. Bequeathed by Ernest Hart, Esq , 1899

[No. 30,446]

Nos 267-289 A miscellaneous group of gold earrings, bangles, plaques, pendants for inlaying, a gold scarab, with ornamental design on the base, etc , of various periods.

No 290. Rectangular gold plate, stamped with hieroglyphics of birds, sceptres, royal dress and sacred symbols. [No. 14,380.]

Nos 291 381 A miscellaneous collection of silver rings, pendants, bangles, figures of gods, etc., of various periods. Among them may be noted :—No 329, a leaden human-headed hawk, with outstretched wings, a rare and interesting object ; No. 379, a metal ægis of Bast, with part of the cord by which it was suspended from the neck of the wearer.

No 382. Sixty-four scarabs, beads, pendants, etc., made of agate, onyx, carnelian, lapis-lazuli, hard green stone, etc., many being set in gold frames of very fine workmanship. They belonged to a princess of the XXIInd dynasty, B.C 2500, and were found at Dahshûr.

Nos. 383, 384   Two gold fish-pendants, B.C. 2500. [Nos. 30,482, 30,483.]

No. 385. Gold soul in the form of a human-headed hawk, with outstretched wings; the feathers were inlaid with paste. [No 14,376.]

Nos. 386, 387. Two gold fish-pendants, inlaid with green stone [Nos 30,484, 30,485.]

Nos 388, 389 Two gold and amethyst pendants for necklaces ; XIIth dynasty [Nos 30,477, 30,478.]

No 390. Silver ring, inscribed with the prenomen of

Åmen-ḥetep IV.   [No. 29,436]

No 392. Silver ring, inscribed with the titles of an official who was a scribe and president of the granaries, a libationer, a prophet of the fourth order, and with the names of **Psammetichus** and **Shashanq** (**Shishak**).   [No. 24,777.]

No 393. Silver ram's head, surmounted by a uræus   [No. 18,300.]

No 394. Silver ring, inscribed with the name and titles of a priestly official.

No. 398.   Copper ring, inscribed [No. 17,740.]

No. 399   Copper ring, inscribed ⌡ 𓂋 ⌣ ⊔
[No. 29,038.]

No. 401.   Silver ring, inscribed with the figure of a goddess seated in a boat.   [No 2,960]

No 403   Silver ring, with rectangular bezel inscribed with the name and titles of I-[em]-hetep 𓊪 ⌐ □ 𓏏 𓆱

[No 29,039]

No. 410.   Copper ring, inscribed with the name of Tchet-hra   𓏤 𓏤   [No. 2951.]

No. 414.   Silver bezel, inscribed with the name of Psammetichus, son of Neith □ ⌡ 𓅢 ⌣ ○ ⊏.

[No 23,853.]

No 427.   Gold banded carnelian ring, the bezel of which is surmounted by the figure of a frog   [No. 2929]

Nos 429-445.   Carnelian rings, the bezels of which are inscribed with figures of sistra, figures of goddesses and amulets, e.g., 𓍯, ⌡, etc   These probably belong to the period of the XXVIth dynasty.

Nos 446-466.   Carnelian scarabs, uninscribed. No 467 Carnelian turtle or tortoise.   Nos 468-560.   Scarabs in mother-of-emerald, lapis-lazuli, amethyst, and miscellaneous figures, amulets, etc   Of special interest are — No. 529.   Lapis-lazuli figure of the god Khnemu, and No 554.   Hand from a hard, green crystalline figure of a man.

On the east side of the case is exhibited a very fine collection of necklaces of hæmatite, garnet, crystal, amethyst, carnelian, agate, and other hard stone beads, which date from about B C. 4200 to the Ptolemaic period   The most interesting are :—

No 561.   Necklace of hæmatite beads , early empire (?).

No 572.   Necklace of garnet beads ; early empire (?).

No. 578   Necklace of round amethyst beads , before the XIIth dynasty.

No 579   Necklace of roughly cut crystal beads of various shapes; VIth dynasty or earlier.

No 582   Necklace of roughly cut amethyst beads, before the XIIth dynasty

No 590   Necklace of amethyst beads, of very fine colours, with a gold hawk pendant.

No 596.   Necklace of amethyst beads of various shapes; early period.

No 599   Necklace of amethyst beads, the ends capped with gold; XIIth dynasty.

No 600.   Necklace of amethyst, having hollow-work gold beads, with *utchat* ⤨ gold pendant

No. 607   Carnelian face, for inlaying in a plaque, very fine work

No. 609   Necklace of carnelian beads, with pendants in the form of the symbol for " good luck " ⚱

No 628   Necklace of round, flat carnelian beads, with serrated edges and pendants ⚱⚱⚱⚱⚱

No 630   Necklace of small carnelian beads, with pendants ⚱⚱⚱⚱⚱.

No 641   Necklace of carnelian, gold and agate beads of various shapes.

TABLE-CASE K On the west side of this case are exhibited large and important collections of objects in **Egyptian porcelain**, glazed blue, green, red, yellow and other colours, belonging to various periods, from about B.C. 1200 to the end of the Ptolemaic period. On the east side will be found a collection of small objects, *e g*, amulets, pendants, ornaments for necklaces, plaques for inlaying, etc, made of **glass** of various colours Noteworthy objects are :—

No. 1 Blue porcelain scarab and figures of the children of Horus, for attaching to the outer swathing of a mummy [No. 20,856] No. 2 Green porcelain amulets, an altar, heads of Horus, crocodile, and two buckles, pierced for

attachment to the swathing of a mummy [No 20,968]
No 3 Porcelain scarab, with outstretched wings, pierced
with holes for sewing to the swathing of a mummy, very
fine work. XXIInd dynasty From Tûna [No 26,229]
No 4 A set of green glazed porcelain amulets consisting
of uræi, pendants, beads, scarabæi, symbolic eye, ring, heart,
figures of Anubis, Isis, Nephthys, Mut, and Thoth, hearts,
emblems of stability, triad consisting of Isis, Horus, and
Nephthys, two fingers, plumes, etc., arranged in the order
in which they were found on a mummy at Tell-Nebesta.
XXVIth dynasty or later Presented by the Egypt Exploration Fund, 1887 [No 20,577] Nos. 5–8. Sets of
figures of the children of Horus, with scarabs, etc., for
attaching to mummies. Fine examples [Nos 26,592,
26,591, 24,755, 22,805] No 9. Four figures of the children
of Horus Fine work. They were found on the mummy
from which came the scarab No 3 [No. 26,230] No. 10.
Porcelain pectoral, glazed green, which was inlaid with red
and yellow paste. The figure represented is the goddess
Nut [No 37,917] No 11 Red porcelain (?) pectoral, with
the head of Hathor, and uræi of the South and North, in
relief. Fine work [No. 7844] Nos 12, 13. Two porcelain
circular plaques, with serrated edges, stamped with demotic
inscriptions [Nos 13,429, 29,157]. No. 14 Blue glazed
porcelain hollow-work pendant, with figures of Thoth and
Rā endowing a king with "life" and "power." On the
reverse are figures of Heru-ur and Menthu-Rā presenting
the king, who is in the form of Horus, with scimitars Very
fine work [No. 14,556] No. 103. Pendant, with symbols
of "life, stability, power," ☥♙♙ [No. 18,065]. No. 104.
Inscribed pendant from the amulet of the *menat* [No.
13,950].

Nos 106 ff A large collection of porcelain *utchats*,
which symbolized the eyes of the sun-god and moon-god,
and were worn with the object of bringing upon the wearer
the "strength," and therefore vigour, of the gods of these
luminaries Interesting examples are :—

No 210 Porcelain *utchat*, inlaid with red paste [No.
23,083] No 223 Quadruple *utchat*, united to two papyrus
sceptres ; the four eyes represent the four cardinal points

[No 7845]. No 254. Porcelain cat, with three *utchats* in relief [No. 7381] No 264 Green porcelain plaque, with *utchats* and emblems of "good luck" ⌇⌇⌇ in blue [No 29,373]. No 265 Porcelain *utchat*, provided with the wings and legs of Horus; in front of the claws is a uræus with disk, and behind it an eye [No. 29,222]. No. 268. Porcelain *utchat*, with four *utchats* and the head of Hathor in relief [No. 7357]. No. 299. *Utchat* with the head of Bes in relief [No. 21,547]. No 329 Porcelain pupil of the eye, with an *utchat* on the flat side, and four rows of eyes on the convex side [No. 30,035] No. 312. *Utchat* surmounted by a figure of a cat [No. 7380] Nos 518 543 Group of eyes for insertion in the faces of mummy coffins; the pupils are of black obsidian, and the eye-lids and sockets are of blue glass [Nos 6911, 6912, etc.]. Nos 544 554 Group of amulets of the **Buckle*** in porcelain. Nos. 555 557. Group of amulets of the **Serpent's head** in porcelain. Nos 558–568. Group of amulets of the **Heart** in porcelain. Nos. 569–574. Group of amulets of the **Menat.** Nos 576 582. Group of amulets of the **Tet** Nos 583, 584. Porcelain **papyrus sceptres** surmounted, the one by the head of the hawk of Horus, and the other by the head of the hawk of Horus, having on his head the lunar crescent and disk, and uræus [Nos. 24,020, 24,021]. Nos 585–608. Group of papyrus sceptres. Nos 609 614. Group of amulets of the **Steps.** This amulet symbolizes :—(1) the throne of Osiris ; (2) the high place on which the sun rested after he had risen for the first time ; (3) the steps on which Shu stood when he raised up the goddess Nut from the embrace of Seb. The meaning of the amulet is, "exaltation to heaven" Nos. 615, 616. Amulets of the **Pillow.** Nos. 617, 618 Amulets of the **Plumes.** Nos 619 622 Amulets of the **sun on the horizon** Nos. 639 643. Figures of Ptah-Seker-Asar, the triune god of the Resurrection, with inscriptions under the feet 🐦🐦🐦 , etc. [Nos. 3614 3617]. No. 741. Porcelain figure of a captive woman. Presented by J. Tylor,

---

* For explanations of these, see the description of the amulets in Table-Case F.

Esq., 1897 [No 29,062]. No. 810. Porcelain bud of a flower, with figures of the winged disk, the ape of Thoth, a winged uræus, and a lotus, in hollow-work [No. 14,586] No. 841. Blue paste face for inlaying in a wall [No. 15,987] No. 855 A group of coloured porcelain lotus flowers, buds, etc., for inlaying. B C. 1450. From Tell el-Amarna Presented by the Rev Greville J. Chester, B A. Nos 863–869. A group of green glazed and black porcelain plaques and tiles, which were found inlaid in the wall of the doorway in the pyramid of King **Tcheser** (B.C. 3900) at Saḳḳâra [No. 2437 ff.] No 873 Circular porcelain plaque for inlaying, ornamented with the design of a spider's web [No. 6134] Nos 892–1374. A large collection of **glass** beads, figures and portions of figures for inlaying, sceptres, bangles, pendants, etc. No. 1063 is a fine example of a face for inlaying in a funeral pectoral, and Nos 1087–1092 are good specimens of **mille-fiori glass.** No 1217 is inscribed " Anubis in the city of embalming "

STANDARD - CASE L. Furniture, chairs, couch, table, etc.

1st Shelf, West Side :—No. 1. Wooden stand made in the form of the upper part of an obelisk. An inscription on one side of the pyramidion shows that it belonged to a priestly official in the temple of Amsu or Min at Panopolis who was called P-senetchem-ab ⬚ ; his father's name was Tches-Âmsu, and he held the office of second prophet of Amsu Pieces of wood were laid across the bars fixed to the sides, and offerings of food, etc., were laid upon them.
[No. 20,866.]

Nos. 2, 3. **Workmen's wooden stools.** From Thebes.
[Nos. 2481, 2482]

2nd Shelf :—No 4. Folding stool with legs terminating in heads of ducks inlaid with ivory The seat, of which portions still remain, was made of leather. XVIIIth dynasty From Thebes. [No 2477]

No 5 **Folding stool** with legs made in the form of the legs of a lion , the seat was made of leather.
[No. 37,406]

Q

No. 6 Leg of a stool or chair made in the form of a man-headed lion, or sphinx The upper portion is ornamented with lotus flower designs, and the lower part is inscribed " all health, all joy of heart, all life and two-fold power " 〖hieroglyphs〗 Late period [No. 24,656.]

On the **floor of the case** are :—

No 7. Framework of a small **bed** or couch, with legs in the form of those of bulls This object is probably unique. From Thebes. [No. 18,196.]

No. 8. Cushion or **pillow** stuffed with the feathers of waterfowl. From Thebes [No 1571.]

No 9 Wooden **toilet box** which belonged to Thuthu, the wife of the scribe Ani. When found the cover was tied on to the box with strands of papyrus and sealed with a clay seal. The inside is divided into four compartments by wooden divisions, which are ornamented with red wood and ebony In these are :—

(i.) Terra-cotta vase containing an unguent of some kind for rubbing over the body.

(ii.) Two alabaster vases containing unguents.

(iii.) A piece of pumice stone for rubbing the body.

(iv.) A double stibium tube bound with leather and provided with two stibium sticks, one wood and the other ivory. One tube contained the powder which was to be smeared on the eyes during the inundation, and the other a medicinal paste or powder to be used in hot weather when the air was filled with sand and dust.

(v.) An ivory comb, with carved back.

(vi.) A bronze "shell" whereon to mix the unguents. The hollow is intended for the finger or thumb.

(vii.) A pair of gazelle skin sandals, with turned up toes ; the outer skin has been tanned of a pink colour.

(viii.) Three red cushions for the elbows. A rare and interesting group of objects XVIIIth dynasty From Thebes. [No. 24,708]

No. 10. Wooden pillar, in the form of a lotus flower, from a canopy or shrine.   [No. 35,763.]

No. 11. Painted wooden stand with bowl.

[No. 2470.]

Toilet Box containing vases of unguents, stibium or eye-paint, a comb, bronze "shell" on which to mix unguents, cushions, and a pair of sandals [No. 24,708.]

1st Shelf, East Side:—No. 12. Painted wooden four-legged stool or **chair**, which was provided with a leather seat. The pattern is intended to represent inlaid ivory buds, etc. The lower part of each leg is concave

Q 2

and is ornamented with a linear design in circles. From Thebes. XXIInd dynasty. [No 2473.]

No 13 Hard wood four-legged stool or **chair**, with portions of the leather seat still remaining. The square holes in which the cross bars are fixed are filled up with plaques of bone or ivory. The lower part of each leg is concave, and is carefully carved in circles. XVIIIth dynasty From Thebes [No. 2474.]

No. 14 Four-legged stool or chair, with ebony legs and cross bars, ornamented and inlaid with ivory, the struts are made of ivory. The leather of the seat was coloured red or pink, and the ivory plaques in the legs were painted red. The lower part of each leg resembles that of the legs of Nos. 12 and 13. XVIIIth dynasty. From Thebes. [No. 2472.]

No. 15. Hard wood **folding stool,** with leather seat. The ends of the leg are in the form of ducks' heads, and are inlaid with ivory and ebony. XIXth dynasty.
[No 29,284]

No 16. Ebony **trinket box,** inlaid on the top and sides with rectangular designs of plaques of blue, glazed porcelain, and ivory stained red; the edges of the cover and legs are ornamented with small squares of ivory, and the buttons round which the fastening was tied are stained red. A fragment of the fastening is still preserved. XIXth dynasty or earlier. [No. 5897.]

No 17. Wooden **three - legged table,** which formed part of the furniture of a tomb. Painted on it is a figure of the goddess "Rennut, the lady of the *ka*" 𓏏𓆑, seated under the branches of a vine laden with grapes. Before her is a table of offerings, on which we see a haunch of some animal, bread, cakes, etc The line of inscription contains a prayer to Amen-Rā, king of the gods, and to Osiris, that they may provide funeral offerings for this table. The deceased was called Pa-per-pa (?) 𓂋𓏤𓂋𓏤. The goddess Rennut was the goddess of the harvest. A rare and interesting object XVIIIth dynasty. From Thebes. [No 2469.]

No. 18   Portion of a chest ornamented with figures of animals, triangles, etc., in relief.   [No 27,391.]

No. 19.   Sheet of glass, on which were painted in gold the figures of the twelve **Signs of the Zodiac.** Græco-Roman period. Presented by the Egypt Exploration Fund, 1885.   [No. 29,137.]

TABLE-CASE M. Terra-cotta **figures of gods, Coptic ostraka,** etc. In the upper portion of this case is a large collection of terra-cotta figures of gods, in which the characteristics of the gods represented are treated after the manner of the art of Egypt in the Græco-Roman period. Many of them were found among the ruins of houses and temples, and many in the tombs round about Alexandria and in the Fayyûm, they appear to have been made for the purpose of warding off the attacks of fiends and demons from the living and the dead. Nearly all are post Christian in date, and some appear to be as late as the IVth century of our era The most noteworthy are :—

No. 1.   Harpocrates seated on a throne supported on lions ; the feet of the god rest on a lotus which springs from the head of a uræus. No. 2. Cippus, with bust of Minerva and torches.   From the Fayyûm.   No. 3. Erotes, or **Cupids,** holding grapes and thyrsus with wreath. No. 6. Tablet, with figure of Harpocrates in relief, supported on the shoulders of two priests, between whom is a lotus standard. No. 7. Satyr bearing grapes No. 9 **Isis,** in the form of a Greek matron, suckling Horus, on her head are her characteristic disk and horns. The supports of her throne are ornamented with rosettes No 11. The goddess **Merseker,** the lady of the funeral mountain, wearing the attributes of Isis, and holding in her right hand a uræus, which is her emblem. No 13 The goddess **Hathor,** or Isis, as Aphrodite Anadyomene No 15. Male figure attended by a Nubian slave carrying a lantern No. 17 Figure of **Canopus,** the pilot of Menelaus, who was buried at Canopus, in Egypt, and was worshipped there under the form of a jar with small feet, a thin neck, and a swollen body. No. 19. Head of Osiris, wearing the Atef crown. No 20   Priest holding up the symbol of the god Canopus. No 21. Isis, holding standard. No. 22. Head of **Jupiter Serapis.** No.

23 Satyr carrying a bull or ox on his shoulders. No. 24 Satyr carrying a lion on his shoulders No. 27 Cupid Cistophoros and Psyche. No. 26 Eros or Cupid with his torch, accompanied by a cock No. 29 Minerva, with shield and torch No. 34. Painted equestrian figure. No 35 Jupiter Serapis and Eagle. No. 36 Eros or Cupid mounted on a bull. No. 37 **Baubo**, a woman of Eleusis, and nurse of Demeter, riding upon a hog No. 41 Nubian holding a rattle, and bearing the figure of a god upon his left shoulder No. 43. Portrait figure of a man wearing a chain or collar. No. 44 Amphoræ with wreaths, in stands No. 45 Head of a Bacchante. No. 46 Vase, in the form of the body of Isis, with side projections in the shape of the feathers of the Atef crown of Osiris, on the front are the horns, disk, and plumes of Isis No. 47 Harpocrates riding on a goose. No. 48 Model of a shield, with the head of Dionysos and a vine wreath in relief. No. 49. Hut surmounted by a crocodile No. 51 Canopus, wearing the attributes of Osiris No. 52 Canephoros, with a flute player and a two-handled amphora. No. 53. Male figure carrying a torch. No. 54 Canephores. No. 55. **Aphrodite** Anadyomene No. 56. **Silenus**, with thyrsus and crater. No 57. Harpocrates (?) leaning against an altar inscribed

A very rare object No. 59 Horus in the dress of a Roman soldier, with shield and spear. Nos. 60-65 Figures of animals No. 71. Male figure and dog No. 69 Grotesque figure No. 101. Black ware bottle in the form of a woman clasping a duck No. 130. Silenus with panther and cornucopiæ. No. 131. The god **Bes**. No. 132. Seated ape, reading a papyrus, a parody on the god I-em-hetep. No. 135 Female figure standing in a doorway, between pillars in the form of Bes supported on lions From Palmyra No. 165. Conical object, ornamented with heads and grapes in relief. No. 167 The god Bes as a warrior. No 187 Aimless, female figure, wearing boss and chains Among the remaining objects are some very good examples of portrait models of heads, both male and female.

On the sloping side of the case, in divisions **1-3**, is an interesting selection of specimens of ostraka and slices of calcareous stone, inscribed in **Coptic.** The texts chosen for exhibition consist of affidavits, legal acknowledgments and undertakings, letters, invoices, contracts, writing exercises, extracts from the Scriptures, and from liturgies, hymns, etc. The period to which most of these belong lies between A.D 550 and 900. The following are the most important :—

No. 1   Affidavit made by three persons that Kyrikos had acknowledged in their presence the receipt of money due to him.   [No. 32,783]

No. 2.   Circular letter from the Bishop Abraham (?) to his people, denouncing the injustice of Psate towards the poor.   [No. 42,782.]

Presented by the Egypt Exploration Fund.

No 3.   Liturgical fragment in Coptic ; containing part of a preface and sanctus from the anaphora of the mass.

[No 32,799.]

No 4   Acknowledgment of the gift of a field from Apa Victor, and engagement to pay the taxes for the same   Signed by five persons ; dated 20th Thoth, 15th year of an indiction.   [No 32,860]

No. 5   Undertaking by Abraham, son of David of Tchēme (Medinet Habu), to look after the camel and its furniture belonging to Apa Iakob   Witnessed by two persons, dated 12th Hathor, 5th year of an indiction

[No 32,794]

No 6   A promise to obey the canons, to learn the gospel of St. John by heart, etc , by three persons who have applied to Bishop Abraham to be ordained deacons

[No 32,789]

Presented by the Egypt Exploration Fund

No 7   Fragment of a writing exercise in Greek, of a religious character, written by Elias   [No 21,091]

No. 8   Religious exercise ; Coptic and Greek hymns.

[No. 35,123.]

No. 9   Letter from the Bishop Abraham to Pesynthios, the Lashane (magistrate), rebuking him for injustice

[No 32,795.]

No. 10. Undertaking by Papas and Photinos, priests, to report the proceedings of Apa Victor to the Bishop (?)
[No. 32,785.]

No. 11   Coptic school exercise in Greek words and names of persons and places.   [No. 26,210]

No. 12. Writing exercise, of a religious character, written by the deacon Petros (?)   [No. 21,271]

No. 13. Blacksmith's invoice of iron rings, chains, collars, etc., which he had supplied. Names wanting.
[No. 21,178]

No. 14 Bilingual (Coptic and Greek) list or account of "damaged sacks."   [No. 32,867.]

No. 15. Coptic abecedarium and copybook. VIIth century.   [No. 26,739]

No. 16. Letter from the "most humble" Pesenthios to his "father" Môyses.   [No. 21,138.]

No. 17. Beginning of an extract from Psalm xcviii., "Sing unto the Lord a new song, etc"   [No. 14,070.]

No. 18   Part of a letter to an unknown person.
[No. 21,087.]

No. 19 Part of the Alexandrine canon of the mass written in corrupt Greek by Apa Eihannes.
[No 5880]

No. 20 Fragment containing part of a Greek hymn and a letter in Coptic, conveying the salutations of Dioskoros to his brother Ounaref, his mother Tnouba, etc.
[No. 5881.]

No. 21 List of measures of corn (?) sent (?) to various persons, whose names are enumerated.   [No 20,025.]

No. 22 Part of a hymn or psalm (?).   [No. 14,248]

No. 23 Letter from Souloumôn Mengera to Apa Karakos, referring to gravestones.   [No. 21,235]

No. 24 List of houses belonging to various persons
[No. 21,430]

No. 25 Part of a letter to Pesynthios, mentioning Samuêl.   [No. 20,012.]

No 26 Letter from the priest Victor, and Matthaios, to Germanos and Isak (Isaac), authorizing them to sow their share of a field, and specifying the rent. Dated in the 4th year of an indiction   [No. 32,840]

No. 27. Letter from the monk Peperporos to a monk Enoch, replying to a former letter, and referring to the matter of Epiphanios   [No 14,210]

No 28. Document referring to the sale of a camel. Dated 2nd Pashans; witnessed by three persons:—Dioskle and Ouanafre of Pallas, and Gergôrios of Remmosh
[No. 14,080]

No. 29 Letter dated the 28th Paôphi, in the 12th year of an indiction, referring to Apa Philotheos having been sent to the writer, and to a payment of $17\frac{1}{2}$ ardebs (of corn ?) having been made to a camel-driver, etc.
[No. 14,134.]

No. 30 Coptic prayer, at end is a fragmentary list of Coptic and Roman months.   [No 5892]

No 31 Letter from Epiphanios to the "lord" Pater-moute, referring to wood, a camel, etc, sent by the latter, and praying that the Lord may bless him and deliver him from the devices of man, and from the snares of the enemy.
[No 14,040]

No 32 Fragment of a letter of religious character, incised.   [No. 35,136]

No 33. Fragment of a religious text written by Shenoute or Papnoute.   [No 5870]

No 34 List of proper names; probably of workmen.
[No. 20,093]

No. 35. Letter from Zebedê to his brother Iôhannes, referring to clothes to be brought by Kalinekos.
[No 16,783]

No 36 Letter of Shenoute, son of Piôb, in the Khastron (*sic*) of Shlout(?), Môyses, son of Severus and Pahôm, son of Dionysios, dwelling in the nome of Ermont, to Shenoute, son of the priest Pham in Ermont, agreeing to pay his wages for having taken charge of the field of Kharitou, without any neglect.   [No. 21,293]

No 37   Part of a letter, in an ornate hand, written to a monk, to ask for advice   [No 21,016]

No. 38   School exercise, consisting of scriptural passages, chiefly relating to Sion   [No 14,030]

No. 39   Fragment of a letter from Maria the nun to Isak (Isaac), "her beloved brother"   [No 21,268]

No 40.   Part of a contract or agreement   [No 31,661]

No 41.   Part of a letter requesting some monks to bless the writers, and to send holy water to them that they may sprinkle their sick beasts with it   [No 21,259]

No. 42   Safe-conduct issued by Souai, the Lashane (magistrate), to Mena.   Written by Niharau the deacon.
[No 32,995.]

No 43   Agreement, drawn up in legal form, between David (?) and Antonios the monk, with regard to articles delivered by the writer in exchange.   [No. 36,294.]
Presented by A H Gardiner, Esq, 1902

No 44   Letter from Isak (Isaac) the monk, enquiring after his "beloved father ' Paam   [No 5865]

No 45   Exercise in writing begging letters by a monk
[No. 32,847]

No 46   Letter from Papnoute to Apa Victor the Presbyter, with regard to his property   [No 20,004]

No 47.   Part of a letter concerning money, and mentioning a sateere (stater) of silver   [No 18,869]

No 48   Authorization from Abraham and Victor to Victor Kyriakos, and to Victor, son of Georgios, with regard to a financial matter.   [No. 31,943]

No 49   An account of measures of corn. straw, and sesame belonging to (?) Theudora (?)   [No. 14,025]

No. 50.   Account of grain   [No. 21,185]

No 51   List of payments or distributions of measures of beans, barley, corn and nuts, to various persons, chiefly church officials   [No. 20,040.]

No. 52.   Receipt for seed-corn " for the work of the ploughs."   No. 21,172.]

No 53   List of measurements of land, in which Greek arithmetical signs, etc., are employed.   [No. 29,750.]

No 54   Letter from Anatôlios and Isak (Isaac) to the holy father Zacharias, mentioning Paam, Victor, and Apa Marouf. VIIIth century.   [No 14,078]

No 55. Acknowledgment of a debt of one holokotinos (solidus) due to Phoibamon the camel-driver, for his pay. Signed by David the monk   [No 21,378]

No 56   Authorization from Pako in respect of rent.
        [No 19,879]

No 57   Receipt for a holokotinos (solidus) paid as tax or rent by Zaêl for the "camels' field," for the ninth year Dated 1st Mekheir, 9th year of an indiction. Signed by Iohannês the monk   VIIIth century A D

        [No 21,150]

No. 58   Receipt for one holokotinos (solidus) paid by Kosmas as an instalment of the yearly tax. Signed by David and Pisraêl   VIIIth century   [No. 20,074.]

No. 59. Acknowledgment by Phoibamôn of a debt owing to Apa David, a monk.   [No 20,039]

No. 60. School exercise in Greek and Coptic grammar ; on the obverse is a portion of a letter addressed to the authorities of a monastery   [No 14,222]

No 61   Reading exercise.   [No. 31,387.]

No 62   Fragment of a school exercise, with rough drawings of animals.   [No 21,291]

No 63   Writing exercise in the form of a letter, and roughly drawn faces, etc   [No. 32,804.]

No 65   Acquittance of Mizael Konstantinos for one holokotinos paid as the first instalment of taxes for the year   Signed by Severus   VIIIth century

        [No. 18,722]

No 66. Writing exercise, for the formation of letters
        [No. 18,816.]

No. 67. Fragment of a letter   [No. 19,379]

No 68. Inscribed fragment with portion of a rough drawing of a bird.   [No. 21,052.]

No. 69.   Fragment of a roughly painted patera with inscription of Theodora (?)   [No. 26,532.]

In **Division 4** are interesting groups of **Coptic crosses, bone pendants, bronze rings, bangles,** etc., presented by the late Rev. J Greville J Chester, 1886. The greater number of them were found at Akhmim, in Upper Egypt, a town which stands close to the site of the ancient city of Apu, called by the Greeks Panopolis   As early as the end of the third century of our era there existed a considerable number of Egyptians who had embraced · Christianity, and were commonly known as Copts, and during the fourth, fifth, and sixth centuries large monasteries and institutions of a somewhat similar character were established in and about the city. The wealth of Panopolis was derived chiefly from linen working and stone cutting, and the rich folk of the city were buried in elaborately embroidered shrouds and winding sheets; it is from the graves of such that the objects in this division have been collected.   The most noteworthy are :—

No 75.   Bone cross.   No. 76. Bronze cross, inlaid with red paste.   No 78. Iron hair-pin, with the figure of a cock at one end.   Nos. 81, 82 Iron bangles, with rectangular inlaid plaques.   No. 84 Fine bronze cross, with inlaid silver boss   No. 85. Wooden dagger, with handle in the form of a Coptic cross.   No 88 Bone pendant, with a figure of a Coptic saint in relief   Nos. 89–104. Group of crosses in metal, glass, bone, mother-of-pearl, etc   No. 105. Tweezers and other implements, on a ring.   Arabic period ?   Nos 106–111. Metal bangles.   Nos 112–115. Metal earrings, with pendants made of glass, etc   Nos 116–126. Group of crosses.   No 127. Mother-of-pearl dove.   No. 128. Mother-of-pearl object, of unknown use.   No. 131. Bronze chain.   Nos. 132 138 Bronze bells, for attaching to garments.   No 150 Bronze hair pins, with round heads. No 151. Bone plaque, compare No 88   No. 152 Mother-of-pearl object, use unknown.   No 153 Bronze ornament from a staff used in religious processions, with model of the seven-branched candlestick which stood in the Jewish Tabernacle   No. 157. Large bronze Coptic cross, with traces of linear ornamentation.   No. 174. Bone amulet on one side is cut the figures of two serpents, which stand one on each side of a fire altai, and on the other is an inscription in three lines, which shows that one of them was called Khnoumis. **BPINTANTHNOΦPINXNOYMIC.** A rare object.

In **Division 5** is a large collection of **terra-cotta moulds** which were used for making amulets, figures of gods, etc, in porcelain and metal, and stamps for bread and cakes made for high days and holidays. Among the latter may be noted Nos 183, 184, 189, 194, 195, and among the former:—No. 179 Figure of Bes. No. 196. Figure of the Bennu bird, which is commonly identified with the phœnix No. 197. Lotus flower. No. 199 A crown made of plumes, horns, and a disk. No. 200. Portion of a *menat*, with ægis of Bast, utchat, uræi, etc. No. 201. The god Anubis wearing the triple crown. No. 202. The god Nefer-Temu No. 209. Mould for bead or similar object, inscribed, "Son of the Sun, Ptah-meri"

No 217. Mould for pendent lion.

In **Division 6** are the following :—

No. 262. **Bronze seal** in the form of a cartouche, with plumes, inscribed . No. 263. Similar seal inscribed "Un-nefer" . No 264. Similar seal inscribed with the name of Heru-sma-taui No. 265 Similar seal inscribed with a figure and the name of Harpocrates. No. 266. Similar seal inscribed with the Egyptian equivalent of "Agathodaimon" . No. 268. Rectangular bronze seal inscribed with emblem of "millions of years," winged disk, palm branches, etc. . No. 269. Bronze seal, inscribed Rā-ka-ānkh .

i e., Ankh-ka-Rā No. 270. Portion of a bronze seal ring, inscribed with the figure of a crocodile No. 271. Bronze stamp, in the form of a hand and wrist, inscribed ⸱. No. 272. Bronze seal inscribed ⸱. No. 275. Bronze stamp with a ram's head, inscribed "house of Amen" ⸱. No 276. Bronze stamp inscribed with a triangular design. No. 277. Bronze wire stamp inscribed with the name of Amen-Rā ⸱. No 280. Stone stamp inscribed "Divine Father, Osiris Un-nefer, *Maāt-Kheru*" ⸱. No. 283. Bronze stamp inscribed with the name of Cnæus Pompeius Felix, **CNPOMPFELICIS** No. 284. Bronze potter's stamp in the shape of a foot, with indistinct symbols. Presented by the Trustees of the Christy Collection, 1865. No. 285. Circular bronze stamp inscribed with Maltese crosses and five letters. No 286. Bronze stamp inscribed "One God" **ЄІС ΘЄΟС** No. 287. Bronze stamp in the form of a cross inscribed **ГІ ΖΑ** No. 291. Green schist mould for an Arabic coin. No 292. Pair of silver bangles, much oxidized. No. 293. Silver wire bangle, each end of which terminates in a uræus wearing a disk. No. 294. Silver wire bangle, each end of which terminates in the flat head of a serpent. Nos 295, 296. Pair of tortoiseshell bangles, period uncertain. No. 310. Blue glazed porcelain bead, of very unusual design. No 311. Thick glass bead. No. 314. Bronze plaque, Pegasus in relief. No 315. Moulds of coins of Constantine and Licinius, A.D. 306-324. Presented by the late Walter Myers, Esq., 1884. Nos. 318-335. Bronze and stone weights, of the Roman and Christian periods.

TABLE - CASE N.   Gnostic amulets and gems.

"Gnostic" is a word used to describe a large number of religious sects, of widely differing views and beliefs, which sprang up in the Eastern provinces of the Roman Empire in the first and second centuries of our era. Many of the founders of Gnostic sects based their systems upon beliefs which were at that time of considerable antiquity, and several of the views held by the Egyptian gnostics were undoubtedly derived from the ancient Egyptian religion, which is made known to us by inscriptions on coffins, papyri, etc. The founders and teachers of **Gnosticism,** a word which is derived from the Greek *Gnosis*, "knowledge," claimed to possess a superiority of knowledge in respect of the science of things divine and celestial, and they regarded the knowledge of God as true perfection. The Gnostics of Egypt adopted into their system the old gods Ptah, Amen, Rā, Thoth, Suchos (Sebek), Aāh, the Moon-god, Osiris, Heru-ur, Anubis, Baba, etc, and the goddesses Neith, Hathor, Isis, Sati, the "Children of Horus," etc. The characteristic god of Gnosticism is "**Abraxas,**" or "Abrasax," and he was intended to represent the ONE who embraced ALL within himself; he represents by his many forms the union of many different ideas and attributes in one figure. His head is that of a cock, his body that of a man, and his legs are serpents; in his right hand he holds a whip, and on his left arm is a shield. The Gnostics of Egypt, like the dynastic Egyptians, attributed magical properties to hæmatite, carnelian, and other stones, which when cut into certain forms, and inscribed with figures of Abraxas and magical symbols and legends, were worn by them as a protection against moral and physical evil. The legends on the stones here exhibited are chiefly the names of Abraxas and his forms, the names of the Five Emanations of God, the names of the Archangels, etc. Many stones are inscribed with the seven vowels, arranged in magical combination and order. The following gems and amulets are noteworthy:—

No. 1. Triangular green stone, with figures of frog-headed and a hawk-headed deities, winged uræus, with pendent "life." The inscription mentions **Bait, Hathor, Akori,** and concludes "Hail, Father of the world! Hail, God in Three Forms"! **XAIΡΕΠΑΤΕΡΚΟϹΜΟΥΧΑΙ-ΡΕΤΡΙΜΟΡΦΕΘΕΟϹ.**

No. 8. Stone inscribed with a figure of the god **Abraxas** holding a palm branch in each hand; near him are two gazelles and two scorpions.

No 11   Abraxas, winged, wearing triple crown, and standing upon a lion. The inscription contains the prayer, " Protect from all evil."

No 12. Stone inscribed with a figure of **Bes** or Abraxas with the attributes of the One God Who comprehendeth all things, standing upon an oval formed by a serpent. The inscription is an address to the deity **IAΩ.**

No. 17. The seven-rayed, man-headed serpent **Khol-khnoubis XOLXNOYBIC**, who is described as the " everlasting sun," **CEMECEIAAM.**

No. 18. The lion-headed serpent **Khnoumis** and the mystic symbol **SSS.**

No. 22. The lion-headed serpent with halo, who is described as " Khnoubis, the driver away of demons."

No. 23. Chrysoprase inscribed with a figure of Khnoubis (or, " Khnoumis, the destroyer of demons ").

No. 25. Bloodstone inscribed with figures of a group of winged beings who stand on a planisphere ; two of them support a crowned mummied figure (Osiris or Christ ?). On the reverse is a figure of the same deity, with eight stars.   On the obverse, below the Gnostic inscription, is inscribed **Π A**, and on the reverse **Π Ω**, the meaning of which seems to be, "**Jah** (*or* **Jehovah**) is Alpha, **Jah** (*or* **Jehovah**) is Omega.**"

No. 28. Bloodstone inscribed with a figure of a six-handed **triad of goddesses** (Isis, Nephthys, and Neith ?), and six stars.

No. 33. Hæmatite plaque inscribed with figures of Khnoumis, and an **ass-headed** deity performing a ceremony at a mystic standard, and the vowels of the Greek alphabet arranged in a magic triangle—

A
Є Є
HHH
I I I I
OOOOO
YYYYYY
ΩΩΩΩΩΩΩ

No. 34. Green jasper oval inscribed with a figure of Jupiter Serapis seated upon a throne, with sides made in the form of winged lions, enclosed within a ring formed by a serpent.

No 36. Crystal oval inscribed with the figure of **Abraxas**, in the form of a cock-headed lion, standing on a prostrate foe.

No. 37. Hæmatite oval inscribed with a figure of Abraxas mounted on a horse; on the reverse is "**Sabaoth**," a name of the One God.

No. 44. Yellow jasper oval inscribed with figures of Abraxas, on the obverse he is lion-headed, and holds a human head in his right hand, and on the reverse he is standing in a chariot which is drawn by serpents.

No 45. Sard inscribed with a six-armed polytheistic figure and the ram-headed god **IA**.

No. 46 Hæmatite plaque inscribed with the figure of a man reaping, on the reverse is the legend **CXIΩN**, *i e.*, "the reaper."

No 49. Jasper plaque inscribed with a figure of Abraxas, cock-headed, and with serpents for legs; on the reverse is the name of the Archangel **Michael**.

No. 50. Hæmatite bezel in a ring inscribed with a figure of Abraxas, who holds a shield whereon is a magical arrangement of Greek vowels.

No. 60. Agate plaque inscribed with a figure of Abraxas holding a shield, on which is inscribed **IAΩ**; on the reverse is a figure of Osiris in mummied form, and the legend **ABΛANAΘAN**, which is said to mean, "Thou art our father."

No. 62. Chrysoprase oval inscribed with a figure of **Abraxas Opheon**; on the reverse is **ZACA**.

No 63. Green jasper oval inscribed with figures of Abraxas and **Harpocrates** seated on a lotus flower.

No 69. Sard inscribed with a figure of Harpocrates, seated upon a lotus flower, a lizard, and a Gnostic inscription enclosed within a ring formed by a serpent.

No 79 Hæmatite plaque inscribed with a figure of **Harpocrates**, who is seated on the head of **Bes**, who

R

stands on a scorpion ; on each side is a seated deity The whole scene is enclosed within a serpent ring, outside which is a Gnostic inscription.

No 87. Hæmatite plaque inscribed with a figure of a knight (St. George?) spearing a foe. The legends read "**Solomon**," the "seal of God."

No. 90. Beryl bezel of a ring inscribed with the figure of a beetle, having two hands and arms and a human head, from which proceed rays of light, and with the figure of a scorpion.

No. 110 Agate oval plaque inscribed with three magical signs enclosed within a serpent ring, and the names of **six Archangels**, viz., Gabriel, Paniel, Ragauel, Thureiel, Souriel, and Michael, and **IAΩ**.

No 123. Yellow jasper plaque inscribed with the figure of a crab holding the crescent moon in one claw ; on the reverse is the legend, "Romula has given birth to Sosipatria," **ΡΩΜΟΥΛΑΕΓΕΝΝΗCΕΝCΩCΙΠΑΤΡΙΑ**.

No. 147. Bloodstone oval plaque inscribed with figures of the chariots of the Sun and Moon, and with the names **Iaô, Sabaoth,** etc.

No. 191. Hæmatite plaque inscribed with a figure of a four-winged trinity, who probably represent the Gnostic form of Sekhet-Bast-Rā, who are figured in the vignette of Chapter CLXIV of the Saite Recension of the Book of the Dead.

No. 201. Chalcedony plaque inscribed with the names of **Michael, Gabriel, Raphael, Iaô,** etc.

No. 231. Jasper oval for inlaying in a ring, inscribed with the scene of the **Crucifixion;** the figures below probably represent the Virgin Mary and Saint John. On the reverse is a Gnostic inscription.

No. 235. Green jasper oval plaque inscribed with a figure of Abraxas, holding a shield on which is inscribed **IAΩ**.

No 251. Obsidian plaque inscribed with a figure of a six-armed trinity ; on one side is Harpocrates, and on the other Khnoumis On the reverse are seven stars enclosed within a serpent ring.

No 252 Hæmatite plaque inscribed with figures of Khnoumis, Iaô, Sabaôth, Harpocrates, Abraxas, and a serpent deity with a star.

No. 323. Bronze pendant, with scene representing a god or knight spearing a prostrate foe. The legend reads, "Thou art the god who vanquishest evil." The being on horseback may be intended for Horus or Saint Michael.

No. 324 Bronze amulet in the form of a pendant, inscribed with Gnostic formulæ.

No 398 Green stone oval inscribed with an ithyphallic, four-armed, four-winged deity, whose head is surmounted by a crown, and who has about it eight rams' heads. In two hands he holds the symbols of the lightning and the thunderbolt, in one he holds a pair of scales, and in another he holds a hatchet, or club. He represents the "God Who comprehendeth All," and stands within a serpent ring

No. 441. Circular agate inscribed with a seven-legged face, seven ears of corn, and fourteen stars

No. 455 Green stone oval plaque inscribed with the figure of a beetle enclosed within a serpent ring, and a Gnostic inscription.

No. 469 Amulet inscribed with a scene representing a woman, who is seated under a tree, and holds in one hand the symbol of life, ⚲, giving birth to a child ; on the reverse is the symbol of " life," and the legend, "One God in heaven." The scene inscribed on the amulet is the Birth of Christ. Presented by H Rider Haggard, Esq., 1887.

WALL-CASES 137–142, 194–204. Stone and alabaster vases. In these cases is displayed a fine representative collection of **funeral vases**, of all periods, in diorite, granite, porphyry, jasper, breccia of various kinds, and in several sorts of " limestone " and delicate alabaster. There is little doubt the predynastic Egyptians, although they appear to have possessed no metal tools, were able to produce stone vases of rude form and poor work, but it is not until the Dynastic period that the largest, finest, and prettiest stone vases appear in the graves of the Egyptians. The custom of depositing stone vases filled with offerings of all kinds was common in Egypt in every period, and it

is certain that it originated among people whose object was
not to offer vases and vessels, but offerings whereon those
who were buried were supposed to live, after they had
entered upon their new life, until such time as they were
able to provide for themselves in the world beyond the
grave   The dynastic Egyptians adopted the custom, and,
having metal tools at their command, they succeeded in
producing vases of most delicate and beautiful forms out of
very hard stones, such as diorite and hæmatite , a true
idea of the variety of forms and of the excellence of the
workmanship can only be obtained by inspecting a number
of the best examples, and this the reader can best do by
examining the unrivalled treasures of this kind in the
National Collection **(Plate VI.)** The following are the
most typical and interesting .—

Wall-Cases 194–197 Nos. 1–20 A group of long
narrow vases in hard, black stone, with lugs , some have
wavy line decorations on their upper parts, and some have
feet. From 'Amrah, near Abydos.
[Nos. 29,926, 32,515, etc]

Nos. 21, 22 Hard stone vases, with rims
[Nos 29,571, 30,366]

No 23   Hard stone bottle, with lugs and rounded
neck   [No 30,369]

No. 24   Flat, hard stone bottle, with flat rim, handle
and spout   [No. 30,741]

Nos 25–28. Four hard stone vases and jugs, with
handles ; one jug has a flat cover   [Nos 36,404, etc]

Nos 29–34. Six black stone unguent vases, with flat
projecting rims   [No. 21,990]

No 35. Green schist bowl in the form of a duck.
[No. 32,177]

No 36   Hard, red stone, flat mortar, with four rectangular projections ; the muller, or grinder, is of unusual
shape   [No 29,301.]

No 37   Black stone bowl, ornamented with heads of
Hathor, the cow of Hathor, papyrus sceptre and plants,
gazelle and young, human figure, etc., in relief. Early
work.   [No 32,554]

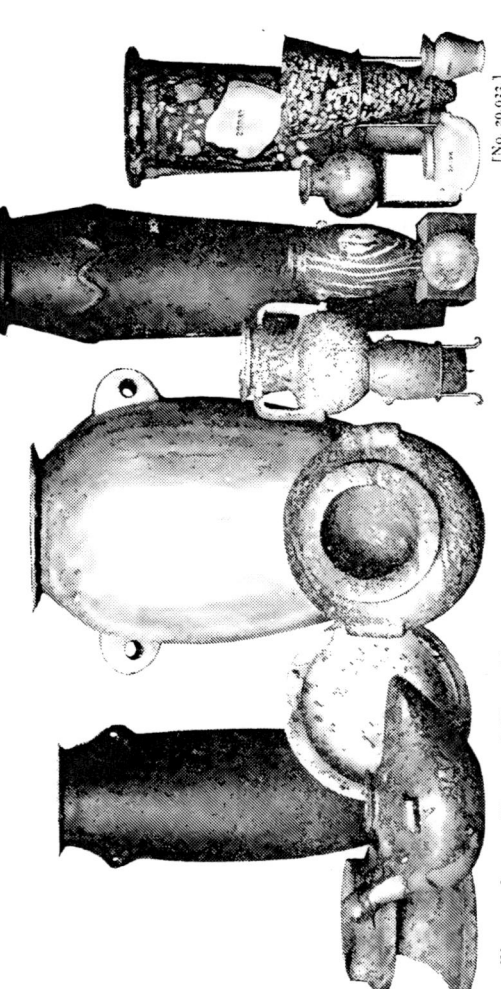

[No. 22,240.]   [No. 32,512.] [No. 4716.]   [No. 35,297.]   [No. 4735.] [No. 36,347.]   [No. 20,921.] [No. 24,416.]   [No. 20,933.]
     [No. 35,366.]   [No. 35,301.]   [No. 26,971.]   [No. 32,152.]   [No. 20,759.] [No. 13,321]

A group of Vases in diorite, granite, red breccia, and other variegated stones chiefly of the period of the first five dynasties.

[To face page 244.]

No. 38   Variegated stone bowl inscribed with the cartouches **Mut-khā-neferu** and **Ámen-ár-ṭās**. XXVIth dynasty.   [No. 4701.]

Nos. 39-42. Hard red stone stibium pot, and three bluish-grey stone stibium vases; one of these [No. 20,759] has handles in the form of apes, and another has handles in the form of serpents [No 12,753]. For a larger vase, in the same kind of stone, see No. 47.

Nos 43-46. A group of mottled black and white stone unguent vases, made of semi-transparent stone.

[Nos. 4707, etc.]

No. 48. Variegated elongated stone vase, with pierced lugs, and a gold rim and cover. A rare object   Fine work   [No. 32,152.]

No. 49. Hard red stone vase, with lugs and rim plated with gold.   [No 30,370.]

No. 50   Red stone cover of a vase sculptured with figures of a lion and a bull in mortal combat. The workmanship of this object is unusually fine and realistic. Period uncertain.   From the neighbourhood of Abydos

[No. 22,866]

In **Wall-Cases 196 and 197** is a fine collection of bowls, vases, jars, etc, in red breccia or " plum-pudding stone "; one of these (No. 35,306) is in the form of a pigeon. The two large, two-handled red breccia bowls, with flat projecting lips, exhibited on the floor of these cases, are extremely fine specimens of their class.   They belong to a series which comprised Nos. 35,698, 35,700, 36,330 (see Wall-Cases Nos. 10-12 on the Landing of the North-West Staircase), and which was found in one of the royal tombs of the Archaic period at Abydos.

On the floor of **Wall-Cases 194 and 195** are examples of large mottled and variegated vases and bowls in hard stone, and a fine specimen of a black, grey, and green mottled table for offerings   [No. 22,832.]

No. 51.   Large grey granite funeral vase inscribed with the cartouche of **Usr-en-Rā**   king of Egypt, B C. 3300.   [No. 32,620]

In **Wall-Cases 137–142 and 198–204** is arranged a large collection of fine examples of alabaster bowls, funeral vases, and vessels of all kinds and of all periods between B.C. 3300 and A.D. 108. A large number of them are noteworthy as much for the delicacy and gracefulness of their forms as for the beauty of the zoned alabaster of which they are made. An examination of their shapes will show that, for the most part, they are modifications, caused by the exigencies of the material of which the vessels are made, of the forms which were in use in the late Predynastic and Archaic periods. The most noteworthy are :—

Nos. 52, 53. A pair of large sepulchral limestone stands which stood one at each end of the bier, and in the hollow upper parts of which incense was burnt. They were made for a priest and "royal libationer" of King **Khufu** (Cheops), king of Egypt, B.C. 3733, called **Ka-ṭep**. The inscription on No. 52 reads

[Nos. 27,339, 27,340.]

No. 54. Massive funeral vase inscribed with the cartouches and titles of **Neb-Maāt-Rā** (Amen-ḥetep III.). From Thebes. [No. 29,479.]

No. 55. Alabaster table, with a complete set of vessels made to hold oils and salves for the high priestly official **Ātená**, who held the rank of *smer uāt*, and performed the duties of "chief reader" to the god Osiris at Abydos.

Alabaster Table, with vessels inscribed with the name of Ātena. [Nos. 4684, etc.]

Alabaster head rest of Ātena. [No. 2523.]

Near the table stands the alabaster pillow or head-rest of Ātená. The name and titles of the deceased, which are found inscribed on each object, were inlaid in green colour. VIth dynasty (?). About B.C. 3200. [Nos. 4684 ff., and 2523.] Close by is a green stone bowl also inscribed with Ātená's name and titles. [No. 4697.]

No. 56. Fragment of an alabaster vase inscribed with the name of **Khāfrā (Khephren)**, king of Egypt, about B.C. 3666. [No. 16,453.]

No. 57. Fine alabaster vase inscribed with the name and titles of **Unás**. [No. 4603.]

No. 58. Alabaster vase inscribed with the Horus name of **Saḥu-Rā**  **Neb-khā-u**, king of Egypt, B.C. 3533.   [No. 29,330.]

No. 59. Alabaster jar inscribed with the name and titles of **Teta** , king of Egypt, about B.C. 3266.   [No. 29,204.]

No. 60. Fragment of an alabaster vase inscribed with the name and titles of Tetä, B.C. 3266.   [No. 22,961.]

Red breccia Bull.   Archaic period.   (The inscription is modern.)
[No. 29,211.]

No. 61. **Red breccia bull** inscribed with the name and titles of Tetá, king of Egypt, B.C. 3266. The object itself is very much older than the reign of Teta, and dates from the Archaic period ; the inscription was added to it a few years ago by a native of Egypt, who hoped by so doing to increase its market value.   [No. 29,211.]

No. 62. Alabaster vase inscribed with the name and titles of **Rā-meri Pepi (I.)**, , king of Egypt, B.C. 3233 ; the inscription is painted green. **(Plate VII.)**   [No. 22,559.]

PLATE VII.

[No. 22,559.]

[No. 4492.]

[No. 22,817.]

[No. 29,204.]

[No. 29,330.]

A group of Alabaster Vases, inscribed with royal names. VIth dynasty.

[To face page 248.]

No 63   Alabaster vase inscribed with the Horus name and name of **Rā-meri, Pepi (I.)**, the hieroglyphics being inlaid in blue   [No 38,074]

No 64   Alabaster vase inscribed with the names and titles of **Mer-en-Rā**, king of Egypt, B.C 3200.

[No. 4493]

No. 65.   Fine large alabaster vase inscribed with the names and titles of **Nefer-ka-Rā, Pepi (II.)**, the polishing of the vase is modern   [No 22,817]

No 66.   Alabaster vase inscribed with the names and titles of **Pepi II.**   [No. 4492]

No 67.   Fragment of a chalcedony vase inscribed with the prenomen of **Usertsen I.**, king of Egypt, B C 2433   [No. 24,118]

No 68   Fragment of a crystalline stone vase inscribed with the name and titles of king **Ápep**; period doubtful   [No. 32,069]

No 69.   Fragment of an alabaster vase inscribed with **Neb-peḥ-Rā**, the prenomen of **Áāḥmes I.**, king of Egypt, B C 1700.   [No. 32,068]

No 70.   Alabaster vase inscribed, in hieroglyphics filled with green paint, with the name of **Maāt-ka-Rā (Ḥāt-shepset)**, queen of Egypt, B.C. 1550   The name of the temple of Dêr al-Baharî, ⌣ ⌣ ⊏⊐, is also mentioned on it   From Dêr al-Baharî   [No 26,282.]

Nos. 71–75   A group of four vases, and one cover of a vase, inscribed with the prenomen of **Ámen-ḥetep II.**, king of Egypt, B C. 1450.

[Nos. 4672, 32,533–32,536.]

No 76   Stone vase inscribed with the names and titles of **Ámen-hetep III.** and **Queen Thi**, about B C 1450, inlaid in glazed porcelain   [No 32,553]

No. 77.   Alabaster pebble inscribed with the name and

titles of **Thothmes III.** (o ⚋ 👁), king of Egypt, B C
1500   [No 18,194]

No 78. Fragment of an alabaster vase inscribed with
the names and titles of **Rameses III.**, king of Egypt,
about B.C. 1200. From Tell-al-Yahûdiyya.

[No 32,071]

No 79 Fragment of an alabaster vase inscribed with
the names and titles of **Rameses IV.**, king of Egypt,
about B C 1166   [No. 2880]

No. 80. Vase inscribed with the name of Ptah-mes, a
sem priest and high priest of Memphis About B C 1200

[No 4640]

No. 81 Zoned alabaster vase inscribed with the name
of **Nub-em-tekh,** 👁 ⸺ 👁, a princess The hieroglyphics were originally inlaid in blue colour [No. 4536]

No 82 Fine zoned alabaster vase, with cover, inscribed with the amount of its fluid capacity, 👁
"eight *hen* and 6 parts of a *hen*" When tested it was
found that this vessel would hold 8½ pints (apothecaries'
fluid measure).   [No 4659.]

No 83. Two-handled alabaster jar ornamented with a
floral design The ends of the handles are in the forms of
heads of ducks Presented by Lord Carlisle, 1887.

[No. 26,242.]

No. 84. Large alabaster vessel inscribed with the
names of Amenartās and Kashta, about B C. 733

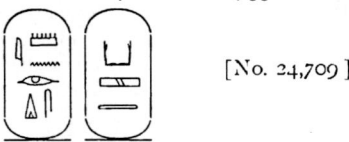

[No. 24,709]

No. 85 Alabaster jar inscribed with the prenomen
and titles of Shabaka, (o 👁 U), king of Egypt, B C. 700

[No. 35,080]

No 86.   Alabastron inscribed with the prenomen of Necho II (o / ⵛ ⵛ), king of Egypt, about B C 633

[No. 4631.]

No. 87.   Alabaster jug in the form of a woman, with one handle.   [No 30,459]

No 88.   Alabaster jug in the form of a kneeling man, with one handle.   [No 29,907]

No 89.   Alabaster vase ornamented with the head of a female in relief.   [No 4535]

No. 90.   Alabaster mortar (?), with four grotesque heads.   Late period.   [No 26,640.]

Nos. 91–93.   Three alabaster vases containing liquid unguent, which was used for anointing the body.

[Nos. 4501, 21,981, 24,418.]

WALL-CASES 143, 144.   On the upper and lower groups of shelves are painted wooden and earthenware models of sepulchral vases in gold, variegated glass and rare stones, belonging to the period between B C. 1700 and 1000   Among these may be noted as typical examples :—

Nos. 1, 2.   Vases of Nebseni, priest of An-her ⵛ ⵛ ⵛ,

[Nos. 30,454, 30,455.]

No. 3.   Gilded vase for *mestemet* ⵛ ⵛ ⵛ, a kind of eye-paint ; made for Rameses II.   [No. 35,274]

No 4.   Gilded vase for *natchu* ⵛ ⵛ ⵛ, a kind of eye-paint ; made for Rameses II.   [No 35,273]

Nos. 5, 6.   Round and conical gilded vases of Rameses II.   [Nos. 35,275, 35,272.]

No. 7.   For purposes of comparison is here exhibited a fine variegated glass vase from the tomb of Amen-hetep II., B.C. 1560.   [No. 36,343.]

On the floor of **Wall-Cases 143 and 144** are three terra-cotta vases, which were found in a tomb of the XIth or XIIth dynasty at Al-Barsha in Upper Egypt in 1903 The mouth of the largest vase has a linen cover, and was originally tied with a cord and sealed ; the fragments of the cord are exhibited in a box by the side of the vase. Presented by F. G. Hilton Price, Esq., F.S.A., 1903.

[Nos. 38,007–38,009.]

WALL-CASES 145–149 contain a representative collection of pottery, dating from the IVth dynasty, B.C. 3700, to the XXth dynasty, B.C. 1000. On the top shelves are examples of vases, etc., which were painted after baking, also specimens of polished red ware of various periods. On the lower group of shelves of Cases 145 and 146 are series of vases, probably of foreign origin, including

[No. 32,240.]   [No. 4740.]   [No. 32,598.]   [No. 36,343.]   [No. 4886.]

A group of Vessels to illustrate the use of variegated stone, painted wood, and coloured glass for sepulchral vessels.

black polished ware, *lekythi* (*i.e.*, bottles), and blackware vases, ornamented with incised designs filled with lime, dating from the XIIIth dynasty, B.C. 2000, to the XIXth dynasty, B.C. 1300. Of special interest are :—

No. 8.   Black ware bottle in the form of a hawk.

[No. 17,046.]

No. 9.   Bottle with incised zig-zag design.

[No. 4809.]

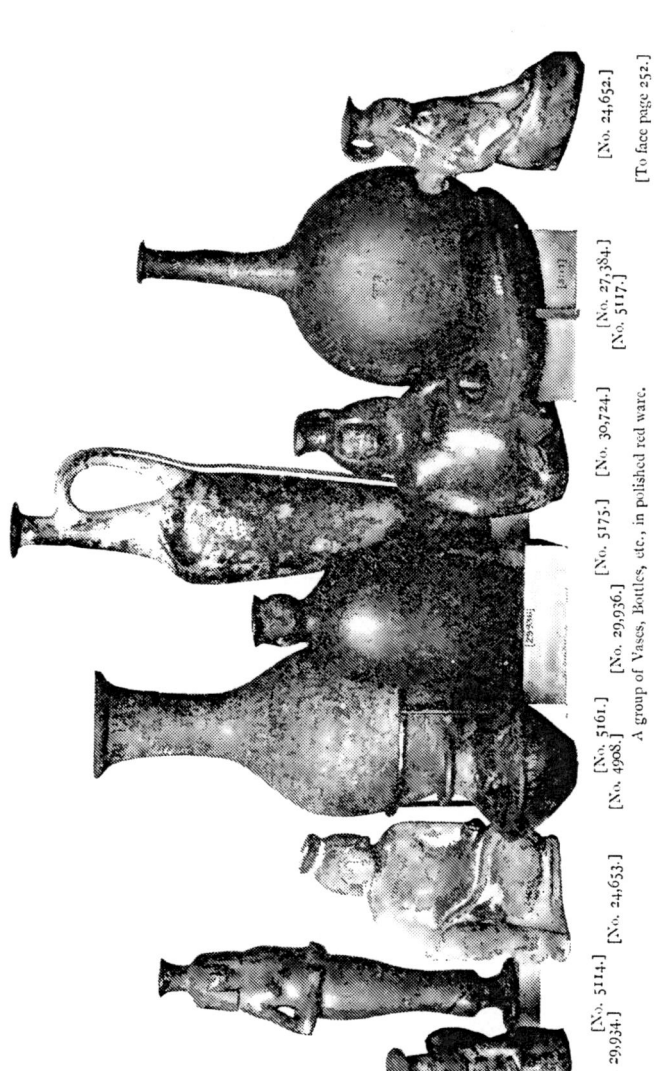

a. 29,934. [No. 5114.] [No. 24,653.] [No. 5161.] [No. 29,936.] [No. 5175.] [No. 30,724.] [No. 27,384.] [No. 24,652.]
[No. 4908.] [No. 5117.]

A group of Vases, Bottles, etc., in polished red ware.

[To face page 252.]

No 10   Black ware cup with incised zig-zag design.
[No. 30,456.]

No. 11.   Two bottles joined, with single handle
[No. 4824.]

No. 12   Yellow ware bottle ornamented with a branch-design, inlaid.   [No. 27,474.]

No. 13   Polished red ware vase of the same type
[No. 36,019.]

Nos 14-22.   A fine series of **false-necked vases**, commonly called **Bugelkannen, or** "pseudamphoræ." These vases are of the well-known Mycenæan type, and were imported into Egypt from Greece. From B.C. 1500 to 1000. No. 16 is of special interest, for it was found in the tomb of a grandson of Pi-netchem, king of Egypt, about B.C. 1050.   [Nos. 22,821, etc.]

No 23   Mycenæan amphora.   [No 4858.]

Nos. 24-33 A group of polished red ware vases and flasks, which have been thought to be of Syrian origin ; the evidence on this point, however, is incomplete XVIIIth dynasty. B C. 1500. [Nos. 36,407, 27,384, etc]

Nos. 34-57 A series of vases of native Egyptian manufacture, chiefly of polished drab ware.
[Nos. 4847, etc.]

Wall-Case 149.   Here is arranged a series of burnished or polished red ware vases, vase-stands, etc., dating from B C 3700 to B C 1400. Of special note are :—

Nos. 58, 59.   Vases with spouts, and necks in the form of human heads.   [Nos 29,936, 29,937.]

No 60.   Vase in the form of a seated man
[No. 24,653.]

No 61   Vase in the form of a seated woman.
[No. 24,652.]

No 62.   Vase in the form of a dwarf carrying a vase on his shoulder.   [No. 29,935.]

No 63   Vase in the form of a standing woman playing a guitar   [No. 5114.]

No 64   Vase in the form of a seated woman   Fine
work and polish   [No. 30,724]

No. 65   Vase in the form of a dwarf squatting and
clasping his knees   [No 29,934]

No 66.   Vase in the form of a wine skin   Made for
Sanni   Inscribed in ink.   XVIIIth dynasty
                                        [No 5117.]

No 67   A group of fine red ware vessels of the IVth
dynasty   These consist of two lamp-stands, a vase stand,
five bowls, one of which has a spout, etc   From Gizeh
and Abydos.   [Nos 5118, etc.]

WALL-CASE 150.   Objects in blue glazed Egyptian
porcelain.

Shelves 1 3.   Group of **vase stands, Canopic jars,
bottles,** etc.   The most important are —No 1   Vase
stand, with a prayer to " Ptah, lord of life," for sepulchral
offerings [No 35,414]   No 2   Portion of a massive
bowl which was inscribed with the name and titles of a
king of Egypt [No 32,597]

Shelves 4 6.   A fine group of vases and jars, cups,
figures of gods, heads of animals,
etc , chiefly of the XVIIIth and
XIXth dynasties   No 1   Plaque,
in the form of a pylon, inscribed
with the names and titles of
Amenemhāt III. and the prince
Ameni.   XIIth dynasty.   From
Thebes   [No 22,879]

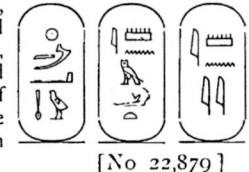

No 2.   Green and black glazed steatite vase inscribed
with the names and titles of **Thothmes I.**
A fine and rare object.   [No. 4762.]

No. 3   Portion of a cobalt-blue glazed
staff-handle (?) inscribed with the name of
Amen-hetep III. [o 𓍹 ⌣] , B.C 1450
                              [No. 24,743]

No. 4   Plaque inscribed with the names and titles of
Amen-hetep III. and **Queen Thi,** for inlaying in the lid of

a box. The hieroglyphics are in dark blue upon a light blue ground This was found with the Tell el-Amarna tablets.   [No 22,878.]

No 5 Cobalt-blue glazed vase inscribed with the name and titles of **Seti I.** ⟨☉ 𓏏 𓅓⟩, B C 1370.

[No 32,637]

No 6 Blue glazed **porcelain boomerang** inscribed with the name of **Amen-ḥetep IV.**, or **Khu-en-Áten**, and ornamented with lotus flowers and *Utchats*, or the eyes of the sun and moon. From Tell el-Amarna

[No 34,213]

Blue porcelain Boomerang, inscribed with the name of
Amen-ḥetep IV   [No. 34,213]

No 7 **False-necked vase** (Bugelkanne, or pseud-mphora), of Mycenæan type, with zig-zag design painted in black. A very fine example About B.C 1300

[No. 25,413]

No. 8. Blue glazed porcelain jug, with one handle, ornamented with diamond patterns and lotus leaves The shape is an imitation of a Mycenæan form About B C 1300   [No. 22,731.]

No. 9. Blue glazed porcelain stibium pot and ape.

[No. 30,452]

No 10 Ushabti figure, inscribed in hieratic, made for the lady Taāaı, XIXth dynasty.   [No 22,789]

No 11. Cobalt-blue glazed ushabti figure, made for Ḥeh, the scribe of the Pharaoh, XVIIIth or XIXth dynasty.   [No 26,720]

On the floor of this case is a very interesting earthen-ware vase painted with figures of camels, trees, etc. Post-Christian period? From Argin, in Nubia. Presented by Somers Clarke, Esq., 1899   [No. 30,712.]

WALL-CASE 151.   Porcelain—*continued*   No. 1. Blue glazed Canopic jar   XXIInd dynasty [No. 9539]. No. 2.   A group of fragments of vases inscribed with the names of **Rameses II., Rameses III.,** and **Seti II., Menephthah.**   XIXth and XXth dynasties, B.C. 1200. From Sarâbit al-Khâdim, in the Peninsula of Sinai [Nos. 13,193, 13,200, 13,201, 37,430, etc.]   No. 3.   Porcelain cover of a vase in the form of Harpocrates [No. 35.055]. No. 4. Figure of Amemit, or " Eater of the dead " [No. 22,030]   No. 5.   Menât amulet with the goddess Hathor [No. 26,232].   No. 6.   The Tet amulet (see page 210), surmounted by horns, plumes, etc. [No. 739].   No. 7. Figure of a cat (modern imitation?) [No. 27,725].   No. 8. Sphinx and cat [No. 11,865].   No. 9.   Figure of a man playing a double reed instrument [No. 26,318].   Nos. 10, 11. Pair of hands for sewing to the swathing of a mummy , (votive offerings?) [Nos. 11,393, 11,395].   No. 12 Cat and kittens [No. 26,239].   No. 13. Standard with the ægis of Khnemu [No. 26,235].   Nos 14–23 Figures of gods and goddesses.—Hâpi [24,413], Shu [No. 411], Nefer-Atmu [No. 35,064], Osiris [No 735], Mentu-Râ [No 344], Bast suckling a king [No. 11,314], Sati [No. 26,237], Bast with two kittens [No. 16,057], polytheistic figure [No. 12,518].   No. 24.   The snake-goddess Neheb-ka [No. 12,055].   Nos. 25, 26 Two fine blue glazed funeral vases inscribed with the name and titles of princess Nesi-Khensu ⟵⟨ ◎ ⟩ [Nos. 13,152, 17,402.]

No. 27.   Fine glazed libation vase, with spout, inscribed with the name and titles of Sheps, a priest and scribe of Amen-Râ, the king of the gods.   [No. 13,151.]

No. 28.   Cobalt and yellow glazed ware vase, orna-mented with a floral design, and inscribed with the name and titles of Rameses II. A very rare and interesting object.   [No. 4796.]

No. 29 Green glazed porcelain head of a giraffe. From Tell el-Amarna. [No. 26,363]

No. 30 Fragment of a green glazed porcelain **boomerang**, inscribed with the names and titles of Rameses II. [No. 14,953.]

No. 31. Portion of a bowl inscribed with the name of prince Khā-em-Uast, who held the office of high-priest of Memphis. About B.C. 1300. [No. 13,169]

WALL-CASE 152. Porcelain—*continued.* No. 32. Blue glazed porcelain jug, with handle, ornamented with a figure of a lady, in relief, making an offering at an altar. The reading of the inscription on the side is doubtful. Ptolemaïc period [No. 37,407]. No. 33. Rhyton, with faces in relief, and the end terminating in a bull's head Greek period [No. 37,452]. No. 34. Blue glazed porcelain figure of the god Bes. Fine colour. This object was probably one of two which formed the supports of a shrine [No. 22,112] No 35. Ape holding a goat [No. 11,910] No 36. Ape holding an *utchat*, symbolic of the moon [No 11,987] No. 37. Cobalt-blue porcelain figure of Ta-urt (Thoueris) [No. 1183]. No. 38. Green porcelain hedgehog; a fine example [No 36,345]. No. 39 Hippopotamus goddess Ta-urt, wearing a disk, horns, and plumes; a fine example [No. 13,162]. No. 40. Hippopotamus; found with the hedgehog of No. 38. The cavities for the teeth were originally filled with metal spikes. A very fine example [No. 36,346] No. 41. Porcelain sow, suckling seven little pigs. This object was a votive offering to Nut, "the great lady, the god-mother" [No. 11,976]. No. 42. Dog-headed ape, glazed in two colours. The species here represented is found at the present day in Central Africa, and is celebrated for its intelligence; such apes chatter loudly from dawn until sunrise, and for this reason the Egyptians believed that they were the spirits of the dawn which saluted the rising sun, and that when the luminary had risen they turned into apes [No. 22,355]. No. 43. Menat with ægis of Bast, and figures of Bes and the *utchat* of the sun in relief [No. 26,231]. No. 44. Similar object, with figures of Neheb-ka and Harpocrates [No. 26,307]. No. 45. The goddess Neith, in the form of a human-headed

S

serpent [No. 11,771]   No. 46. Kneeling woman suckling her child at her right breast, on the back, in relief, is the figure of a man (?) rising out of a basket or net   Fine work [24,412]   No. 47. Green glazed steatite box in the form of a sepulchral chest [No. 23,056].   No. 48. Seated figure of Thununa, overseer of the cattle of Amen-Rā in the reign of Thothmes III   On his knees is the figure of the prince Temi, B.C. 1550 [No. 35,400]   No. 49. Green glazed porcelain bangle or amulet [No. 24,686].   No. 49a   Fine blue glazed pectoral ornamented with a figure of Anubis, and drawings of the Buckle and Ṭet (see p. 210).   [No. 24,705]   No. 50 Pendent *utchat* with inlaid eye [No. 26,300].   Nos. 51a–c *Utchat*, with figures of two lions on the brow, and the figure of an animal in relief on the side [No 22,838].   Porcelain plaques with *utchats* in relief [Nos. 24,684, 24,685]

Ushabti figure of king Seti I.
[No 22,818]

WALL-CASES 153, 154. Porcelain—*continued* A fine group of glazed porcelain ushabtiu figures, among which may be specially mentioned :—

No. 52. Portion of an ushabti figure of Ḥui an official of Amen-Rā   XVIIIth dynasty [No. 34,185] No. 53 Ushabti figure of Sa-Amen, an official of Amen-Rā [No 34,180]   No. 54   Portion of an ushabti figure of

Pa-Rāmessu [No. 34,184]. No. 55. Ushabti figure of Māā [No. 9044]. Nos. 56, 57. **Ushabtiu figures of Seti I.,** king of Egypt, B.C. 1370 [Nos. 8895, 22,818]. Nos. 58-62. Blue glazed porcelain ushabtiu figures of members of the family of the **priest-kings** of Thebes, viz.:—The princess **Nesi-khensu** [No. 24,397], **Pi-netchem** [No. 30,400], queen **Ḥent-taui** [No. 30,398], queen **Maāt-ka-Rā** [No. 16,989], and **Ast-em-khebit** [No. 24,396]. No. 63. Ushabti figure of the lady Bakthi [No. 29,406]. No. 64. Ushabti figure of **Nesi-ta-neb-asher**, inscribed with a version of the VIth Chapter of the Book of the Dead. All the above are very fine examples of the work of the periods to which they belong. [No. 24,398.] Nos. 65-70. A group of ushabtiu figures inscribed for Tchanehebu, son of Nefert-ith, a superintendent of the royal barges [Nos. 34,278, etc.]. No. 71. Blue glazed porcelain rectangular tile or plaque, with a representation of the royal scribe Åmen-em-åpt adoring Osiris. XIXth dynasty [No. 6133]. No. 72. Portion of a white glazed vase with the name and titles of queen **Nefer-ith** inlaid in blue glaze [No. 23,226]. No. 73. Large blue glazed porcelain bowl, ornamented with figures of a lake and lotus flowers in black outline. A very fine example [No. 4790]. Nos. 74-78. A group of small green and blue glazed porcelain bowls, ornamented with designs of lotus flowers and fish in black outline [No. 22,730, 22,788, 29,217, 29,940, 32,591]. Nos. 79-86. A group of blue glazed porcelain bowls, ornamented with designs of lotus flowers and running water [Nos. 13,153, 22,737, 24,678, 29,216, 29,939, 32,590, 35,415, 36,409]. No. 87. Bowl ornamented with a

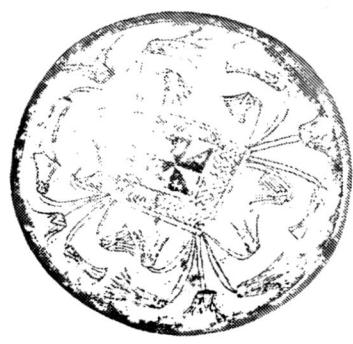

Blue glazed porcelain Bowl. [No. 4790.]

figure of a calf (Hathor) standing in a boat which is moored among lotus flowers [No 35,120] No 88. Bowl ornamented with figures of the head of Hathor and lotus flowers [No. 29,359]. Nos. 89, 90. Two glazed porcelain snakes which formed cases to hold mummied snakes [Nos 25,359, 30,453]. No. 91. Blue glazed porcelain vase in the form of a fish. Fine example [No. 24,410] No. 92. Portion of a lid of a box ornamented with figures of a gazelle and branches [No 26,387]. No. 93 Glazed steatite spoon (?) or bowl, in the form of a gazelle lying down [No 26,817] No. 94 Porcelain vessel in the form of a flower [No. 24,687]. No. 95. Model of a bowl with spout [No. 17,081]. Nos. 96, 97. Bowls with figures of couchant lions on the flat lip [Nos. 22,016, 34,887] No. 97a. Small bowl with spout, and figures of three frogs on the flat lip [No 24,689]. No. 97b. Blue glazed porcelain beard, from a coffin [No 6894]. No. 98. Portion of a blue glazed porcelain wig [No. 14,950] No. 99. Blue glazed porcelain head-dress from a statue of a king, with bands and uræi inlaid with plaques of carnelian and light-blue stone, set in a gilded border [No. 2280]

WALL-CASES 155, 156. Porcelain—*continued*. No. 100 Large glazed porcelain jug with the figure of a queen or princess making an offering at an altar. The handle is ornamented with bearded male heads, and traces of gold leaf indicate that portions of the woman's figure were gilded Ptolemaic period [No. 37,408] No. 101. Blue porcelain headless figure of a god holding a caduceus [No 1418] No. 102 Blue porcelain jackal (?) Roman period [No 22,761]. No. 103 Green porcelain flat figure of the goddess Isis (?), for inlaying [No. 32,196]. No. 104. Aphrodite Anadyomene. Roman period. From the Fayyûm [No. 34,208]. No 105. Portion of a glazed plaque, with a figure of a Roman galley in relief [No. 12,527] Nos. 106–109. Four porcelain balls glazed black and blue [Nos. 34,919, etc] No. 110. Glazed plaque for inlaying, stamped with the names and titles of **Sha-shanq I.**, about B.C. 960. On the reverse a prince called Tchet-Heru-auf-ānkh, and a princess are mentioned [No. 26,811] No. 111. Oval porcelain ornament with figures of

Khnemu, uræi, crocodiles, ape, etc. [No. 22,889]. No. 112. Blue porcelain spindle whorl [No. 34,215] No. 113. Green porcelain hollow-work spindle whorl. A fine example [No 34,216]. No. 114. Porcelain plaque for attaching to the breast of a mummy, with a figure of Anubis bending over the dead body as it lies on the bier. Christian period [No. 22,874]. No. 115. **Ushabti figure of Sôtêr**, a sailor, with the inscription in Greek. Roman period [No. 30,769] No. 116 Portion of a green glazed porcelain **draught-board** [No. 34,927]. No. 117. Head of an eagle [No. 34,905]. Nos. 118, 119. Two glazed porcelain ink-pots. Roman period [Nos. 22,015. 27,387]. No. 120. Green glazed porcelain bangle [No. 26,241]. Nos 121, 122. Two vases in the form of a **hedgehog** [Nos. 4764, 13,177]. No. 123. Dark blue porcelain model of the hieroglyph for " heaven," ⊏═╕ *pet* [No. 2050]. No. 124. Green porcelain bell [No. 15,748] No 125. Portion of a figure of Isis reclining on crocodiles. Roman period [No. 2392]. No. 126. Cippus of Horus [No. 11,821]. No. 127. Neck of a porcelain vase ornamented with figures of Erotes (Cupids) playing musical instruments. Roman period From the Fayyûm [No. 35,059]. No. 128. Green glazed porcelain ornament for a necklace, with figures of gods and goddesses in relief Very fine work. From Tûna [No. 26,303]. No. 129. Similar ornament with figures of Harpocrates with uræi, and Isis seated on a throne among lotus flowers [No. 26,233]. Nos. 130-132. Blue and green porcelain figures of the god Bes, standing on a papyrus column, suckling a young Bes; at his feet sits an ape. These figures seem to be parodies of the well-known figures of Isis suckling Horus [Nos. 11,820, 26,267. 27,375]. Nos. 133-138. A group of figures of Bes, chiefly of the late dynastic and Ptolemaïc periods.

Arranged on a sloping board standing on the floor of **Wall-Cases Nos. 151-156** is a fine collection of **tiles** and fragments, glazed in many colours, from Tell el-Yahûdiyyeh, the site of the famous city. about 20 miles from Cairo, which was built by **Onias, the high-priest,** about B.C. 160. These tiles, rosettes, etc., formed part of an extensive decoration of the walls of a chamber in a temple, which was rebuilt by Rameses III., about B.C. 1200, in honour of the god Temu. This temple seems to have existed in the time of Seti I., about B.C. 1370, and it was one of the most important in the Delta; it is probable that a temple occupied the site so far back as the XIIth dynasty. Several of the specimens here exhibited display the great skill of the Egyptians in glazing tiles under the XVIIIth and XIXth dynasties, and of especial interest are the figures of captives [Nos. 326, 330, 339-341, 350], the ornamental borders, rosettes, etc. [Nos. 148 249].

WALL-CASE 157. Porcelain objects of the **Saite** period, etc No 139. Glazed porcelain hawk for inlaying Fine work [No. 1835]. No. 140. Porcelain vase, in the shape of a small figure of an animal on the pedestal. From Memphis. About B.C. 600 [No. 4765]. No. 141. Vase inscribed with the name of **Nekau (Necho)** ~~~ 𓏏𓃭𓅂, king of Egypt, about B.C. 600 [No 24,238] No. 142. Glazed porcelain jug with the prenomen of **Amāsis II.** (o𓆓𓎟), inscribed in dark blue glaze [No. 13,175]. No 143. Part of a menat (see p. 210) inscribed with the name of **Apries** (o𓋹𓎟), king of Egypt, about B.C. 580 [No. 37,360] No 144. Upper portion of a porcelain model of a sistrum [No. 34,190]. No 145 Handle of a porcelain model of a sistrum inscribed with the names and titles of **Amāsis II.** 𓏏𓌳𓏤 (o𓆓𓎟) 𓆓𓏏𓄿 (𓈖𓅓𓏏𓊖) 𓃀 𓎡, king of Egypt, about B.C. 572 [No. 34,201] No 146. Portion of the handle of a porcelain model of a sistrum, inscribed with the prenomen of **Psammetichus II.** (o𓎡𓎟), king of Egypt, about B.C. 596 [No. 34,203.] No. 147. Fine greyish white glazed ushabti figure of Tcha-Heru-ta 𓆓𓏤 𓃀𓏤 ═, inscribed with the VIth Chapter of the Book of the Dead. XXVIth dynasty [No. 8971]. No. 148. Porcelain figure of **Ptah-Seker-Āsār**, with ram's head turned behind him XXXth dynasty. Presented by the Marquess of Northampton [No. 109].

WALL-CASES 158-164. Earthenware amphoræ, jars, vases, etc., of the Saïte and Ptolemaïc periods Worthy of note are:—No 149 Rough vase ornamented with a grotesque head of the god Bes [No. 14,957] No. 150. Two-handled vase ornamented with a grotesque head of the god **Bes** [No. 5091] No 151 The god Bes, wearing plumes, standing on a pedestal [No 22,378] Nos 152–160. A group of terra-cotta vases ornamented with the head of Bes [No. 5098, etc] No 161 Flat vase, with neck in the form of a lotus flower, with seated apes at each side ; on the side is inscribed the wish that Ptah, Sekhet, Nefer-Temu, and Neith may "open a happy year," *i e*, give a "**Happy New Year**" to the owner of the vase [No 4767]. No 162. Vase of similar shape, ornamented on one side with a figure of the cow of Hathor and lotus flowers in outline On the flat edge is a series of rosettes, and above these is inscribed, " May Isis open a happy year for its owner," and " May Amen-Rā open a happy year for its owner." [No. 24,651] No. 163 Small vase, of similar shape, with an inscription for the New Year [No 32,592] No 164 Glazed porcelain in the shape of a human-headed bird [No. 32,593]. No 165. Neck of a large two-handled wine-jar, with plaster sealing stamped with the prenomen of **Amāsis II.**, king of Egypt, about B C. 572 [No. 22,356]. No. 166. Portion of a plaster sealing of a wine jar stamped with the name of King **Psammetichus** [No 23,791]. Nos. 166*a–f*. Six large terra-cotta vases, inscribed in Coptic and Demotic [Nos 36,501, etc]

WALL-CASES 165-170. Here is exhibited a large miscellaneous collection of **terra-cotta vases**, jugs, bowls, cups, saucers, etc., which belong chiefly to the Saïte and Ptolemaïc periods, *i.e*, from about B C 600 to B C. 50 On the **top shelf** is a series of vases inscribed in rude hieratic characters with the names of drugs, medicines, unguents, etc.; they probably belonged to an apothecary's store, and were found in a chamber near a tomb of the VIth dynasty at Aswân in 1887. Among the objects on the **three middle shelves** are of interest.—No. 167. Red terra-cotta three-handled vase inscribed with the name Amen-em-uaa [No 38,432]   Nos 168-170   Portions of the handles of jars stamped with the name of the temple in the city of Khut Aten, to which they belonged [Nos. 23,306, etc.]   Nos 171-174   A group of four jars, inscribed with the names of the substances which they contained, each vase has the original mud cover on it, and on one of them is a portion of the linen with which it was tied up [Nos. 4948-4951].   Nos. 175-182. A group of small terra-cotta vases inscribed in hieratic and demotic, of various periods between B.C. 1200 and A D. 100 [Nos 21,713, etc]   No 183 Terra-cotta vase ornamented with a covering of blue glazed porcelain bead-work [No 38,433]   Nos 184, 185. Two red terra-cotta bowls inscribed in hieratic.   XVIIIth or XIXth dynasty [Nos 32,614, 32,615]   No 186 Red terra-cotta bowl, the outside of which is inscribed in hieratic   XXth–XXIInd dynasty [No 30,361].   No. 187. Portion of a flat bowl inscribed in Coptic [No. 27,718]   No 188 Buff-coloured bowl, ornamented on the inside with a floral design   Late period [No. 21,998]   No 189. Vase in the form of a pigeon [No 38,436].   No 190 Vase in the form of a duck [No. 38,437]   On the **floor of the case** are :—A series of terra-cotta two-handled jars, small sepulchral vases, plaster stamps, etc.   Among the smaller objects may be mentioned :—No. 191   Cover of an amphora stamped with the prenomen of Amen-hetep III., king of Egypt, B.C 1450 [No. 38,438]   No. 192   Portion of a vase inscribed with the name of Tetau [No. 38,435]

No 193. Jar-sealing stamped with the name of Rameses II [No. 38,434].   No 194. Jar-sealing made of clay and linen ; the sealing is stamped with ten impressions of a scarab [No. 22,002]   No. 195   Half of a mould for making small, two-handled terra-cotta vases, with sides ornamented with a two-headed winged serpent, having a serpent at the tip of each wing [No. 23,350].   Nos 196-203. Eight plaster and terra-cotta stamps of the Roman and Coptic periods ; after A.D 100 [Nos. 20,917, etc]

WALL-CASES 171–174 Earthenware and terra-cotta vessels chiefly of the Græco-Roman period, B C 200–A D. 150. **Top Shelf:**—No. 204. Bowl with figure of Osiris standing on Maāt and four serpents [No 5138]. No. 205 Similar bowl, with figure of Osiris [No 5139]. No. 206 Similar bowl, with figure of Ur-hekau [No 5142] No 207 Similar bowl with figure of Amen-Rā, king of the gods [No. 5141]. Nos 208–209. Similar bowls, with figures of two deities standing in a boat floating on the celestial Nile [Nos. 5135, 5140]. Nos 210, 211 Similar bowls, with figures of ten gods and goddesses painted on each in white outline [Nos 5136, 5137] **Third Shelf:**—No 212. Terra-cotta platter ornamented with the figure of a fish painted in white outline [No 36,035] No 213. Similar platter painted in black, with figures of pods of some vegetable, and wavy lines to represent water [No 36,036] Nos 214–216. A group of three dark, earthenware, flat, two-handled vases, ornamented with rosettes, bands, etc ; each has two handles, and two projections at the base on which it could be set upright. On No 214 are incised the hieroglyphics

[Nos. 30,445; 32,049, 36,032]. Nos. 217–219 A group of glazed ware, two-handled vases, ornamented with grotesque faces of Bes and other deities [Nos. 15,476, etc] No. 220. Black ware jug in the form of a pig [No 15,475] No. 221 Red ware vase in the form of a seated man [No 21,876] **Fourth Shelf:**—No 222 Earthenware pilgrim bottle found in clearing out a water wheel pit near Eastern Semneh, i e , Kummeh. Presented by Somers Clarke, Esq , 1899 [No. 30,709] No. 223 Terra-cotta basket [No 30,726]. No. 224 Red terra-cotta water bottle ornamented with figures of a fish, a tree, and a man leading an animal into a house or stable [No 5248]. No. 225 Red terra-cotta jar with ribbed ornamentation and a spout terminating in the head of an animal [No 35,358].

WALL-CASE 175. Unbaked Bricks. Here is a group of typical sun-dried bricks, many of which are stamped with the names of kings of the XVIIIth and

XIXth dynasties, B.C. 1700 to B.C. 1300. The art of brick-making appears to have been introduced into Egypt by the people who entered the land in the late predynastic period, and who eventually conquered it and settled down in the country. They came from some part of Western Asia, and it is thought that they may have been related to the dwellers in Southern Babylonia, where the art of brick-making had attained a high pitch of perfection. Babylonia contained large masses of a peculiar kind of clay, which was eminently suited for the making of bricks, and the earliest Babylonian bricks known to us are baked, and stamped with the names of the kings who had them made. The mud of Egypt was not very suitable for the making of bricks of a large size, hence Egyptian bricks are relatively small, and it was found necessary to mix chopped straw (*teben*) and reeds, hair, etc., with the mud in order to bind it together. The Egyptians never succeeded in making such large, well-shaped bricks as the Babylonians and Assyrians, and want of fuel prevented them from burning their bricks on a large scale. No. 2 is stamped with the name and titles of **Åmen-ḥetep III.**, B.C. 1450 [No. 6016]. Nos. 3 and 15 bear the name of the high-priest of Åmen, Pa - ren - nefer [Nos. 6023, 6024]. Nos. 5, 11, 24, bear the name of

Sun-dried mud brick stamped with the name of Rameses II. [No. 6020.]

Thothmes III., and come from Thebes [Nos 6011–6013] Nos 6, 12, 14, 17, 21, bear the name of **Rameses II.** [Nos. 6118-6022] No 7 bears the name of a "steward of Amen" called Thothmes [No 483] Nos 9 and 13 bear the name of **Thothmes I.** [Nos 6009, 6010], Nos. 18, 19, 22, 23 came from the Pyramids of Hawâra Dahshûr, Illahûn [Nos 6005–6008] Several of the above bricks were presented by Lord Prudhoe in 1835, Col Howard Vyse and J. S. Perring, Esq, in 1840, and Sir J Gardner Wilkinson

WALL-CASES 176-181. On the top shelf are several examples of heads of **portrait figures**, and portions of statues of the Græco-Roman period, which have been found at Alexandria and at various places in the Delta.

On **shelves 2-4** are arranged groups of bronze figures of Egyptian and **Greek gods and Heroes** of the Græco-Roman period. The most interesting are —1 Bust of a queen wearing tiara, necklace and pectoral [No. 36,050] No 2. Draped figure of an emperor or philosopher [No. 36,049] No. 3. Upper part of a figure of **Aphrodite,** A D. 200 [No. 12,272] No. 4. Bust of **Diana, or Luna** [No. 36,068]. No 5 Bust of a monarch [No. 36,067]. No 6 Head of **Herakles** [No. 36,066] No 7. Head of **Zeus Serapis** [No. 24,768] No. 8. Emblema in the shape of a bust of **Serapis** [No 12,271]. No. 9. Aphrodite, wearing the disk, plumes, and horns of Isis, and holding a mirror in her left hand [No. 32,584] No 10. Bronze figure of Aphrodite. The eyes are of silver inlaid [No 36,075] No 11. Lamp, in the form of Eros holding a wine skin From Alexandria [No. 36,071] No. 12 Figure of **Harpocrates** holding a cornucopia [No. 36,077] No 13 Massive bronze figure of Horus attired as a Roman soldier [No. 36,062]. No. 14 Cock-headed **Gnostic figure**, arrayed in Roman military attire. Presented by Maj.-General A. W. N. Meyrick, 1878 [No. 36,052]. No. 15. Bronze figure of **Canopus**, emblem of **Osiris-Serapis**, wearing the disk and plumes of the Atef crown, and pectoral [No. 26,264] No 16. Bronze figure of the god I-em-hetep (**Imouth: Asklêpios**) [No 579] No 17 Weight from a steelyard, in the form of a bust of a man wearing a helmet surmounted by a disk and a cluster of lotus flowers [No. 36,055]. No. 18. Bronze figure of the god Bes [No. 36,060]. No. 19 Bronze figure of the god Amen-Rā, wearing disk and plumes, and holding the emblem of life in his left hand. Round his neck is a necklace, with a pendent pectoral, and on his right wrist is a bracelet [No 27,356]. No. 20 Kneeling figure of a man holding an altar before him. The wings at the back show that it formed an ornamental support for some object like a box [No 37,642]. No. 21. Portion of a handle of a swinging lamp [No. 38,530] No. 22 Deep bronze collar, inscribed with three ovals containing figures of gods, and three lines of hieroglyphics [No. 38,528]. No. 23. Bronze model of a fire altar [No. 38,541]. No. 24. Bronze jug ornamented with a human head wearing a tiara [No. 38,520]. No 25. Bronze figure of **Ptolemy Alexander**, having the attributes of the genius of Alexandria. From Alexandria [No. 38,442]. No. 26. Bronze figure of **Cleopatra Selene**, having the attributes of the goddess **Fortuna.** From Alexandria [No. 38,443]. No. 27. **Bronze weight** of the Coptic period (3 lbs. 2 25 oz. Troy) [No. 6193]. No. 28 Bronze weight of the Coptic period (2 lbs. 7 25 oz. Troy) [No. 6192].

On the shelves and slope in the lower part of **Wall-Cases 176-180** are collections of terra-cotta and bronze **lamps,** and miscellaneous pieces of inscribed stones from the walls of temples. Among the lamps may be specially noted.—No. 1. Portion of a lamp with the name of **Victor** in relief [No. 38,158]. No. 2. Lamp with the name of **Abbâ Joseph,** the Bishop, upon it in relief [No. 23,330]. No. 3 Mentioning the name of one Peter [No. 20,777]. No. 4. Lamp, with handle, mentioning the name of Abbâ Joseph [No. 22,829]. No. 5. Lamp mentioning the name of **Mark, the Evangelist** [No. 23,329]. No. 6. Portion of a lamp, with handle, ornamented with a cross in relief [No 23,331]. No 7. Lamp in the form of a bust of Serapis [No 38,419]. No. 8. Lamp in the form of a bust of Osiris [No. 38,425]. No. 9. Lamp, with two nozzles, supported by a figure of Bes From the Fayyûm [No 15,485]. No. 10. Lamp in the form of Minerva seated in a bath [No. 12,744] Nos. 11-16. Terra-cotta lamps, each with the figure of a frog upon it in relief [Nos. 5187, 21,948, etc]   Nos 17, 18 Terra-cotta lamps, each with the figure of a dog upon it in relief [Nos 24,703, 38,450].   No. 18a Lamp, with figures of a dog and mythical animals in relief [No 38,470] No 19 Lamp with figures of horses and a mounted soldier in relief [No. 38,469].   No. 20. Lamp, with the figure of a horse in relief [No. 38,471].   No. 21. Lamp in the form of an elephant's head [No 38,423] No. 22. Lamp with the figure of a winged gryphon in relief [No 38,473]   No 23. Lamp, ornamented with several figures of animals in relief [No. 20,785]   No. 24 Rectangular lamp, with places for ten wicks [No. 38,418] No 25 Lamp, with three nozzles [No 5227]   No. 26 Triangular lamp, with places for ten wicks [No 38,416] No 27. Lamp, with upright handle, ornamented with the figure of a woman in relief [No 38,477]   No. 28 Lamp, with four nozzles [No. 38,417]   No 29 Circular lamp, with six projecting nozzles [No 38,141]. No 30. Lamp, with two nozzles, ornamented with figures of **Jupiter, Serapis** and **Europa** (?) on a bull [No. 38 412] Nos. 31, 32 Lamp handles, ornamented with mythological scenes in relief [Nos. 38,542, 38,543] No 33 Bronze lamp, with the figure of a mouse on the cover [No. 38,444]   No 34. Bronze lamp, with the cover on a hinge [No 38,445]. No 35. Bronze lamp in the form of a horse [No 38,446] No 36 Bronze lamp, with handle in the form of the neck and head of an animal [No 5335]   All the above mentioned lamps belong to the Græco-Roman and Christian periods   Nos 37 and 38, which are of glazed terra-cotta, belong probably to the Christian or Arabic period [Nos 4803, 38,475]   No 39. Lamp in the form of a negro's head, late period [No 15,478]

Nos 40-57.   A group of terra-cotta two-handled, **pilgrim-flasks,** or bottles, which were made near the shrine of **Mâr Minâ,** or **Saint Menas,** which lay about nine miles from Alexandria   They were used for holding oil which had been blessed, either by contact with the relics of the saint, or by a blessing pronounced by the abbot of the time, and they were suspended by strings Menas appears to have been born at Mareotis, and he suffered martyrdom under the Emperor Galerius at Alexandria ; before he died he begged that his body after death might be placed on a camel, and that the animal might be turned loose into the desert. This was duly done, but his body was found by miraculous means, and was buried near Alexandria. In commemoration of these things the greater number of these flasks have figures of the saint and a camel, or camels, upon them, in relief; a halo encircles the saint's head, and his hands are raised in benediction. Many of the bottles are inscribed in Greek ΕΥΛΟΓΙΑ ΤΟΥ ΑΓΙΟΥ ΜΗΝΑ, or simply ΤΟΥ ΑΓΙΟΥ ΜΗΝΑ, or Ο ΑΓΙΟC ΜΗΝΑC. The most characteristic examples of the flasks of Mâr Minâ are Nos 40 and 41 ; No. 42 is of interest, for whilst the figure of the saint is wanting, the familiar Greek inscription is given within a circular ornamental border [No. 17,083, etc.].

In **Wall-Cases 180 and 181** are examples of **Roman keys**, a **hinge** of a small door, and **bronze cases for door-pivots**, etc. Of interest are:—No 58. Bronze bolt, with a lion's head. Presented by Professor Petrie [No 16,038]. No 59 Bronze chain, composed of large, flat, circular links, with bronze pendent figure of Harpocrates [No 38,544] No 60 Disk or patera, with handle and emblemata in the form of busts of Serapis and Isis [No 38,526]. Nos. 61–66. Six **iron keys** [No 23,346, etc] No 67. Bronze pivot case from a large door, inscribed with the names of the queen **Tefnut**, the high-priestess of Amen, **Shep-en-Apt**, a royal princess, and the high-priestess **Amenartâs** About B C 600 [No 36,301]. Bronze pivot case, from a door [No. 15,738].

On the floor of **Wall-Cases 181 and 182** is a large collection of **weights** made of stone, porcelain, etc. The largest, No. 68, came from Memphis, and weighs about 121 lb Presented by Colonel A. Bagnold, R.E., in 1887 [No. 20,652]. No. 69. Rectangular weight inscribed with the prenomen of **Amen-ḥetep I.**, B.C 1700 ⟨cartouche⟩ [No 38,546] No 70 Basalt duck-weight inscribed with the prenomen of **Psammetichus I.**, B C. 666 ⟨cartouche⟩ [No. 27,394]. No 71. Circular weight inscribed with the prenomen of **Amâsis II.** ⟨cartouche⟩ [No. 38,545].

WALL-CASES 182–187. On the **top shelf** is a collection of **baskets** of various shapes and sizes, which were placed in the tombs to hold bread cakes, dates, and other fruit, etc. ; the oldest of them date from the period of the XVIIIth dynasty, about B.C 1600. Of interest are :— No 1 Vase-shaped basket ornamented with a floral design in coloured grass or papyrus [No. 38,552]. No 2. Small hollow-work basket, with blue glazed porcelain beads arranged in zig-zag rows [No. 16,058]. No. 3. Basket, with circular, conical cover, and strengthened with a network cord [No. 6346] No 4. Oval basket, with a coloured design woven into it [No. 6312].

On the **second shelf** are arranged large typical collections of **toilet objects**, including **bronze mirrors** and **razors, tubes and pots for stibium**, or eye-paint (*kohl*), **combs, hair-tweezers**, handles of **fans**, etc., of various periods, chiefly from the XVIIIth dynasty to the Coptic period, *i.e.*, from B.C. 1600 to A.D. 500. Among the mirrors may be mentioned those with ivory or bone handles [Nos. 1–6] ; No. 7. Mirror, with a wooden handle, in the form of a lotus flower, No. 8. Mirror with a wooden handle in the form of the perch of the hawk of **Horus** [No 2732] No. 9. Mirror of unusual size and shape, with a wooden handle in the form of the god **Bes** [No. 37,176]. No 10. Mirror, with a wooden handle in the form of a lotus flower, and ornamented with gold bands [No. 37,175]. No 11 Mirror, of unusual shape, with a handle in the form of a lotus column surmounted by a head of Bes [No. 2737]. No. 12. Mirror, the lotus handle of which is surmounted by two hawks [No. 32,583]. No 13. Mirror, with lotus handle surmounted by four uræi [No 20,756] Nos. 14, 15. Mirrors, with handles ornamented with Hathor heads [Nos. 29,428, 37,174]. Nos. 16, 17. Mirrors, having handles in the forms of women with raised extended hands and arms [Nos. 20,773, 37,173] No. 18 Bronze mirror, with green glazed steatite handle in the form of a lotus column, on the upper part of which is an inscription showing that it was made for **Menthu-em-hāt**, the son of **Ḥeq-áb**,

These names suggest that this mirror was made during the XIth or XIIth dynasty, or

perhaps a little earlier [No. 2736]. Nos. 19, 20. Handles
of fans, or fly-flappers [Nos. 5509, 5510]. No. 21. Portion
of the handle of a fan inscribed with the name of **Nebseni,**

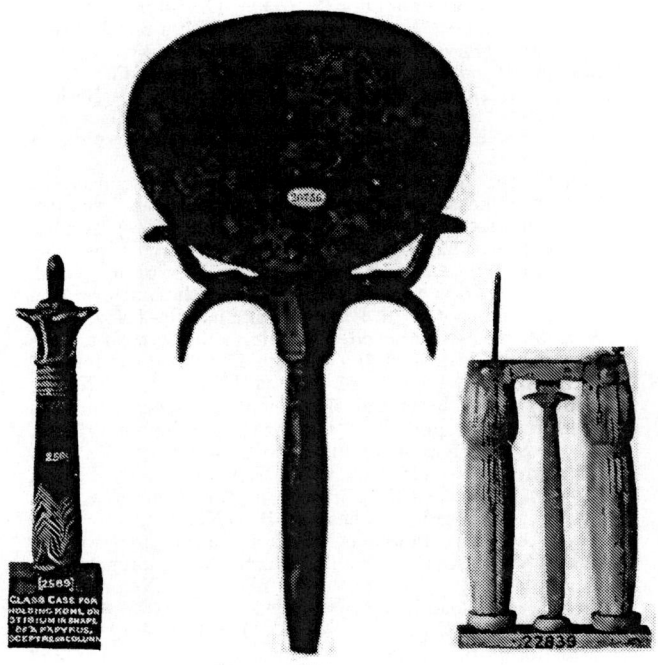

Fig. 1.   Fig. 3.   Fig. 2.
Bronze Mirror and Tubes for Eye-Paint.

the inspector of the goldsmiths of Amen, [hieroglyphs] [hieroglyphs]. XVIIIth dynasty [No. 37,172].

Among the tubes and pots for eye-paint the following are of interest :—No 22 Porcelain tube inscribed with the names of **Amen-ḥetep III.** and **Queen Thi,** B C. 1450 [No. 27,236]. Nos 23, 24. Porcelain tubes inscribed with the names of **King Tutānkh-Amen** and **Queen Ānkh-sen-Amen,** B.C. 1400 [Nos. 2573, 27,376]. No 25. Variegated glass tube in the form of a lotus column (see fig. 1), with needle [No. 2589]. No. 26. Marble stibium pot inscribed with the name of Paatenu (?) [hieroglyphs] [No. 37,192]. No 27 Hæmatite stibium pot, the upper part of which is plated with gold [No. 32,151]. No. 28. Stibium pot, with cover, on four-legged stand [No. 29,931]. No 29 Opaque blue glass stibium pot, with cover, edged with gold. XVIIIth dynasty [No 24,391]. No. 30 Green glazed steatite stibium pot, with hollow-work side, on four-legged stand [No 37,234] No. 31. Stibium tube, in the form of a man, made of lapis-lazuli and gold ; the bone needle is ornamented with a gold band, on which is the emblem of "life" in relief [No. 30,481] No. 32. Ivory stibium tube in the form of **Bes** [No 2571]. No. 33. Bone stibium tube ornamented with annules and zig-zag patterns [No. 6181]. No 34 **Reed stibium tube,** with needle, and leather case in which it was carried [No 12,539]. No 35 Green glazed steatite ape holding a stibium tube [No. 21,895]. No 36 Steatite stibium pot, with **two tubes** [No. 30,052]. No. 37. Wooden stibium pot, with two tubes, double cover, and needle [No 2597]. No. 38. **Obsidian stibium pot,** with **two tubes,** and ornamented with a figure of Bes in relief [No. 2599] No 39 Ivory stibium pot and needle (see fig 2), with two tubes in the shape of lotus columns [No. 22,839] No. 40. Wooden stibium pot, with two tubes, inscribed with the names of **Amen-ḥetep III.** and **Queen Thi** [No. 37,202]. No. 41. Bone stibium tubes ornamented with female figures in relief [No. 30,464] No 42. Terra-cotta stibium pot in the form of the **triple crown,** with **three tubes** ; the needle is surmounted by a figure of the hawk of Horus [No 2612]. No. 43. Green glazed steatite stibium pot, with **four tubes,** inscribed with the signs for "life, good luck, stability" [hieroglyphs], and the name of its owner, the scribe Aāḥ-mes

𓈖𓏤 [No. 2606] No. 44. Stibium case made of wood inlaid with ivory, with four tubes [No. 18,176] No. 45 Stone stibium pot, with four tubes [No. 37,191] No. 46 Wooden stibium case, with **four tubes**, three of which held kinds of eye-paint which were suitable for particular seasons of the year One tube held the eye-paint for use in the spring, another held that for use in the summer, and a third held that for use in the period of the Inundation, a fourth tube held a kind which is said to be "good" for every day, 𓄿𓅓 . This case was made for the scribe Aāh-mes [No. 27,196]. No. 47 Stibium case, with four tubes; inscribed with the name of **Amen-mes** 𓇋𓏠𓈖𓄿 [No. 2609] No. 48 Stibium case in the form of a hippopotamus, with four tubes [No. 27,371] No. 49 Wooden **comb** ornamented with the figure of a horse [No. 21,893] No. 50 Wooden comb with the back in the form of an animal [No. 2678] No. 51 Wooden double comb, having teeth of two sizes, with a figure of a dog in the handle in hollow-work [No. 25,260] No. 52 Similar comb, but of larger size, with a figure of a camel in the handle in hollow-work [No. 26,683] Nos. 53 62. A group of wooden combs, some having teeth of two sizes [No 2681, etc] No. 63 Bronze comb [No 24,633] No. 64 Handle of a bone comb, with the figure of a goose [No 20,993] No 65 Bone comb, with ornamental handle [No 18,666] No. 66 Bronze **razor** (?), with handle in the form of an oryx [No 20,761] No. 67. Bronze razor (?), with handle in the form of a man riding a horse [No. 36,314]. Nos 68 73 A group of bronze razors, one of which (No 68) is inscribed with the prenomen of Thothmes III. 𓇳𓐰𓏏 [No 17,087, etc] No. 74. Pair of bronze **forceps**, with ends in the form of fishes With them is the wooden last by which they were kept in shape [No 37,206] Nos 75-79 Bronze and iron **tweezers** [No. 37,215, etc.]. No. 80. Bronze implement, with pointed ends, and case for the same [No 20,776]

On the same shelf is a collection of painted **porcelain bottles inscribed in Chinese characters**, with short extracts from the writings of poets; they appear to have been used for scent, unguent of some kind, or snuff, and were not found in the ancient tombs of Egypt, as was once supposed, but among the ruins of buildings and graves along the old caravan route from the Red Sea to Kena on the Nile, which passes through the valley now known as Wâdi Hammâmât. It was formerly thought that some of these bottles dated from the XVIIIth dynasty, but the late Sir Wollaston Franks, K.C B., was able to show that the kind of porcelain of which they are made was not known before the XIIIth century of our era, and it is now tolerably certain that they were brought from China by the Arab traders, who travelled between China and India and Western Africa, in the XVth, or even XVIth century.

No. 81. Porcelain bottle inscribed in Chinese with the words, " Only in the midst of this mountain " (or, " Alone in this mountain "), which are taken from a poem by Kea Taou, who flourished from A D. 831–887. This bottle was found at Nimrûd on the Tigris [No. 93,098] Nos. 82, 83 Porcelain bottles inscribed in Chinese with the words, " The opening flowers have opened in another year," which are taken from a poem by Ying-wuh, who flourished from A D. 702–795 * [Nos. 24,695, 35,444]. No 84. Porcelain bottle inscribed in Chinese, " The clear moon shines amidst the firs " [and the sap becomes amber in a thousand years]; the author of these words was Wang Wei, who flourished in the first half of the VIIIth century of our era [No. 37,239]. Nos. 85–88. Porcelain bottles with Chinese inscriptions, which have not yet been deciphered [No. 35,443, etc.].

On the **wall of the case,** mounted on boards, is a collection of bronze, ivory, and wood **hair pins and studs,** and **needles for stibium pots** and tubes.

On the **third shelf** the principal objects of interest are :— No. 1 Bronze bowl containing **pieces of blue colour** used for painting papyri [No 5556] Nos. 2–9 Pieces of **ochres** of various colours, red, blue, green, yellow, used for writing and

---

* On the inscriptions on Chinese bottles of this class, see *Transactions of the China Branch of the Royal Asiatic Society,* Part III., 1851–52, Hongkong, 1853, p. 45 ff.

painting on papyri [Nos 38,269, etc] Nos 10, 11 **Mullers and slabs** for grinding paint [Nos 5548, 23,337 8] No 12 Alabaster slab, with seven circular hollows for holding portions of paint or unguent ; above each the name of the substance it was intended to hold is given in hieroglyphics This object was made for the nobleman and priestly official Atenā ⟨ ⟩ From Abydos [No 6123] Nos 13, 14. Two slabs, with similar hollows and inscriptions , the names of their owners are not given [Nos 6122, 29,421]. No 15 Alabaster slab, with six crystal and black stone bottles and vases, and two stone instruments, the use of which is unknown [No. 5526] No. 16. Wooden **plaque,** with rounded top, ornamented with a design in outline, in which **Amen-hetep I.** is seen standing in his chariot [No. 2429] No. 17. Portion of a **box** which was made for an official of Pepi I VIth dynasty [No. 5910]. No. 18. Portion of an inscribed wooden object which was made for a priest called Amen-sa [No 38,550]. No 19. Wooden **box,** with portion of a lid with a long hinge [No 5906] No 20 Rectangular case made of papyrus leaves and stalks [No 5918]. Nos. 21–24 Semicircular case or box, with carved designs inlaid with white paint, and portions of other cases similar in shape, inlaid with bone leaves [No. 5921, etc.]. No. 25 Portion of a wooden and ivory box, ornamented with a design of lotus flowers painted in red and green [No 38,283]. Nos. 26–29 Wooden figures which formed the ornamentation of the sides of a funeral chest [No 23,178, etc] No 30 Part of the fastening of a funeral chest, inscribed with the prenomen of **Amen-hetep III.** [No. 38,282]. Nos 31–33 Wooden unguent boxes, ornamented with incised floral designs Very fine work [No. 5921, etc.] No 34. Circular box, with unguent [No 5923] No 35 Wooden box in the form of a hippopotamus [No 22,825] No. 36. Painted funeral chest, with four compartments, and two baskets [No 21,818] No 37 Wooden funeral chest, with a dedicatory inscription to Osiris [No. 5907]. No. 38. Portion of a box inlaid with plaques and flowers in light and dark blue porcelain [No. 38,252] No. 39 Portion of a box made for the scribe Tehuti-hetep [No. 30,801]. No 40 Portion of a box made in

the form of two animals [No 30,800] No. 41. Ebony and
acacia wood box, with ivory fastenings painted pink [No
23,057]. No. 42. Model of a sepulchral box inlaid with a
chequer pattern in ivory, ebony, and acacia wood [No
20,784] No. 43. Hard wood toilet box, of which the cover
is surmounted by a woman-headed sphinx, and the sides
are ornamented with delicately cut figures of gods in relief.
The inside is in the form of a cartouche Ptolemaic period
[No. 29,598] No 44 Wooden box in the form of a duck
[No. 29,367] No. 45. Wooden box, veneered with ivory,
and ornamented with ivory panels, on which are cut figures
of gods and goddesses, birds, flowers, etc. Several of the
designs are painted. A rare and fine example of late
Roman funeral chests [No 5555]. No. 46. Wooden box,
with rounded cover, ornamented with bands of ivory incised
with annules [No. 5901] No. 47. Rectangular **toilet box**
ornamented with incised lines and annules. From the
Fayyûm. Early Coptic period [No. 37,349]

On the floor of **Wall-Cases Nos. 182-187**, are ·—Nos.
1, 2. Portions of **pillars** ornamented with **disks of porcelain** painted with rosettes, and with buds and flowers
[Nos. 38,273, 4]. Nos. 3, 4. Architectural ornaments inscribed with the names of Rameses III. [Nos. 11,753, 38,277].

No. 5. Brown **stone weight** inscribed $\overset{\text{o}}{\underset{\cap\cap\cap}{\cap\cap\cap}}$ [No. 23,065].

No. 6. Portion of a **tree trunk** found in the masonry of
the Great Pyramid at Abûsir Presented by Col. H. Vyse
and J. S. Perring, Esq, 1839 [No. 38,259]. No. 7 Palm
leaf capital and abacus from a model of a pillar. Presented
by F G Hilton Price, Esq, 1903 [No. 37,900]. Nos 8-10
Pieces of **petrified wood** from the remains of a forest near
Wâdî Halfa Presented by Colonel Holled Smith, 1887
[Nos. 38,260-38,262] No. 11. Bronze architectural ornament in the form of a lion's head [No. 38,280]. No. 12.
Wooden stand for holding a sepulchral vase [No 2471]
No. 13 Stand for funeral offerings made of reeds and
papyrus [No. 6302]. No 14 Rectangular seat from a
stool, made of plaited papyrus, covered with leather on
which is painted a rectangular design in red, white, and
blue [No. 2517]

WALL-CASES 188–190.   Furniture, wooden models, etc.   On the **upper shelf** and on the floor of these cases are:—No. 1. **Stool** in wood, painted white, with framework sides and concave seat ; an interesting specimen [No. 2476]. No. 2. Portion of the upper framework of a stool, with

remains of the seat, which was made of palm fibre covered with leather [No. 2475].   Nos. 3, 4. Two wooden legs from a throne made in the form of the head and fore paws of a lion [Nos. 2518, 2519].   No. 5. Wooden **chair**, with sloping back, and seat made of plaited string [No. 2479]. No. 6. Leg of a chair or throne, the upper part of which is in the form of the woman-headed serpent M e r s e k e r t , which was made for Nefer-Merä(?) [No. 2559].   No. 7. Portions of the framework of a **bronze ceremonial seat**, or chair; much restored.   Presented by Walter Myers, Esq., F.S.A., 1884 [No. 13,513].   No. 8. Low chair, with legs in the form of lion's paws, and straight back, inlaid with ivory and ebony in panels set in acacia wood ;   the seat is made of plaited string [No. 2480].

On the **second shelf** are :—No. 9. Right arm and hand from a large wooden statue ; on the wrist is cut the royal prenomen, Rä-tcheser-kheper-setep-en-Rä (Ḥeru-em-ḥeb?), and other characters, which were inlaid with coloured paste, or porcelain [No. 36,427].   No. 10. **Group of wooden**

figures on a stand One carries a wine jar on his head, two are kneading or treading out some substance in jars, another stands before a circular table or bench, etc [No 36,423] No 11 **House,** within which is a group of figures engaged in cooking food, and packing it, and carrying it away in rectangular baskets [No 30,719] No 12. Model of a man engaged in mixing dough(?) in a bowl [No. 23,348]. No 13. Stone model of a woman rolling dough on a board [No 2378] No 14 Wooden model of a man squatting and fanning a fire [No 29,596] No 15 Model of a woman carrying a rectangular basket on her head with bread cakes, joints of meat, etc [No 30,716] No 16. Group of models of butchers who are engaged in slaying and cutting up animals [No 30,718]

WALL-CASES 191–193. Here is exhibited an interesting collection of large and small **portrait figures,** chiefly in wood and bronze, which belong to various periods between B C 2600 and A D 100 ; nearly all of them were found in tombs. The most interesting are :—

No 17. Wooden figure of **Kuatep,** a high priestly official who flourished about B C 2600 (see pages 72 and 114) From Al-Barsha [No 30,715]

No. 18 Painted wooden figure of a lady of the family of Kuatep [No. 29,595.]

No 19 Painted wooden figure of a lady of the family of Kuatep, who carries a bundle on her head. Very fine work. [No 20,867.]

No. 20 **Model of a bull** belonging to Kuatep, with a disk and plumes between his horns , he is followed by his keeper. Fine work [No 24,713]

No. 21 Painted wooden figure of a lady of the family of a kinsman of Kuatep, who was buried in the mountain near the modern Al-Barsha. XIth or XIIth dynasty, B C. 2600–2500. [No 22,541]

No 22 Wooden figure of a high official, wearing a full wig and an elaborately pleated garment XIXth dynasty [No. 2320.]

No. 23   Bronze kneeling figure of **Rameses II**, wearing the crown of the South, and making an offering of two vases of wine.   XIXth dynasty, B.C. 1300

[No. 32,747.]

No. 24.   Painted wooden figure of the priestess Re-Shat (?)-pet ⌒ 𓏢𓉐 𓏢 𓂝 ⌇ 𓍿   XXth dynasty.

[No. 2376.]

No. 25   Figure of a woman carrying a sepulchral chest on her head, she wears large earrings, and a long tress of hair falls by each side of her face.   [No. 32,767.]

No. 26   Wooden figure of a woman carrying a cat.

[No. 32,732.]

No. 27.   Wooden figure of a woman wearing a full-bottomed wig, carrying a cat   [No 32,733.]

No 28   Wooden figure of a king, with moveable arms, carrying a vessel with a handle in one hand, and an undefined object in the other.   [No. 2325.]

No. 29.   Porcelain figure of a woman carrying one gazelle on her neck and shoulders, and leading another by its horns   After the XXIInd dynasty   [No. 2369.]

No 30.   Wooden figure of a king or prince, with his collar and tunic gilded   [No. 2335.]

No. 31.   Bronze figure of a king.   After the XXIInd dynasty.   [No 2276.]

No 32.   Bronze figure of a king, with featherwork tunic inlaid with gold, in the character of An-Her.   Fine work

[No 2277.]

No 33.   Bronze figure of a king (**Tirhakah?**), wearing double plumes, in the character of the god An-Her-Shu.   XXVth dynasty.   About B.C. 700   [No. 32,761.]

No 34   Votive bronze figure of a god wearing the triple crown, and standing upon a sledge with runners; it was dedicated to the god by Heru-sa-Ast.   [No. 32,746.]

No. 35.   Wooden sepulchral figures of Heru and Uah-áb-Rā-meri-Ptah; both officials were attached to the service of the god " Ptah-Sekei-Asar, lord of the hidden shrine."   XXVIth dynasty   [No. 32,731]

No 36   Wooden figure of the lady Bet-en-Reshep, wearing a necklace of coloured porcelain beads   This figure was made to commemorate the deceased lady at the expense of her son. XXVIth dynasty.   [No. 32,774]

No 37.   Wooden figure of Thetá, a man of very high rank, and a high priestly official, the eyes are inlaid with obsidian and white stone.   XXVIth dynasty
[No 29,594]

No 38   Bronze hands and arms which were originally fixed on the head of a statue, to indicate that it was the *ka* or "double" of the deceased.   [No. 27,389]

No. 39.   Green glazed inscribed steatite roll or seal, which was originally held in the hand of a statue of Queen Ámenártás, about B.C. 725.   In one cartouche is the name of the Queen **Mut-khāu-neferu**, and in the other is the name of the "High-priestess Amenartás". A rare object   [No 29,212.]

On the north and south walls of this room are two painted plaster casts, which illustrate scenes in the Syrian, Libyan, and Nubian wars of Rameses II.   They were taken by the late Mr Joseph Bonomi from the walls of the rock-hewn temple which Rameses II built near Kalâbsha to commemorate his victories.   On the north wall are the following scenes :—

I Rameses sitting under a canopy, and wearing a crown with disk, plumes, and four pendent uræi ; near his feet lies his favourite lion.   In the upper register one of his sons is leading a number of fettered men into his presence, and in the lower register a company of men are tendering their homage to him

II Rameses slaying a member of a Libyan tribe ; above his head is the vulture, the emblem of the king's protecting goddess.

III   Rameses in his chariot charging the Libyans

IV   Rameses slaying Libyans in one of their fortresses

V.   A son of Rameses II bringing Syrian prisoners into the king's presence.

On the **south wall** are the following scenes :—

I   Rameses and his two sons, Amen-her-unami-f and Khā-em-Uast, in their chariots, charging the Nubians.

II   Rameses, seated under a canopy, receiving gifts of gold rings, leopard skins, prisoners, apes, panthers, giraffes, oxen, gazelle, ostriches, ebony, bows, feathers, fans, chairs of state, tusks of elephants, a lion, an antelope, etc., all these things must have been brought from the Northern Sûdân.

INDEX.

292   INDEX.

BIBLIOLIFE

Old Books Deserve a New Life

www.bibliolife.com

Did you know that you can get most of our titles in our trademark **EasyScript**[TM] print format? **EasyScript**[TM] provides readers with a larger than average typeface, for a reading experience that's easier on the eyes.

Did you know that we have an ever-growing collection of books in many languages?

Order online:
www.bibliolife.com/store

Or to exclusively browse our **EasyScript**[TM] collection:
www.bibliogrande.com

At BiblioLife, we aim to make knowledge more accessible by making thousands of titles available to you – quickly and affordably.

Contact us:
BiblioLife
PO Box 21206
Charleston, SC 29413

Lightning Source UK Ltd.
Milton Keynes UK
UKOW04f0113160114

224644UK00003B/57/P